From Brand Vision to Brand Evaluation

From Brand Vision to Brand Evaluation

The strategic process of growing and strengthening brands

Second Edition

Leslie de Chernatony

AMSTERDAM • BOSTON • HEIDELBERG • LONDON • NEW YORK • OXFORD
PARIS • SAN DIEGO • SAN FRANCISCO • SINGAPORE • SYDNEY • TOKYO

Butterworth–Heinemann is an imprint of Elsevier

Butterworth-Heinemann is an imprint of Elsevier
Linacre House, Jordan Hill, Oxford OX2 8DP
30 Corporate Drive, Suite 400, Burlington, MA 01803, USA

First edition 2001
Second edition 2006

British Library Cataloguing in Publication Data
A catalogue record for this book is available from the British Library

Library of Congress Cataloguing in Publication Data
A catalogue record for this book is available from the Library of Congress

ISBN-13: 978-0-7506-6749-4
ISBN-10: 0-7506-6749-4

For information on all Butterworth-Heinemann publications
visit our web site at http://books.elsevier.com

Typeset by Charon Tec Ltd, Chennai, India
www.charontec.com
Printed and bound in Great Britain by MPG Books Ltd, Cornwall

06 07 08 09 10   10 9 8 7 6 5 4 3 2 1

Working together to grow
libraries in developing countries

www.elsevier.com | www.bookaid.org | www.sabre.org

ELSEVIER   BOOK AID
             International   Sabre Foundation

To Carolyn, Gemma and Russell, with love

Contents

Part Two: Planning for Integrated Brands

Part Three: Employing the Brand-building Process

6 Setting brand objectives 171

7 Auditing the brandsphere 185

8 Synthesizing the nature of a brand 223

Preface

Since the first edition of this book managers and academics have become more attuned to the need not just to focus branding activity on customers, but rather to take a more balanced perspective – in particular paying more attention to staff as brand-builders. More is being spoken about internal brand-building, and a growing number of brand success stories are being attributed to the importance of the brand-ambassador role of staff. Organizations internationally, developing either products or services in consumer and business-to-business sectors, are increasingly perturbed by the way that technology is shortening the sustainability of any competitive advantage from brands' functional advantages. Recognizing that brands are clusters of functional and emotional values resulting in promises about unique and welcomed experiences, interest is growing in the importance of sustainable emotional values and the associated brand experiences. More managers are now seeking to harmonize the way that the values from staff contribute to the brand experience, integrating this with clever use of customer communications.

Within this context there are a notable number of organizations internationally that are adopting more corporate, rather than line-branding, strategies. This is not a strategy that emphasizes the name of the corporation; rather, it draws on corporate heritage to integrate a brand vision with an appropriate organizational culture that enthusiastically embraces the contribution staff make through being the living embodiments of the brand and thereby enabling customers to have trusted and welcomed experiences. Contributions to brand differentiation result from an amalgam of the way that employees' knowledge and skills contribute to *what* the customer receives (functional values) along with the way that employees' behaviour and feelings give rise to *how* the brand is received (emotional values). Competencies plus organizational culture are drivers of sustainable brand differentiation, which are being harnessed by forward-thinking, successful corporations. Brand management both defines an externally centred promise and considers how staff inside the organization can be orchestrated to ensure vibrant commitment to delivering the promise.

No longer are staff being recruited just because of their intellect and functional knowledge. In addition, they are being recruited according to the extent to which their values align with the values of the brands they will be supporting, and whether they wish to proudly strive towards the brand's vision. Customers are more sophisticated, and can see through staff who pay lip service to a brand's values, doing little more than acting out a branding role. They welcome interaction with staff who genuinely believe in what a brand stands for and are committed to its delivery. When co-ordinating the activities of individuals, less effort is demanded in supervising employees whose values align with their brand's values.

Brand management goes beyond solely focusing on customers, and is increasingly adopting a more balanced approach of satisfying stakeholders. The classical model of a source inside an organization instigating and controlling communication with customers has gone. Instead, customers learn about brands, amongst other ways, through communicating with their peers and other stakeholders, and by selectively using marketer controlled media; then they may decide with which parts of the organization they want to communicate. To ensure their brand is perceived as an integrated offering, managers are striving to ensure that staff speak and act with the same voice and spirit about the brand. By managers being more open with staff, providing them with more brand information, and through having the confidence to empower staff who are aligned with the brand's values, employees are more likely to present a coherent message about their brand. Moreover, by recognizing that the brand-building process starts at the staff recruitment stage and continues through the brand induction, training and appraisal stages, closer integration helps ensure a more coherent approach to internal brand management.

In the new branding world, where the challenge is co-ordination, brand management is less about a brand manager and rather about a brand's team. This may be composed of individuals with diverse functional backgrounds, representing a variety of departments inside and outside an organization. Successful brands are more likely to emerge when mechanisms are developed to ensure that all members of the brand's team have values that are aligned with the brand and differences in perceptions about the brand are rapidly surfaced and resolved.

Thus, this book is about:

• having a more balanced perspective that looks both inside and outside an organization to satisfy stakeholders' needs, and

- developing integrated brands through a planning process that seeks to bring about a brand vision through an appropriate organizational culture with stretching objectives, which results in a novel brand essence, coherently enacted to meet the regularly monitored performance metrics.

Workshops run internationally on the thinking contained in the first edition of this book showed that the ideas and the model for growing and strengthening brands worked. Regardless of the continent or the sector, managers spoke about the need for a holistic, pan-company approach to brand management that satisfied both internal and external stakeholders. These comments were also echoed in my classes with MBA and MSc students who were taking a career break to strengthen their management competencies. However, as time progressed, further research, learning from applying the ideas with managers, and the helpful feedback from key audiences stimulated the intention to revise the first edition. The result is a refreshed text that augments the principles of the first edition with new material. Each chapter has been updated, the examples, exercises and readings supplemented and new advertisements included.

Years of working with students (both undergraduate and postgraduate) and managers has brought home the importance of enabling them to internalize ideas. Explaining new concepts is part of the process, but another contributor is getting people to apply the ideas to particular problems. This book follows this philosophy by raising questions in the activities sections in each chapter, then proposing, in the discussion sections, possible ideas for moving matters forward. At the end of each chapter, exercises have been devised to enable readers put more of the ideas into practice.

This book is intended for both business school students and managers. It is grounded in a considerable literature that draws on numerous disciplines. By pulling on such a rich literature, it has been possible not only to acknowledge the work of many respected writers, but also then to build on this to develop the logic behind the systematic brand planning model. At the end of each chapter is a references and further reading section for those who wish to delve deeper into the supporting literature.

A theory is only as good as its applicability. As such, throughout this book there are examples and advertisements that strive to bring the material to life. Generalizability is a further consideration in the adoption of a brand-building model, and the ideas within this book can be applied in consumer, business-to-business, product and services sectors, as well as in both for-profit and not-for-profit sectors.

This book is divided into three parts.

Part One: The Changed Notion of Brand Management consists of the first two chapters, which lay the foundations for the move away from classical brand thinking.

Chapter 1 presents the case for managing brands by adopting both external and internal perspectives. A unifying definition of a brand is proposed and the move to team-based brand management is explored.

Chapter 2 reviews the spectrum of brand interpretations to enable people to realize that in the same organization there may be different interpretations of a brand, resulting in sub-optimal use of branding resources. It considers how different interpretations can be surfaced in order to have a more coherent approach.

Part Two: Planning for Integrated Brands focuses, in Chapter 3, on the need for an integrated branding programme. It considers instances where inconsistencies can arise in branding programmes and reviews some models to minimize inconsistencies. The sequential, iterative process for building and sustaining brands is overviewed.

Part Three: Employing the Brand-building Process goes through each block of the process for building and sustaining brands, explaining the key issues and considering their applications.

Chapter 4 focuses on the three elements of a powerful brand vision, i.e. an envisioned future, the brand purpose and the brand values. Ways to surface these three elements and encourage coherence are explored.

Chapter 5 acknowledges the impact organizational culture can have on the nature of the brand, considers how to characterize an organization's culture, discusses how to align staff with the desired culture and explores the culture characteristics associated with enhanced brand performance.

Chapter 6 discusses the importance of setting long- and short-term objectives, and the use of catalytic mechanisms to focus employees' attention on achieving these.

Chapter 7 reviews the five forces in the brandsphere that enhance or impede brand success, i.e. the corporation, distributors, customers, competitors and the macro-environment, and considers how to assess the favourability of these forces to capitalize on opportunities.

Chapter 8 considers how the core nature of a brand can be summarized through the five levels of the brand pyramid, and a crisp statement of the brand essence. Alternative models are presented. The integration between the brand pyramid and the brand's positioning and personality is discussed.

Chapter 9 explores some of the factors critical to ensuring the brand promise comes true. Mechanistic then staff implementation considerations are reviewed. The detailed form of the brand is clarified using the eight components of the atomic model of the brand.

Chapter 10 considers how a brand's progress can be evaluated.

Acknowledgements

I am most grateful to Karen Duffy, who provided superb secretarial support, and for the assistance Susan Cottam provided in selecting relevant press advertisements.

The ultimate thanks go to my wife Carolyn and to our daughter Gemma and son Russell, who gave me their gift of time to complete this new edition.

Professor Leslie de Chernatony

About the author

Leslie de Chernatony is Professor of Brand Marketing and Director of the Centre for Research in Brand Marketing at the Birmingham Business School, University of Birmingham, Edgbaston, Birmingham B15 2TT, England. Prior to his academic career he spent seven years working in the marketing departments of various major blue-chip organizations. He is Visiting Professor at Thammasat University in Bangkok and the University of Lugano in Switzerland and held a Visiting Professorship at the Madrid Business School.

With a doctorate in brand marketing, Professor de Chernatony won several research grants that have enabled him to lead a team investigating the factors and processes associated with successful brands. He has numerous articles on brand management in European, American and Asian journals, and is a frequent presenter at international conferences. His papers have won best paper awards in journals and at conferences. Leslie's other books on brand management include *Creating Powerful Brands*, published by Elsevier (with Professor M. McDonald), and *Brand Management*, published by Ashgate. His books have been translated into Chinese, Polish and Slovenian.

A Fellow of the Chartered Institute of Marketing and a Fellow of the Market Research Society, he acts as a brand consultant and has advised organizations internationally about more effective brand strategies. He runs acclaimed brand management workshops throughout the UK, Europe, North America, the Middle East, Asia and the Far East. Leslie is an experienced expert witness in commercial and competition cases involving brand issues that have gone to court.

Leslie can be contacted at L.dechernatony@bham.ac.uk

Part One

The Changed Notion of Brand Management

Chapter 1

A balanced perspective on brands

Summary

The purpose of this chapter is to introduce the reader to the concept of brands from both the external perspective as well as the internal perspective. It opens by showing that brands are valuable to both organizations and customers. In essence brands are clusters of functional and emotional values, and traditionally brand management has taken an external focus, concentrating on meeting customers' needs. With the growth of the services sector and the greater interaction between customers and staff, this chapter argues for a more balanced perspective on brand management, in particular aligning employees' values with the brand values so they are able and committed to deliver the brand's values. A unifying definition of the brand is advanced, and key aspects of this definition are explained. Finally, the move to team-based brand management is explored.

Why the interest in brands?

If this business were to be split up, I would be glad to take the brands, trademarks and goodwill and you could have all the bricks and mortar – and I would fare better than you.

(John Stuart, Former Chairman of Quaker Oats Ltd)

This quotation is an apt way of opening a book about brand-building, since it makes the point that brands are valuable assets and if they are well managed they can provide a guaranteed stream of future income. By reading the business press, you are no doubt aware of the financial value of brands. As Interbrand (Perrier 1997) showed, there are three types of assets that provide the sources of earnings: tangible assets, brands and other intangible assets (for example, for an airline this could be landing rights at particular airports). Depending on the market, up to 70 per cent of the earnings can be attributed to the brand (Lindemann 2003).

Well-managed brands drive respected reputations and, as Fombrun and van Riel (2004) have documented, favourable reputations result in higher financial returns. Stakeholders grow to respect strong brands. In a time-pressured society, if a brand has consistently delivered satisfaction its customers are likely to become confident that they can minimize their search activity, abdicating choice to a low cluster of brands per category. In part this explains why Ed Burke, former CEO of Johnson & Johnson, was quoted as saying 'A brand is the net present value of the cumulative trust that the owners' past marketing efforts have earned from consumers.'

Through well-conceived and effectively managed brands, firms are able to build favourable reputations which enhance the confidence of staff, buyers and users. Even in times of difficulty, firms reap the benefits of well-developed brands. As John Charlton Collins once remarked, 'In prosperity our friends know us; in adversity we know our friends.' Powerful brands such as Mars and Tylenol quickly regained their dominant positions, not only due to the rapid actions of recall programmes after discovering illegal tampering had taken place in the production process, but because of the respect these brands had built up through years of careful nurturing.

The problem is that some corporations overlook the value of a brand's reputation, failing to realize that trust takes time to build and needs to be managed. Customer confidence results from repeated brand interactions characterized by consistency and a perception that the brand cares for the customer. On one occasion Coca-Cola didn't give sufficient attention to trust and was slow to recall its products in Belgium, where people were becoming ill after consuming a batch that did not meet the corporation's strict guidelines. Larkin (2003) estimated that the tardy product recall reduced the brand's performance by $103 m and dented consumers' trust in the brand.

Brands don't just command respect because of their value to corporations. They do so because they add to the quality of life.

Think about the type of clothes you wear or the car you drive. These are making non-verbal statements about you as a person. People choose brands not just because of their utility, but because for some products and services they project aspects of the users' personalities. Think about when you wander through a museum and how seeing particular brands helps you to define that period of society – for example, the way that in the 1950s the Hoover vacuum cleaner started to lift the burden of house cleaning, the way that the Mini added a sparkle of excitement to driving in the 1960s, the Filofax added a new twist to diary management during the 1980s, the Apple Mac made a statement about users' creativity in the 1990s and eBay changed the rules of buying and selling in the new millennium. Consider how brands help people perpetuate their particular beliefs. When people give donations to specific charities, it is not just to appease their feelings of sorrow or even guilt. They give to particular charities because they believe more strongly in the *values* of that charity rather than competing charities. Think about how brands help people feel more at ease with others through the cultural norms they reinforce – for example, giving Moët et Chandon champagne at a celebration party. Also think about the way that brands act as pressure groups (such as Greenpeace, Co-op Bank), helping people to push for a better environment through their 'economic voting behaviour'. Anholt and van Gelder (2003) show how brands can contribute to a better society through improved working conditions for employees and investing in local communities.

A balanced perspective on brands

The theory of brand-building is couched within marketing theory. It has been argued by Vargo and Lusch (2004) that a new dominant logic for marketing has emerged, shifting the focus from tangible to intangible resources, from frozen value to co-created value and from transactions to relationships.

Brands are powerful entities because they blend functional, performance-based values with emotional values – so while the Jaguar may compete with other brands of cars on the rationally evaluated performance value, it may be bought because of the emotional value of prestige. When a newly appointed director was asked why he had chosen a Jaguar as his company car, the importance of the emotional value can be appreciated from his reply: 'because I can'.

As is becoming more apparent to many organizations, brands' unique functional values can soon be understood by competitors, who are capable of not just emulating the functional advantage, but also then surpassing it. To lever their brand investments, once managers have created consumer trust in their brand's functional superiority, they then seek to build consumers' appreciation of particular emotional values. However, it is stressed that to thrive, firms must ensure their systems deliver the desired level of functional-based satisfaction. Barwise and Meehan (2004) have argued that many organizations have not taken sufficient care in delivering the necessary category of functional levels of satisfaction in their quest to offer differentiation through emotional values.

In view of the importance of values it is worth clarifying this term, which will be covered in greater depth later in this book. One of the clearest definitions of values is from Rokeach (1973: 5), who defines a value as 'an enduring belief that a specific mode of conduct or end-state of existence is personally or socially preferable to an opposite or converse mode of conduct or end-state of existence'. Examples of a brand's functional values could include security, creativity, convenience, simplicity and adaptability, while examples of emotional values might include integrity, dignity, friendliness, conservatism and independence. One of the reasons for the interest in values is that consumers choose brands on the basis of the way these values fit their lifestyles and enable them to satisfy their needs.

Traditionally, advertising has been a particularly powerful way of communicating a brand's functional values, as well as building and communicating its emotional values. In an era where the services sector exceeds the importance of the manufacturing sector, people's impressions of brands are more strongly influenced by the staff they interact with. Their behaviour, style of dress, tone of voice, beliefs and attitudes create a picture in consumers' minds about the brand's values. The difference between competing brands in today's environment is not so much based on 'what customers receive' (i.e. functionalism) but rather on 'how customers receive it' (i.e. placing more importance on emotional values). Historically CEOs were seen as the embodiment of brands, yet today all staff, particularly customer-facing staff, are the brand's visual representations, influencing customers' views about how they are receiving the brand. While advertising remains a powerful brand-building and communicating tool, the challenge firms face is ensuring that their staff deliver the promises expected from the advertising.

Southwest Airlines is a good example of a corporate brand which realized that if the externally advertised promise of the brand is about offering greater freedom (through travel), this needed to be not only understood by staff, but also enacted through the way the organization internally echoed to its staff the concept of freedom. A series of projects were undertaken with staff. Freedom was interpreted inside the organization to relate to health, financial security, work–life balance and learning, amongst other factors. New policies were instigated to support these aspects of the organization, and an internal programme was run around the theme 'Freedom starts with me'. By taking an external promise and translating it internally so staff understood it, the staff were more committed to delivering the promise. Alas, there are organizations that devise innovative external promises but don't put the effort into translating these internally to enable staff to understand and become committed to their delivery.

Traditionally, firms have emphasized the importance of knowledge and skills when recruiting staff, since these are key in delivering functional values. Yet if staff are the visual manifestation of brands, their individual values will be perceived as those of the brand. One of the challenges of brand management is ensuring that staff have values that concur with those of the firm's brands. It is difficult to shift someone's values, and firms such as First Direct have developed staff recruitment policies that place considerable emphasis on recruiting staff whose values align with the brand's values. Training can enhance the ability of staff to deliver the functional values, but to enable the emotional values to be genuinely delivered, rather than superficially acted out, recruitment policies need to be based on alignment between staff and brand values.

Thus brand management, or managing promises, is not primarily about focusing on customers. Instead, a more balanced perspective is needed by also focusing on staff. If staff are genuinely committed to a set of values, they are more likely to deliver the brand's promise. By contrast, where firms place more emphasis on telling their staff about desired values, employees will be less committed and will be regarded as actors; consumers will see through these phoney values, losing confidence in brands.

Successful branding through bridging the external promise internally

From earlier research (de Chernatony and Dall'Olmo Riley 1998) it was concluded that every brand exists by virtue of a continuous process whereby senior managers specify core values that are enacted by the organization's staff, and interpreted and redefined by customers whose changing behaviour influences managers' views about more appropriate ways for staff to live the brand's values. A brand therefore represents a dynamic interface between an organization's actions and customers' interpretations. It can be regarded as a cluster of functional and emotional values which promises a unique and welcomed experience. The success of a brand depends on the extent to which there is harmony between the managerially defined values, effective implementation of values by staff and appreciation of these values amongst customers.

This perspective of a brand is universally applicable across contexts within which offerings (e.g. corporations, countries, politicians, products, services, etc.) are branded. In each case, the value-providing and value-seeking interactions lead to ongoing interactions between staff and external stakeholders. As Ambler and Barrow (1996) noted, longevity of these interactions depends upon favourable associations driving stakeholders' perceptions about the trustworthiness of the organization delivering their promise.

From this perspective, the characteristics of a brand can be appreciated through the brand triangle, shown in Figure 1.1.

When someone chooses a brand (whether the stakeholder is a potential car customer, or a new graduate assessing career options) they are initially concerned with rationally assessed functional values, then with emotional values. In the case of a consumer assessing a car the key functional value may be the car's power from a technologically advanced engine, and for a graduate evaluating a corporation it may be the firm's commitment to training. The rational values are linked to emotional values which in the case of the car may relate to confidence, and for the prospective employee could be responsibility. To simplify the brand, a promise is proposed to stakeholders enabling them to rapidly

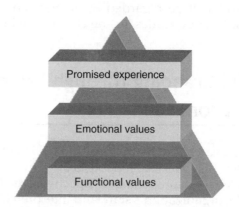

Figure 1.1   *Brand triangle*

appreciate, at a holistic level, how the brand can enhance their experience. Thus the promise to the car consumer may be that of an exciting form of transport, while for the corporation targeting new graduates it could be a growing career.

The brand triangle has categorized values at the two levels of functional and emotional values, since this facilitates a rapid appreciation of the brand's characteristics and reflects the way other researchers and consultants characterize brands. The model is influenced by Park *et al.*'s (1986) functional, emotional and experiential views about the brand concept.

A brand's strength is influenced by the extent to which the internal and external components of the brand triangle are congruent. For example, an outdoor clothing company may have durability as one of its functional values. Consumers appreciate this because the clothing doesn't easily tear, and staff welcome this value because they enjoy being part of a team that survives against harsh competitive pressures. The associated emotional value of caring appeals to consumers, since they enjoy feeling that the firm has their wishes at the heart of its activities. Likewise, staff are grateful for a corporate policy that cares for their well-being. The promised experience for the consumer from these two values is confident progress, specifically strengthening their confidence to walk in the less frequented mountain areas. Likewise, the promised experience for staff is also confident progress, in this case the enhanced certainty of developing a long-term challenging career. Due to the way that the management team has worked to align the internal and external interpretation of the brand, it does not suffer from schizophrenic characteristics – there is a continual linkage between the internal and external components of the brand.

Thus, to encourage brand success, managers should not focus solely on characterizing their brand externally. Rather, they are more likely to gain staff commitment if they consider how the brand triangle translates into the internal environment and then devise internal strategies to enable staff to understand better the desired brand promise, just as Southwest Airlines did. By aligning the external promise internally there is a greater likelihood of the desired brand promise being delivered.

Staff and brand-building

By thinking about brands as both external and internal flags, managers have banners around which they can stake a claim to a particular promise, and then use the flag to rally staff. This can make everyone aware of the type of behaviour expected of them. The flag's unique design represents the cluster of values characterizing the brand, and thereby the culture of the organization, which helps everyone to act consistently in a particular manner. As staff become more geographically dispersed the culture acts as an invisible glue, linking disparate employees and enabling them to deal with customers in a similar manner, based on their adherence to an internalized set of values.

Staff look to strong leaders for guidance, and powerful brands are characterized by enthusiastic leaders who have a passionate belief in a few values. By managers not just talking about these values but also living them, employees appreciate how genuine these values are and are more likely to be committed to delivering them. An example highlighting this was provided by Kotter and Heskett (1992: 71). It is one thing to exhort staff to satisfy customers, but if staff are to be committed to this value they need to see managers acting in this way. When Coors introduced a newly designed can-top, customers complained. Its response was to tell its distributors, 'since we produce the best beer available, we are confident that our customers will find a way to get round it'. This type of management response does not fit comfortably with claims about satisfying customers, and would not instil enthusiasm for customers amongst staff.

Placing more emphasis on internal brand management through aligning the staff's values with brand values minimizes the often cited problem of variable quality between employees. It facilities unified behaviour and minimizes surprises as customers encounter variants on the brand promise from different employees. A further advantage of shifting the focus of brand management and looking inside the organization is that it gives rise to a corporate persona with a deeply felt set of values, enabling the brand to have a clear attitude. Increasingly, consumers want to know more about what's behind a brand, to see if the corporation has principles. Classic examples of organizations developing their brands internally include the Co-operative Bank, the Body Shop, Walt Disney and Hilton International. For these companies, years of internal debate have led to a clear set of values providing principles about how staff should behave when delivering the brand's promise. These deep-rooted values give brands distinctive attitudes that attract customers who empathize with these.

Our journey in this book takes a more balanced perspective regarding brand-building, as it bridges the external and internal perspectives. The journey will be a planned one with a route map to appreciate how to grow brands. As Chapter 3 shows, a systematic process has been devised that indicates the stages involved in creating and sustaining strong brands, and this book will explore each of these stages. This, however, does not reduce branding to 'painting by numbers' since, while it covers the sequential blocks of activities, it still necessitates creativity within each block to give the brand its magic sparkle. However, before we travel through the different stages of the systematic process of brand-building, the concept of brands needs clarifying.

The multifaceted nature of brands

Research has shown that brands are multifaceted concepts, and to talk about 'a brand' sometimes overlooks the richness of this concept. A particularly useful tool that helps managers to appreciate the nature of brands is the 'branding iceberg'. In workshops, managers are asked to define the term brand and their comments are written on a whiteboard to stimulate discussion. Depending on the managers present, possible comments might include 'they are names or logos used to differentiate a firm's offering', or 'they are a guarantee of a consistent level of quality'. An iceberg (as in Figure 1.2) is then drawn, with 15 per cent visible above the water and 85 per cent invisible beneath the water, and the comments are placed above or below the water level according to their customer visibility. This enables at least two points to be made. The first is that managers often talk about the visible part of brands (the name or logo) rather than the unseen value-adding processes inside the organization that give brands their competitive advantages. The comment about the brand being 'a guarantee' comes about because, particularly for product-based

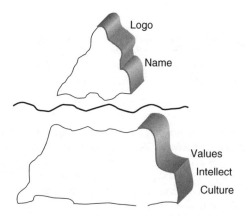

Figure 1.2   *The branding iceberg (after Davidson 1997)*

brands, the organization has systems unseen to the customer that ensure reliable quality levels. The second point is that when probing to identify the elements below the water, these start to encompass not just marketing factors but also company-wide factors such as committed staff, a well-respected research and development department, helpful customer services staff, well-conceived logistics process etc. It is only by taking a planned perspective that the roles of these diverse domains can be integrated to ensure the brand is a holistic entity, whereby the claims implicit in the visible components are backed by the invisible systems. This is why this book is concerned with a planned approach to brand-building. Unless everyone in the organization is aware of precisely what the brand stands for, there is a danger that staff in different departments may be pulling in different directions. As the RMS *Titanic* found, there is a significant impact from the unseen part of the iceberg, and it behoves management to ensure that the brand's strength is not diluted through an unco-ordinated series of internal activities. Furthermore, there need to be checks to ensure integration between the externally advertised claims for the brand and the understanding, ability and commitment of staff to deliver these claims.

The exercise can be concluded by getting the managers to recognize that two critical assets, internal to the organization and unseen by consumers, are the core competencies and organizational culture that shape the brand. The core competencies enable the managers to preserve the brand's functional advantage and to devise the positioning strategy using the brand's functional values. The organizational culture characterizes the corporate personality that enables the brand's team to develop a personality strategy for their brand, metaphorically representing the brand's emotional values.

Activity 1.1

Think about a brand in your organization, or one you have experience of. Why might the strength of that brand not be at its maximum?

Discussion

There could be a pensions brand that makes the claim externally of being simple to understand and simple to purchase. Yet if the managers inside the organization are infrequently in contact with consumers, what the managers regard as being 'simple' may not match consumers' views. By running internal workshops with staff from different departments, their views about what 'simplicity' means can be surfaced and debated, and a consensus view reached about how to enact this brand claim. For example, amongst the sales team, simplicity could mean spending longer listening to consumers and then providing straightforward information and uncomplicated products. For the IT staff, simplicity could mean developing computer systems that their internal customers find simple to use. In the case of the HR department, simplicity could mean planned induction programmes that enable new staff to recognize that one of their roles is to consider how they can make any consumer communication simpler to understand.

As will be explored in more detail in Chapter 2, there are several different interpretations of the brand, and brand strategists often draw on a number of ideas in their conceptualizations. The definition that is adhered to in this text was originally devised by de Chernatony and McDonald (2003), based on both the academic literature and numerous branding workshops over the years with senior managers and graduate students.

The definition subscribed to is:

> *A successful brand is an identifiable product, service, person or place, augmented in such a way that the buyer or user perceives relevant, unique, sustainable added values which match their needs most closely.*

> (de Chernatony and McDonald 2003)

The definition starts by focusing on *successful brands*. To develop a brand takes time and money, and is in effect an investment which, if properly managed, should produce healthy rewards. Unfortunately some organizations do not take a sufficiently long-term view of brand-building and, because they do not achieve rewards early on, cut back on investment. In fact, in markets where there are powerful retailers with strong own labels some manufacturers have taken a short-term view on their brand investment, been unable to achieve sufficient returns from their brand and changed their brand strategy to become an own-label supplier to the retailer.

The next important term in the definition is *identifiable*. There are many roles brands play – for example, building confidence or enabling consumers to communicate, non-verbally, aspects of their personality to others. However, there has been a tendency for managers to stress rapid identification. The reason for stressing brands as being effective recognition devices, and therefore differentiating devices, arises in part because of the confusion with the term 'trademark'. A trademark is any sign capable of being represented graphically that is capable of distinguishing one organization's goods or services from another's. As Blackett (1998) notes, this could consist of words (e.g. Kodak), letters (e.g. RTZ), numbers (e.g. No. 5), symbols (e.g. the leaping jaguar of Jaguar Cars), signatures (e.g. Ford) or shapes (e.g. the pyramid shape of Toblerone chocolate). What differentiates a brand from a trademark is the presence of functional and emotional values.

Organizations need to work hard to encourage consumers to associate a trademark with their brand. Powerful examples include the 'swoosh' of Nike, the 'golden arches' of McDonald's, the briskly walking gentleman of Johnnie Walker, Michelin's Bibendum character, and the BMW roundel.

Some organizations have registered the shape of their brand or its container as a trademark and have used this in their advertising so that when seeing the shape the public then associates this with a cluster of values. The most well-known example of advertising drawing consumers' attention to a shape and reinforcing the link between the shape and brand values is the Coca-Cola bottle. The challenge is not just to create awareness of the trademark, but also to then make effective use of communication opportunities to link the trademark with the brand's values.

Other organizations have registered their logos as trademarks and display these in their brand advertising to facilitate the association consumers are being encouraged to make between the logo and the brand values. Furthermore, the logo is often selected to be congruent with the nature of the brand. Examples of this are Microsoft's 'window', BT's 'trumpeting and listening person' and Shell's 'seashell'.

Where an organization develops a trademark that is descriptive of the brand (e.g. Timex) or focuses on the appearance of the brand (e.g. the 'mountain' shape of Toblerone), the organization educates the trade and consumers by continually featuring the trademark in all forms of promotional activity. In the early stages of the brand's launch there is an emphasis on facilitating the trade and consumers in appreciating how the trademark links back to the values of the brand. Subsequent promotional work reinforces the recognition and association of the trademark with the brand. By contrast, where the trademark is an invented logo that does not automatically relate to the brand category, or is a non-descriptive word, considerably more emphasis is needed in the promotional activity to raise the public's awareness of the trademark and to aid the public's association of the trademark with the brand and its values. Having created this knowledge amongst the public, the organization can then reinforce awareness and appreciation of the trademark.

Regardless of the form of the trademark (e.g. word, shape or logo), it must be prominently displayed – whether in advertising, packaging, point-of-sale material or the product itself. The challenge is to use all the communication tools (e.g. advertising, packaging, etc.) not only to gain consumers' awareness of the trademark but also to then link the trademark with the brand's values so that consumers recognize the brand as being distinct and make the desired associations between the trademark and brand values.

Brands can be based around *products*, as exemplified by Coca-Cola, which over a number of years has been estimated to be one of the most valuable global brands (Lindemann 2003).

In developed economies, *services* typically account for nearly three-quarters of the GDP. For example, the UK services sector accounts for over 70 per cent of production income and almost 80 per cent of employment. Some services organizations are awakening to the importance of brands, seeking to learn from the experience of marketers in product sectors. Successful services brands are emerging through adding value to the consumption experience – for example, British Airways striving for a seamless service in their global alliances, or American Express with their emphasis on global service.

However, in 2004 only 28 per cent of the Interbrand top 100 global brands were services brands. Part of the reason for the low proportion of services brands has been the historical reliance on the brand-building models that have worked so well in the fast-moving consumer goods sector. These place significant emphasis upon customers, as they can rely on internal quality-control systems that are geared to consistently delivering functional attributes from manufacturing processes. As is now becoming more evident (de Chernatony *et al.* 2003), services brands need to be based on models that take a more balanced view, looking at both employees and customers. More work is being done to recruit staff whose values align with the brand, to educate staff about the brand, and to help staff consistently deliver the desired brand values. This more balanced perspective is a theme that this book explores.

Brands have been built around *people*. David Beckham's football success has attracted many corporations' interest, and he has been used to endorse a variety of brands whose values align with his. In America, the marketing activities supporting political parties as they fight election campaigns draw on the values of their party's leader. It is now increasingly common to see politicians, pop stars, company chairs and entertainers being groomed by advisors to ensure their success as brands.

Places such as countries and cities have been, and are being, developed as brands. One only has to think of the way that the images of countries add to the image of product categories to recognize the importance of place branding – for example, French perfume, Scottish whisky and German cars. However, one of the challenges is to ensure that the stereotypical perception of a place does not become outdated. With the economic revival of cities or countries, and political changes, key stakeholders may be difficult to attract owing to their views regarding the place's image not matching its identity.

Anholt (2003) developed a model to help appreciate the brand characteristics of places, and a modified version of this is shown in Figure 1.3. Certain places have built a reputation for a particular category of brands – for example, Japan and consumer electronics, Stilton and cheese, and Cambridge with its university colleges. Places are differentiated by the foreign and domestic policies they follow – for example, Moscow versus Washington. The strategies places follow to attract particular types of commerce lead to different commercial images – for example, the hi-tech perception of 'Silicon Valley' in California. Locations have engendered particular cultures, in part influenced by the heritage legacy; examples include Stratford-upon-Avon and Shakespeare's plays, and Sri Lanka with the population's love of cricket. Finally, each place attracts a different type of person – consider the chic, affluent, fun-loving residents of the London suburb of Chelsea, and the time-pressured, action-driven people in the City of London.

When developing places as brands, some of the key issues include identifying how a brand promise can be developed that matches the aspirations of all the interested stakeholders, then ensuring a consistency of delivery. Inherent in this process is the tension that is likely to occur – for example, between the tourist authorities working to project an image about environmental splendour, and the government's desire to attract particular industries.

Schultz (1999) presents an interesting example of how Hawaii benefited from managers developing a clear understanding of it as a brand. During the late 1990s, Hawaii's tourism declined due to economic problems in Asia and Japan. To respond to this, the

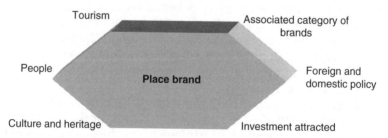

Figure 1.3 *Understanding a place's brand characteristics (adapted from Anholt 2003)*

Hawaii Tourism Authority was challenged with developing an integrated brand strategy. Numerous groups, such as hotels, resorts and retailers, were trying to get tourists' attention, often promoting Hawaii differently.

The process started by identifying the Hawaii brand as being a superior holiday based on natural beauty, diversity of experience, and the warmth and hospitality of the 'Aloha Spirit'. A programme was then developed for the tourism and travel business community, explaining the nature of the Hawaii brand and helping them to understand their roles in delivering the brand promise to meet visitors' expectations – for example, development and training seminars were held in departure cities to enhance knowledge and enthusiasm amongst travel agents. Those agents who passed an examination received continuing education and accreditation as Hawaii Destination Specialists. This entitled them to newsletters, familiarization trips, database-building programs, and receipt of qualified consumer referrals from enquiries to the Hawaii Visitors and Convention Bureau call centre and website matched by postal code.

Readers particularly interested in destination brands might also like to read Morgan and Pritchard's (1999) consideration of Wales and Australia as brands.

To move from a commodity to a brand, the core offering needs to be *augmented with values* that staff strive to reinforce. If a branded washing machine has the functional value of reliability, there should be a coordinated, integrated approach within the organization to deliver this promise. Thus it is not just a case of the R&D department developing a leading-edge self-diagnosing fault chip that displays a number on the panel for the consumer to then inform the service call centre; it should also encompass an effective system that enables an engineer to visit the customer, with the appropriate replacement part, within twelve hours of the customer's call to the service call centre.

The definition talks about *relevant* values, since in some organizations the values and the implementation of these values are more relevant to managers than to consumers. Sometimes values are stated in such generic terms that they become problematic – for example, quality. To a consumer looking at brands of kitchen furniture, quality may relate to the type of material used, the aesthetics and the fit of the different items. Yet talking on one occasion to a director of a firm manufacturing kitchen kits revealed a different view. His interpretation of quality was that if any of the items were dropped from a height of four metres, they should not break. While he was devising quality-control tests around this view of quality, his lack of contact with consumers was leading the organization to develop the brand with a poor match to its consumers' needs.

Activity 1.2

Take one of your organization's brands, or a brand with which you are familiar. Identify some of its brand values, then consider how these values have been implemented from the perspective of staff and consumers.

Discussion

An example here is a DVD brand that comes with a remote control. One of the values is 'modernity'. From the consumer's perspective, this relates to the equipment incorporating the most up-to-date technology – which therefore leads to quality recordings and some time elapsing before the brand needs replacing because the technology is outdated. A clue about how the organization interprets this may be found from the remote control, which has so many features and buttons that it appears to be targeted at NASA scientists! Unfortunately, for some consumers this enactment of the brand's value results in extra features that are not particularly welcome.

Another key word in our definition is *sustainable*. With a much deeper understanding of technology in product-based brands and better appreciation of process delivery in service-based brands, it is difficult to sustain a brand's functional values for notable periods of times. One has only to consider the continual leapfrogging in the PC market to appreciate the problem of sustaining functionalism. Alternatively, in the case of the airline market, think about the short time that British Airways had the advantage of its automated checking-in booths before other airlines, such as SAS, introduced similar booths.

It is more difficult to copy a brand's emotional added values. Starbucks Coffee has become a successful business not just based on its obsession with excellence in coffee, but also because of its values of trust and community. This has generated what Howard Schultz, Chairman and CEO, describes as a 'third place' – i.e. a location between work and home that has become a gathering place. The inspiration for this chain came when Schultz was on holiday in Italy and was struck by the sense of community in Italian cafés. To reinforce this experience, staff (or, as Starbucks calls them, partners) are trained to understand thoroughly the nuances of coffee and to become inspired to help deliver what Schultz refers to as 'an extension of people's front porch'. It is a great testimony to the power of employees as ambassadors for this brand that contributes to its sustainable emotional values.

Structuring to manage brands

One of the most common ways of structuring a department to manage brands was the brand management system devised by

Procter & Gamble in the 1930s. Under this system, a manager was made responsible for a low number of brands. Managers acted as central coordinators for all the marketing activity supporting their brand, and had responsibility for developing and implementing the brand marketing plans. However, the 1990s proved particularly challenging owing to such factors as more sophisticated, demanding and micro-segmented consumers, the growth of multimedia technologies, new distribution channels, and globalization. The traditional brand management system was not sufficiently able to respond to these challenges, and many firms reorganized the way they structured their departments.

A common theme in this restructuring was the move to brands being managed by teams rather than individuals. The popularity of a team-based approach to brand management arises from the notion that improved performance is more likely to occur from the group's combined capabilities to identify and solve problems. The precise structure of the team varies by organization – for example, George *et al.* (1994) identified structures whereby integrators are appointed because they understand the drivers of brand profitability. These integrators work across the value chain to develop customer-focused brand strategies, and lead cross-functional teams responsible for implementing these strategies.

Veloutsou and Panigyrakis (2001) showed that while the brand team can be regarded as consisting of internal (e.g. from marketing, sales, production, HR and finance) and external (e.g. advisors from consultancies) staff, a more helpful categorization is that of strategists/implementers, supporters, facilitators and incidentals. The strategists/implementers are the heart of the team and, as the name implies, devise the strategy and direct the team. The supporters, typically R&D, HR and production, provide the necessary resources for the brand. The facilitators, e.g. market research and finance, provide *ad hoc* services. The incidentals are an extension to the core team, e.g. legal advisors, joining for specific tasks.

Whatever the structure adopted, the multidisciplinary team operates on a boundary-spanning basis, coordinating and transmitting information so value can be created. Members of the team jointly lobby for resources and act as catalysts for change, reflecting the increasingly demanding needs of experienced customers. Ancona *et al.* (2002) have identified that teams are likely to succeed if they:

- don't just focus their activities internally, but also take heed of the dynamic external environment
- have extensive ties internally and externally
- operate through three types of team membership – i.e. the core tier devising strategy, the operational tier undertaking

the ongoing work, and the outer-net tier joining the team for *ad hoc* projects needing specialized expertise
- have flexible membership, with people leaving and joining over the brand's life
- employ effective coordination mechanisms, such as integrative meetings, transparent decision-making and shared timelines.

The team approach is better suited to today's more competitive environment, and should be able to respond faster and in a more coordinated manner. Throughout this book reference is frequently made to the 'brand team', to reflect this form of brand management. The larger number of people working on the brand provides a more comprehensive representation of their organization's competencies. However, as explored in Chapter 2, because of the larger number of people directing and implementing the brand strategy there is a greater likelihood of diverse assumptions about the nature of their brand – and unless these differing assumptions are surfaced, all the departments may not be pulling together.

Conclusions

Brands are valuable to organizations and customers. Their wealth-generating capabilities result from the way organizations seek to add value to customers' lives. Essentially, brands are clusters of functional and emotional values. Traditionally brand management has focused externally, seeking to understand customer behaviour so that a unique mix of values can be devised to enhance customers' lifestyles. However, with the growth of the services sector and the importance of service in product-based brands, customers' increased levels of interaction with staff provide them with a powerful clue about brands' values. It is therefore argued that a more balanced perspective is needed, whereby brand management is as much about managing the brand internally (i.e. the role of staff) as it is about managing it externally (matching customers' needs). As staff are seen by customers as a manifestation of the brand, it is important they have the knowledge, skills and organizational support to deliver the functional brand values. Furthermore, by recruiting staff who genuinely believe in the brand's values, and therefore have their values aligned with those of the brand, managers need to enable these committed employees to behave in a way that reinforces the desired emotional values of the brand.

Brand management, or promise management, entails adopting a planned programme that bridges the staff's capabilities and enthusiasm with the customers' expectations. Effective brand management is about harnessing the organization's values and intellect in such a way that a unified value-enhancing process can deliver a sustainably unique offer that customers welcome from both a rational and psycho-social perspective. As a result of the pan-company approach needed to build and sustain brands, a team-based approach is commonly seen when firms structure their brand management processes.

Brand marketing action checklist

This chapter contains ideas and frameworks that can help organizations to strengthen their brands. To capitalize upon your brand's potential, undertaking some of the following exercises can be beneficial in helping you to put these ideas into practice.

1. Taking one of your organization's brands, write down what you believe, in order of importance, are your brand's functional and emotional values.

   Brand ....

Functional values	Emotional values
1.	1. ....
2.	2. ....
3.	3. ....

   Do each of the functional values support the emotional values? For example, does talking about a washing detergent that uses an abrasive agent to get clothes clean, then regarding one of its emotional values as caring, raise doubt about internal brand consistency?

2. For the same brand, find job advertisements and further particulars used to recruit staff to work on the brand. Do the advertisements and the paperwork supporting these posts talk about the types of values staff should have? In view of the benefits of having staff whose values concur with those of the brand, if you are not taking applicants' values into consideration during the recruitment process, there is an opportunity to consider doing so.

   From the job advertisements and any further particulars about the job, write down what appear to be the three key functional values and the three key emotional values being sought from the applicants, in order of importance. If you have problems eliciting these, talk with other colleagues.

Brand ....

Staff's functional values	Staff's emotional values
1.	1. ....
2.	2. ....
3.	3. ....

Now compare the values you have elicited about staff with those of the brand. Do the same values emerge? Are the priorities the same?

If there is a situation where there are differences between the most important values of staff and of the brand, this is indicative of a pressing need for action to ensure greater alignment.

3. Take on the role of a 'mystery shopper' and experience the various encounters involved in being a customer. Complete the grid below, starting with the very first encounter (1) and continuing with each subsequent encounter in chronological order until the brand purchase has been completed.

Brand ....

Encounter	Title of employee interacted with	Implications about brand's values
1.		
2.		
3.		
4.		

Reflect upon:
- the extent to which there is congruence between the inferred values across all the encounters
- the degree of congruence between the most frequently noted values from these encounters and the brand's values, as stated in the brand plan.

If there are discrepancies, it is worth undertaking more of these mystery shopper events through a market research agency to gain a better appreciation of the size of the problem and undertake suitable corrective action.

4. By liaising with colleagues who are responsible for arranging induction and training programmes, evaluate what is being done to help staff to understand the brand's values and to behave in a way that supports them.

Are there:

- 'credit cards' with the brand's values that are given to all new staff?
- short videos and brief brochures that clarify the brand's values?
- workshops that present scenarios of interactions with customers and force employees to play out a particular response, after which these actions are debated to appreciate whether the employee response reinforced the brand's value?

5.   Arrange for your team to meet, preferably in a room away from their desks. Take one of your brand's values and, using a flip chart, write this clearly. Then ask your team what this value means in terms of their day-to-day behaviour. Write each of the comments on the flip chart without any evaluation. Once all the replies have been obtained, choose one of the comments and discuss it, seeking agreement amongst your team about whether this really supports the brand's value. Use several examples to encourage debate, which should enable the team to appreciate desired brand-supporting styles of behaviour. Undertaking this activity on a regular basis, discussing the other values, is one way of enabling the team better to support the brand.

6.   Convene a workshop with members of the brand's team to identify the core values of your brand. In the workshop, ask your colleagues to think back over time and to identify serious challenges and crises that the brand has faced. Record the challenges/crises with approximate dates on a flip chart. Ask the group what brand actions were taken for each of these individual challenges, and again record these on the flip chart. For each of the actions, consider what values underpinned them. After this questioning, a grid should emerge as below:

Challenges/crisis (with date)	Actions taken	Values underpinning the responses
1.	....	....
2.	....	....
3.	....	....
4.	....	....

Try to group similar categories of values together, then consider the following:

- What are the frequently emerging values?
- Do these values concur with the espoused brand values?

The fact that the organization has acted in a particular way says more about the importance of the emergent (rather than the espoused) brand values. This exercise elicits the emergent, rather than espoused, brand values. These emergent values have guided managers' strategies, and by surfacing these values the team has a better appreciation of their taken-for-granted views regarding the brand's values. A debate should resolve the issue of what the real values of the brand are.

References and further reading

Ambler, T. and Barrow, S. (1996). The employer brand. *Journal of Brand Management*, **4** (3), 185–206.

Ancona, D., Bresman, H. and Kaeufer, K. (2002). The comparative advantage of X-teams. *MIT Sloan Management Review*, **Spring**, 33–9.

Anholt, S. (2003). Branding places and nations In *Brands and Branding* (Clifton, R. and Simmons, J. eds). London: The Economist.

Anholt, S. and van Gelder, S. (2003). Branding for good? In *Beyond Branding* (Ind, N., ed.). London: Kogan Page.

Barwise, P. and Meehan, S. (2004). *Simply Better*. Boston MA: Harvard Business School Press.

Blackett, T. (1998). *Trademarks*. Basingstoke: Macmillan.

Clifton, R. and Maughan, E. (eds) (2000). *The Future of Brands*. Basingstoke: Macmillan.

Davidson, H. (1997). *Even More Offensive Marketing*. London: Penguin.

de Chernatony, L. (1993). Categorising brands: evolutionary processes underpinned by two key dimensions. *Journal of Marketing Management*, **9** (2), 173–88.

de Chernatony, L. and Dall'Olmo Riley, F. (1998). Defining a 'brand': beyond the literature with experts' interpretations. *Journal of Marketing Management*, **14** (5), 417–43.

de Chernatony, L. and McDonald, M. (2003). *Creating Powerful Brands in Consumer, Service and Industrial Markets*, 3rd edn. Oxford: Butterworth-Heinemann.

de Chernatony, L., Drury, S. and Segal-Horn, S. (2003). Building a services brand: stages, people and orientations. *The Service Industries Journal*, **23** (3), 1–21.

Fombrun, C. (1996). *Reputation: Realizing Value from Corporate Image*. Boston MA: Harvard Business School Press.

Fombrun, C. and van Riel, C. (2004). *Fame & Fortune*. Upper Saddle River NJ: Pearson Education.

George, M., Freeling, A. and Court, D. (1994). Reinventing the marketing organisation. *The McKinsey Quarterly*, **4**, 43–62.

Heskett, J. (1987). Lessons in the service sector. *Harvard Business Review*, **March/April**, 51–61.

Katsanis, L. P. (1999). Some effects of changes in brand management systems: issues and implications. *International Marketing Review*, **16** (6), 518–32.

Kotler, P. and Gertner, D. (2002). Countries as brand product and beyond: a place marketing and brand management perspective. *Journal of Brand Management*, **9** (4–5), 249–61.

Kotter, J. and Heskett, J. (1992). *Corporate Culture and Performance*. New York: The Free Press.

Larkin, J. (2003). *Strategic Reputation Risk Management*. Basingstoke: Palgrave Macmillan.

Lindemann, J. (2003). Brand valuation. In *Brands and Branding* (Clifton, R. and Simmons, J. eds). London: The Economist.

Lovelock, C., Vandermerwe, S. and Lewis, B. (1999). *Services Marketing*. London: Prentice Hall.

Low, G. and Fullerton, R. (1994). Brands, brand management, and the brand manager system: a critical–historical evaluation. *Journal of Market Research*, **31**, 173–90.

Morgan, N. and Pritchard, A. (1999). Building destination brands: the cases of Wales and Australia. *Journal of Brand Management*, **7** (2), 103–18.

Park, C., Jaworski, B. and MacInnis, D. (1986). Strategic brand concept – image management. *Journal of Marketing*, **50**, 135–45.

Perrier, R. (ed.) (1997). *Brand Valuation*. London: Premier Books.

Rokeach, M. (1973). *The Nature of Human Values*. New York: The Free Press.

Schultz, D. (1999). IMC in Hawaii: no plan is an island. *Marketing News*, **13 September**, 18.

Vargo, S. and Lusch, R. (2004). Evolving to a new dominant logic for marketing. *Journal of Marketing*, **68** (1), 1–17.

Veloutsou, C. and Panigyrakis, G. (2001). Brand teams and brand management structure in pharmaceutical and other fast moving consumer goods companies. *Journal of Strategic Marketing*, **9**, 233–51.

Chapter 2

The diverse interpretations of 'brand'

Summary

The purpose of this chapter is to explain the variety of interpretations about brands. Building on interviews with leading-edge brand consultants, the diverse interpretations of brands are clarified, according to whether the interpretation is predominantly input-based (i.e. facilitating managers' plans to use resources more effectively), output-based (i.e. customers' interpretations) or time-based (reflecting brands' evolutionary processes). Drawing on knowledge management, a process is described to enable managers to surface their individual interpretations of their brand and, through reaching consensus, identify more coherent brand-supporting processes.

Spectrum of brand interpretations

A review of the literature and interviews with leading-edge consultants advising clients about their brands showed a variety of interpretations about brands (de Chernatony and Dall'Olmo Riley 1998). Table 2.1 shows the variety of interpretations encountered that will be considered.

To facilitate appreciating the variety of interpretations, these have been placed into three categories. The categories are based on whether the perspective is input-based (i.e. stressing branding as a particular way of managers directing resources to influence

Table 2.1   *Different interpretations of 'brand'*

Input perspective	Output perspective
Logo	Image
Legal instrument	Relationship
Company	*Time perspective*
Shorthand	Evolving entity
Risk reducer	
Positioning	
Personality	
Cluster of values	
Vision	
Adding value	
Identity	

customers), output-based (i.e. consumers' interpretations and consideration of the way brands enable consumers to achieve more) or time-based (recognizing their evolutionary nature).

Brands are complex offerings that are conceived in brand plans, but ultimately they reside in consumers' minds. Brands exist mainly by virtue of a continuous process whereby the co-ordinated activities across an organization concerned with delivering a cluster of values are interpreted and internalized by customers in such a way that enhances their existence and, through the organization responding to feedback, enhances the likelihood of brand success. Figure 2.1 shows how the unified nature of brands evolves through balancing the input and output perspectives on brands.

If a brand is conceived solely in terms of either an input or an output perspective, this can lead to an unbalanced strategy

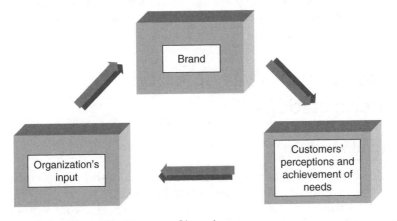

Figure 2.1   *The unified nature of brands*

and weaken the chances of longevity. Just as marketers are active participants in the branding process, so are consumers, who are far from passive recipients. As was once so lucidly argued by Meadows (1983), branding is not something done to consumers, but rather something they do things with. Brands are perceived in a particular way by consumers, sometimes differently from that intended by marketers. They take on meaning because of the way they enable consumers to perform different roles.

The success of the Apple brand is not just due to its 'input' activities through proclaiming 'Think different' in its advertising. Rather, because also of an 'output' perspective it liberates consumers to enhance their lifestyles through enabling them to use its PCs and iPods in ways which consumers tailor for themselves.

The model of the unified nature of brands in Figure 2.1 provides the foundation for brand management through minimizing gaps. With a clear appreciation of the vision for the brand, a cluster of functional and emotional values can be devised and delivered through co-ordinated, pan-company processes. This leads to the development of a positioning statement to communicate the brand's functional values, and a personality to act as a metaphor for the brand's emotional values. Ideally, these should be perceived by customers as congruent with their self-image, matching their functional and emotional needs and thus generating goodwill from a trusted relationship that grows customer confidence in the brand over time. By monitoring customers' perceptions of the brand, the organization's input can be either rectified, closing any gaps with customers' perceptions, or reinforced through stressing the issues of particular relevance to the target customers.

In view of the points raised so far, one of the characteristics of a healthy brand is that the brand's team has a conceptualization of the brand that encompasses several of the themes in Table 2.1. Some of these themes are overlapping, as will become evident.

Input perspectives on brand interpretations

Brand as a logo

One of the more established definitions of a brand was proposed by the American Marketing Association (AMA) in 1960. This stresses the importance of the brand's logo and visual signifiers primarily as a basis for differentiation purposes, i.e.

> *A name, term sign, symbol or design, or a combination of them, intended to identify the goods or services of one seller or group of sellers and to differentiate them from those of competitors.*

The unique shape of Coca-Cola's bottle, the distinctive 'golden arches' of McDonald's, the blue and white roundel of BMW and the spectrum-coloured, part-eaten apple of the Apple PC are notable examples of brands instantly identifiable through their logos.

Organizations invest considerable resources on their logos as they become powerful recognition devices, speeding brand selection. Good logos, as Henderson and Cote (1998) argue, should:

- speed brand recognition through provoking memory
- give rise to recognition about a familiar set of associations linked to the correct brand
- favourably influence a brand selection decision.

While this interpretation represents an important ingredient of brand-building, it should not be the primary emphasis. Brand differentiation is more than making a brand distinctive – at its most basic, it's finding an attribute important to customers and then seeking to sustain this unique characteristic in a profitable manner. Developing the logo for the brand should be done strategically, rather than tactically. In other words, the vision of what the brand is to become should drive ideas about the core essence of the nature of the brand, which should then be used as the brief for designers. Whether the colour or the type of font is appropriate can then be judged against how these will help the brand on its journey.

Brand as legal instrument

One of the simpler interpretations of a brand is that of ensuring a legally enforceable statement of ownership. Branding represents an investment, and thus organizations seek legal ownership of title as protection against imitators. As part of its brand strategy, Absolute Vodka stresses the importance of continually monitoring competitors' brand activity, so it can quickly stop any firm adopting the name or bottle design.

It is estimated (Browne 2005) that counterfeit goods account for nearly 7 per cent of world trade, ranging from spare parts for cars and aeroplanes, to mobile phones, clothes, music and pharmaceuticals. Growth in counterfeiting is in part due to the popularity of Internet shopping, which makes it easier to pass fakes off as originals.

Effective trademark registration offers some legal protection for brands, as discussed in Chapter 1, but 'look-alike' own labels in retailing exemplify the problem of being over-reliant on legislation as a barrier against competitors (e.g. Davies 1998; Lomax *et al.* 1999). Kapferer (1995) devised an innovative procedure to help evaluate the extent to which a competitor is infringing a brand's equity. Consumers are invited to sit in front of a PC screen and are presented with an unfocused picture of the packaging of the copycat product. They are asked if can state what the brand is. Then, in an incremental manner, the picture gradually becomes clearer. At each step of increasing clarity, consumers are asked if they can state the brand. The measure of confusion is based on the proportion of consumers who state they have seen the original brand when actually they have seen the copy.

Various other ways to assess consumer confusion between the authentic brand and a look-alike have emerged (Mitchell and Kearney 2002). Shoppers have been interviewed at the point of sale immediately after purchasing a look-alike, but before consuming the brand. Another approach has been to show respondents pictures of pairs of products for several seconds and ask for rating of similarity, probing to reveal consumers' perceptions of similarity. The fact that there are such diverse methods reflects the way that each court case is judged within its particular context.

Brand as company

One way of considering the nature of a brand is to think about the spectrum shown in Figure 2.2.

At one extreme is corporate branding, where any branding is solely based on the corporation. This is typically seen in financial services (e.g. AXA, HSBC), where the corporation dominates in any branding strategy and where the corporate values are thought capable of stretching across the diverse product groups. At the other extreme, the brand has a unique name and is not easily recognized as being associated with a particular corporation. For example, Ariel Color washing powder and Fairy Liquid washing detergent are both from Procter & Gamble, while Cif and Comfort are both from Unilever. This can only be appreciated by looking

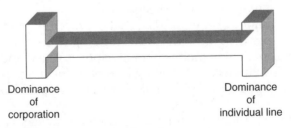

Dominance   Dominance
of   of
corporation   individual line

Figure 2.2   *Corporate versus line branding*

carefully at the label. In this case, managers believe there is so little synergy between the corporation's values and the different clusters of unique values for each of the individual brands that, rather than diluting the values of the corporation, the individual brands are free-standing. Between these extreme positions exist brands that place differing emphasis on seeking corporate endorsement.

Considering a corporate brand solely from a nomenclature basis overlooks the rich meaning of this concept. A corporate brand is a projection of the amalgamated values of a corporation that enable it to build coherent, trusted relationships with stakeholders. Besides unifying staff, a corporate brand signals expectations to staff about desired forms of behaviour through a set of values that bond an organization. A successful corporate brand flags to stakeholders a set of principles that the organization stands for and that add value to the ongoing relationships.

If the corporate brand has gained respect from its stakeholders it leads to a partnership mentally, whereby each stakeholder does not take a price-driven, short-term transaction perspective but rather adopts a more flexible attitude, recognizing that both parties need a win–win outcome. From time to time either the corporation or its stakeholders entrusts a process or a decision to the other party, confidently knowing that the principled corporation's behaviour will be consistent with its espoused values.

Corporate brands stand for something that is unique to each corporation. They have strong leaders who nurture value-adding communities. Transparency is critical in gaining a sense of fairness and community. No single stakeholder should be seen as adopting a 'power stance', dictating the agenda; rather, a more balanced perspective is adopted, based around targeting and attracting stakeholders who welcome similar values to those of the corporation.

Ultimately, corporate brands should inspire staff to treat their stakeholders in a consistently similar manner. The outcome should be stakeholder confidence in extending their purchasing to a broader range from the seller's portfolio. By being focused on understanding what the corporate brand stands for and the way it projects its values, external stakeholders and staff should gain pride from their partnered approach to growing each other.

For a variety of reasons there has been a move towards corporate branding – for example, the need to curtail the increasing costs of promoting individual line brands; as a response to increased distributor power; to engender greater stakeholder confidence; and the prevalence of category management, where priority is given to promoting product sectors to retailers rather than individual line brands. Mitchell (1997) provides a more complete picture. We have moved from the industrial age, which stressed tangible assets, to the information age, which seeks to exploit intangibles such as ideas, knowledge and information. The new branding model is therefore one that emphasizes value through employees' involvement in relationship-building. Internally brand management is becoming culture management, and externally it is customer interface management. In the new branding model, corporate branding internally signals messages about the desired culture and externally it reduces the information overload problems from line branding, decreasing customers' information processing costs. Corporate branding facilitates consumers' desires to look deeper into the brand and assess the nature of the corporation. A further reason for corporate branding is that, through building respect and trust with one of the corporation's offerings, consumers are more likely to accept the corporation's promises about other offerings.

Corporate branding thus provides the strategic focus for a clear positioning, facilitates greater cohesion in communication programmes, enables staff better to understand the type of organization they work for, and thus provides inspiration about desired styles of behaviour.

Managing corporate brands needs a different approach to classic line branding. Individual line branding primarily focuses on consumers and distributors, and few staff interact with consumers. By contrast, corporate branding is about multiple stakeholders interacting with many staff from numerous departments, and important objectives are ensuring a consistent message and uniform delivery across all stakeholder groups. In line branding, consumers mainly assess the brand's values from advertising, packaging, distribution and the people using the brand. Yet in corporate branding, while values are partly inferred from corporate communication campaigns, stakeholders' interactions with staff are also important.

In the early days of some corporate brands (e.g. Virgin, Body Shop and Walt Disney), strong-personality entrepreneurs had a philosophy about their brand making the world a better place and recruited staff with similar values to theirs. With a low number of staff in regular contact with each other, stakeholders were likely to perceive a consistent corporate brand. Success resulted in growth and more staff. The more successful firms communicated their brand philosophy through a culture that enshrined particular core values, allowing peripheral values and practices to adapt over time. New staff could appreciate from the culture how to contribute as brand-builders. In less successful corporations, new managers were uncomfortable with the issues of corporate culture and brand visions, and over time lost sense of their core values. New staff were less confident about the corporation's core values and different styles of behaviour evolved, causing disparate perceptions amongst stakeholders. These changes over time can be appreciated from Figures 2.3 and 2.4.

In corporate branding, staff are not only vital contributors to the brand's values, but also represent evaluative brand cues. As such, the HR director should be regarded a key member of the brand's team, since he or she devises policy that impacts on brand-building – such as recruitment, induction, training and reward systems. At Waterstone's, the marketing director's view is 'Recruitment is a branding exercise, it's part of the management of the corporate brand' (Ind 1998: 325). For successful

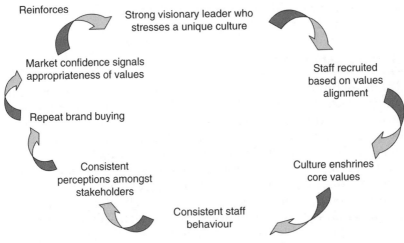

Figure 2.3 *The virtuous circle of corporate branding (based on Kotter and Heskett 1992)*

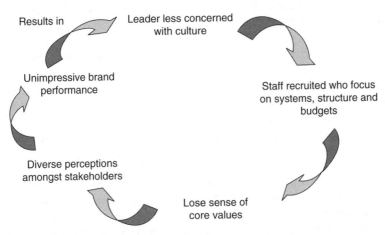

Figure 2.4 *The vicious circle of corporate branding (based on Kotter and Heskett 1992)*

corporate branding, staff must understand the brand's vision and be totally committed to delivering it, and greater emphasis should be placed on internal communication.

In corporate branding, the CEO is responsible for the corporate brand's health. The CEO's leadership therefore needs to enable all employees to recognize the importance of the corporation's core values. An advantage of focusing everything behind a common name is not only to provide clear direction for staff, but also to achieve a coherent focus for the portfolio and communicate a consistent message to all stakeholders. The disadvantage is that problems with the organization's reputation – for example, Shell and its controversial involvement in Nigeria in the 1990s – can taint the image of the whole portfolio.

Brand as shorthand

There are finite limits to our ability to seek, process and evaluate information. Yet surfing the web or considering other forms of advertising quickly makes us aware of the emphasis many organizations place on the quantity rather than the quality of information. To protect their limited cognitive capabilities, people have developed methods for processing such large quantities of information. Miller (1956) carried out research into the way the mind encodes information and his research, along with that of Jacoby *et al.* (1977) and Bettman (1979), helps us to appreciate what happens. If we compare the mind with the way computers work, we can evaluate the quantity of information facing a consumer in terms of the number of 'bits'. All the information on the packaging of a branded grocery item would represent in excess of 100 bits of information. Researchers have shown that the mind can only simultaneously process between five and nine bits of information.

To cope with the deluge of marketing information, the mind aggregates bits of information into larger groups, or 'chunks', which contain more information. An analogy may be useful. Novice yachtsmen learning Morse code initially hear 'dit' and 'dot' as information bits. With experience, they organize these bits of information into chunks (letters), then mentally build these chunks into larger chunks (words). In a similar manner, when exposed to a new brand of convenience food, the first scanning of the label may reveal an array of wholesome ingredients with few additives. These are grouped into a chunk interpreted as 'natural ingredients'. Further scanning may show a high price printed on a highly attractive, multicoloured label. This is grouped with the earlier 'natural ingredients' chunk to form a larger chunk, interpreted as 'certainly a high-quality offering'. This aggregation of increasingly large chunks continues until final eye scanning reveals an unknown brand name, but on seeing that it comes from a well-known organization (e.g. Nestlé, Heinz, etc.) the consumer then aggregates this with the earlier chunks to infer that this is a premium brand: quality content in a well-presented container, selling at a high price through a reputable retailer, from a respected manufacturer known for quality. Were a consumer not to purchase this new brand of convenience food, but later that day to see an advertisement for the brand, he or she would be able to recall the brand's attributes rapidly, since the brand name would enable fast accessing of a highly informative chunk in the memory.

The task facing the marketer is to facilitate the way consumers process information about brands, such that ever larger chunks can be built in the memory which, when fully formed, can then be rapidly accessed through associations from brand names. Frequent exposure to advertisements containing a few claims about the brand should help the chunking process. What is important, however, is to reinforce attributes with the brand name rather than continually repeating the brand name without at the same time associating the appropriate attributes with it.

Conceiving brands as shorthand devices forces managers to think about the way they emphasize quality of information rather than quantity of information in any brand communication. As our minds cannot cope with more than seven bits of information at once, one test to apply to any brand communication is whether there are more than seven bits of information contained in it. Furthermore, given the target market's experience and brand understanding, is the brand being presented in a manner whereby the communication reflects the understanding of the marketing team, rather than consumers? It is likely that the marketing team will have sophisticated capabilities to understand brands in the category, and may well be attentive to subtle distinctions. However, due to their lower levels of involvement and less well-formed heuristics to decode brand information, such detail may be lost on consumers.

Brand as risk reducer

When people choose between brands they do not always base their decision on choosing the brand that maximizes their utility, as economic theory suggests. Rather, there are situations where consumers perceive risk – for example, the perceived risk of friends disapproving of a particular style of clothing. It is not uncommon to find consumers choosing between competing brands according to the extent to which they perceive least risk. Bauer (1960: 389–98) was one of the first writers to suggest this notion, and a stream of research has since evolved showing the importance of perceived risk – i.e. the uncertainty consumers have that buying a particular brand will result in a favourable outcome.

While risk can be conceived as an objective concept, consumers use their perceptual processes to make any assessment. As such, due to their diverse backgrounds and the context in which they make assessments, it is likely that the perceived risk in choosing a brand will vary between consumers.

Customers perceive risk along several dimensions, such as:

- performance risk (will the brand meet the functional specifications?)
- financial risk (will the customer get good value for money from the brand?)
- time risk (will more time have to be spent evaluating unknown brands, and if the brand proves inappropriate, how much time will the customer have wasted?)
- social risk (what associations will the customer's peer group link with him or her as a result of the brand choice, and will this enhance or weaken their views about the customer?)
- psychological risk (does the customer feel right with the brand in so far as it matches his or her self-image?).

Brands are more likely to succeed when the brand team delves deeper to understand what dimensions of perceived risk customers are most concerned about. From this analysis a way needs to be found of presenting the brand to minimize customers' perceptions of risk along the dimensions that particularly concern them. For example, if research surfaced that potential car buyers were reticent about considering a new car brand because of its futuristic design, it would be wise to consider a communications strategy that seeks to reduce social risk through the use of peer group endorsement.

Activity 2.1

Scan advertisements to see how organizations are using the concept of the brand as a risk reducer, and evaluate which dimensions of perceived risk the brand is majoring upon.

Discussion

HP once ran a successful campaign for their PCs showing a picture of a man, balanced on his head, on a plank that was attached to the window almost at the top of a skyscraper. The caption read 'And for his next trick he'll buy a PC without proper support'. This campaign was concerned primarily with heightening awareness of performance risk, and presented the HP brand as a risk reducer.

Building trust through brands is a strategy many firms have followed. Dell's brand investment makes it difficult for new entrants to match the image they have for rapidly and efficiently fulfilling telephone and Internet orders. Buyers perceive risk when purchasing a new brand for the first time, and look for ways of reducing it. One way they reduce this is through trust in respected colleagues. Thus when a GP becomes aware of a colleague prescribing a new drug, and hears of its success, the GP is more likely to prescribe it.

To capitalize on the brand as a risk reducer, marketers should segment customers by similar risk perceptions. If any one of the segments has sufficient customers and if the firm is profitably capable of developing the brand as a risk reducer to meet the segment's needs, this strategy should be considered.

Brand as positioning

Another perspective managers adopt when interpreting brands is in terms of positioning, i.e. ensuring that customers instantly associate a brand with a particular functional benefit or a very low number of functional benefits – for example, BMW for performance and Volvo for safety. In the information age, people are bombarded with large amounts of data and choice. For example, it has been estimated that the weekend edition of a quality newspaper has more information than someone would have been exposed to during their lifetime in the seventeenth century. In a grocery superstore, the customer is faced with over 30 000 lines. To cope with this notable quantity of data, people's perceptual processes take over. In effect, these raise 'barriers' protecting the mind against accepting just any type of data, and perceptual vigilance then focuses attention on particular data that are selectively comprehended and retained in the memory. One of the implications of the perceptual process is that customers may interpret a brand in a different way from that intended by the organization. For this reason, some managers interpret a brand as a device that enables them to establish a key functional association in the customer's mind.

Successful brands represent a point of view, and their positioning reinforces this. For example, innocent, the healthy drink company that sells smoothies, questioned why healthy subsistence had to be dull and boring. The company stands for putting fun back into a healthy diet, with its frequently changing labels that are designed to raise a smile. Virgin is positioned as the challenger that questions whether consumers are being fairly treated, regardless of the market. Identifying a brand's differential advantage is but one part of a process that needs to establish the brand in the customer's mind.

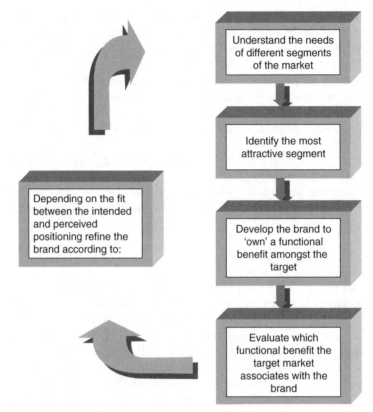

Figure 2.5   *A balanced perspective on brand positioning*

Good positioning is about anchoring a brand to a category so a consumer has a reference point. Within the category it is important that the brand then has the characterizing factors to be a valid part of that category. Thus for banks, a new entrant would need to match the security, performance and convenience that all customers expect. The issue then becomes finding a customer-relevant advantage that hopefully can be sustainably differentiated. It is here that First Direct succeeded with its refreshing approach to conversing with customers and being genuinely service focused.

There are several characteristics of a powerful brand positioning strategy. First, it should be centred ideally around one functional attribute or, if necessary, a couple, since the more attributes included the more difficult it is to get these registered in customers' minds. Secondly, it should be recognized, as Ries and Trout (1986) stressed, that positioning is not what is done to a brand, but rather what results in the customer's mind. In other words, it is myopic to just focus on brand development; rather, there should be a balanced perspective, evaluating what the customer registers about the brand, then fine-tuning the brand until there is better alignment between the intended positioning and the resultant positioning (see Figure 2.5).

Thirdly, the brand positioning should focus on functional benefits valued by customers, rather than those valued by managers. It is too easy to focus on features that have more to do with reflecting the organization's competencies, rather than taking time to involve the customer in the development process.

Activity 2.2

Consider a brand in your organization's portfolio, or one with which you and your team are familiar, and get the brand's team to write down the primary benefit members believe this brand delivers. Either using consumer insight reports, or through talking with consumers, identify the primary benefit customers are seeking. To what extent does your brand meet the customer's need?

Discussion

A tool that helps managers to appreciate the extent to which they have an effective brand positioning strategy is the matrix shown in Figure 2.6.

Following through from the activity, the brand team, or the key brand strategist, needs to identify the brands against which their own brand competes, then for all of these brands, including the organization's brand, they need to consider what the key benefits are that are being offered to the target market. By then referring back to the market research database, or undertaking some market research with customers, insight is provided about how much customers appreciate each of the benefits. By then plotting the location of the brand on the matrix, managers can evaluate the effectiveness of their brand positioning.

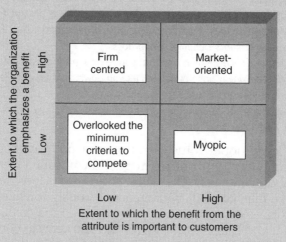

Figure 2.6 *Evaluating the effectiveness of the brand positioning*

In the two broad categories used to categorize brand interpretations, the interpretation of a brand as a positioning device has been grouped into the input perspective since this reflects managers' views of the brand as a strategic tool. For successful brand positioning there needs to be both an input and an output perspective.

Brand as personality

With advancing technology and sufficient investment, competitors can emulate and surpass the functional advantage of a leading brand. One way to sustain a brand's uniqueness is through enrobing it with emotional values, which users sometimes welcome beyond the brand's functional utility. Customers rarely undertake a thorough review of a brand to identify its emotional values, as can be appreciated from the early discussion about perceptual processes. By using the metaphor of the brand as a personality, manifest sometimes through a celebrity in brand advertisements, customers find it much easier to appreciate the emotional values of the brand. Furthermore, with experience of the brand, customers develop their views about the brand and to help them express this they personify brands. A good example of the way consumers personify brands, based on their opinions about their emotional values, is when British Airways and Air France stopped using Concorde in October 2003. An array of celebrities was invited onto the last scheduled flight, and Jeremy Clarkson then wrote:

> And what was that last flight all about? Why were so many people taking photographs and why, after 27 years, did every single one of Heathrow's 30,000 employees turn out to watch it do what it was designed to do?
> I like to think that a machine does have a heart and a soul. I like to think of them as ordinary people think of dogs.
> Think of Concorde as a dog that you've had in the family for 27 years. Think of the way it has never once let you down. And how thrilled it is when you feed it and pet it and take it out for a walk.
> And now try to imagine how that dog would feel if you locked it up one night. And never went back.

A brand's emotional values are also inferred from its design and packaging, along with other marketer-controlled clues such as pricing and the type of outlet selling the brand. However, it should be realized that, particularly for conspicuously consumed brands, people form impressions according to the type of people using the brand, and this is less easy for the marketer to control. There are some examples of successfully capitalizing on the people consuming a brand – for example, the launch of the alcopop drink

Hooch in Sweden. One of the emotional values of this brand is a distinctively independent attitude. In its early days, staff from the Swedish importer went to popular holiday skiing slopes and watched young skiers. Those who had a more flamboyant skiing style were approached and asked if they would like to invite friends to a party that evening at a local bar where Hooch was being promoted. This proved to be a successful way of getting the brand associated in its early days with people whose emotional values echoed those of the brand.

Interpretation of brands has given rise to a considerable amount of research into brands as symbolic devices with personalities that users welcome. When choosing between competing brands, customers assess the fit between the personalities of competing brands and the personality they wish to project, as shown in Figure 2.7.

According to the situation they are in, this may be

- the self they believe they are (for example, the brands of clothing selected by a manager for daily wear in the office)
- the self they desire to be (for example, the brand of suit worn by a young graduate going for interviews immediately after completing a degree)

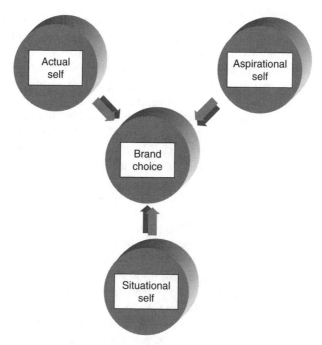

Figure 2.7   *Choosing a brand to match self*

- the situational self (for example, the brands of clothing worn by a young man who is to meet for the first time the parents of his fiancée)
- the rejected self (for example, rejecting an automotive brand because the consumer perceives it as being brash and does not want to have this type of association).

When seeking to communicate the emotional values of the brand, it is therefore important to understand the emotional role potential customers expect of the brand.

Brand as a cluster of values

In this interpretation, a brand is considered as a cluster of values. For example, Sir Richard Branson declared that the Virgin brand is a cluster of five values – quality, innovation, value for money, fun, and a sense of challenge. When evaluating the extension of the Virgin brand into new markets, at least four of the five core values must still be appropriate before the extension is authorized. Conceiving a brand as a cluster of values provides a basis for making the brand different from others. Thus while there are several brands of off-road four-wheel-drive vehicles, Land Rover is distinctive because of its values of individualism, authenticity and freedom.

One of the key reasons for the interest in values is because they influence behaviour, as can be appreciated from Figure 2.8.

As a result of the society and the peer groups people come into regular contact with, they develop their individual values. These lead to anticipation of particular types of outcomes, albeit varying by situation. For example, people with the value of honesty may leave their door unlocked at home because they live in close proximity with neighbours who share the same value, yet when staying in a hotel they lock the bedroom door because of uncertainty about the values of other guests. Ultimately, though, values affect brand choice.

Consider the example of a lady who has a value of wanting to be fashionable. She is going out for dinner with her husband, and will be meeting his colleagues for the first time. As such, when going through her dresses in the wardrobe her choice is based on rejecting those dresses that are over a year old, and because of the company she will be keeping she also rejects those that are not conservative in style. If at the end of the evening she is complemented on her good taste in clothes, this will reinforce her association between the chosen dress and the value of being fashionable. One of the reasons for the success of First Direct bank was because, in its early days, its values of customer respect,

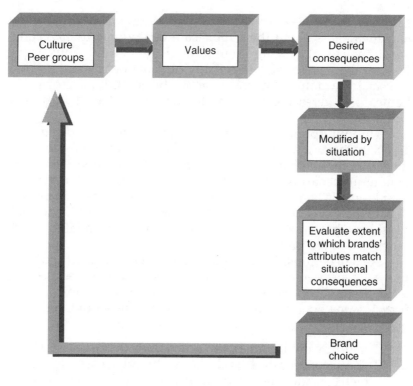

Figure 2.8   *How values influence behaviour (after Gutman 1982)*

openness and getting it right first time resonated with the values appreciated by numerous people.

The challenge managers face when interpreting brands as clusters of values is understanding which values are particularly important to their target market, then ensuring they are able to deliver these. If some staff do not believe in these values, this will show in their behaviour and consumers will change to another brand.

Brand as vision

Another perspective noted about managers' interpretations of brands is akin to a beacon whose rays provide a clear sense of direction for the traveller. In other words, brands are about a vision senior managers have for making the world a better place. As James Dean once said, 'Dream as if you'll live for ever, live as if you'll die today.' Within a brand's context it's a case of working to envision exhilarating futures then seeking to enjoy the challenge of bringing that future about. As a result of this vision, a role can be defined for the brand. Within this perspective, brand management is about the senior team taking time to envision a world they want to bring about through their brand. Thus Apple PCs are about enabling more creativity, Benetton is about a world of social harmony, Amazon is about bringing bookshops into homes, and Versace is about a pleasurable life based on beauty and joy.

This interpretation is more strategic, and its adoption is associated with a more courageous brand's team. Gone are incremental extrapolations, and instead the team takes time to envision long-term scenarios that they boldly want to bring about through their brand. When thinking about brands in these terms, managers debate the envisioned future they want to bring about, and then consider what they must do differently to enable them to unroll the future to the present.

As will be considered in more detail in subsequent chapters, the visionary perspective on branding is important because this is the first issue managers must address when developing a new brand. A powerful brand vision is one that consists of three interlinked components:

1. The future environment the brand aims to bring about
2. The purpose for the brand – i.e. the brand's reason for being, which considers how the brand will make its environment a better place
3. The values that will characterize the brand and enable it to satisfy the purpose.

Without a well-defined vision a brand could be in danger of drifting, and when faced with an unforeseen threat a short-term solution may result which could shift the brand's direction. A good brand vision spurs managers, staff and consumers towards greater things. Nike's consumer advertising campaign once proclaimed, 'You didn't win silver. You lost gold'. This is a good example of the way the brand vision encourages its stakeholders to set their standards high and stretch themselves.

Brand as adding value

This perspective on brands is akin to considering the extra benefits over and beyond the basic product or service that are added and which buyers value. These extra benefits could either be functionally based, albeit more difficult to sustain over time, or emotionally based. A functional example is provided by a garage in a commuting town north of London, which displays a banner proclaiming, 'We go the extra mile'. They do so through providing an extra service to customers who bring their cars to the garage for maintenance, driving their customers to and from the train station a mile away. By contrast, different brands of watches tell different stories about who the owner is. This emotional component of a fine chronometer can account for a notable part of the price.

Added value is a relative concept that enables customers to make a purchase on the basis of superiority over competing brands. It is about recognizing how new clusters of benefits from the brand enable customers to have greater gains relative to smaller increases in sacrifices (e.g. money, search time, etc.). It can also be judged by customers in terms of how the brand has improved over time – for example, the pleasant surprise a car owner experiences when trading in a car for a newer model of the same marque. Interviews with branding consultants (de Chernatony *et al.* 2000) showed that unless there has been a breakthrough in technology creating a new market, added values should not be conceived in terms relative to the core commodity form but rather relative to competition or time.

As a result of the saying 'value is in the eyes of the beholder', if a brand is to thrive then its added values need to be relevant to customers and not just to managers. For example, an engineer may believe that he or she has helped in the branding process by developing a computer chip which repeatedly tells an unbelted car driver 'your belt is not fastened'. Yet hearing caravanning enthusiasts say they would pay to have this removed as it's so irritating when jumping in and out of a car reversing a caravan onto a small pitch at a campsite provides some indication of its worth to customers!

One way to identify added-value opportunities is to accompany customers both on their shopping trip and when they are using the brand. This enables identification of the stages they go through when choosing and using a brand. By then talking with customers about each of the incidents, and getting them to identify what they liked and disliked, and how different brands provide different benefits at each of the stages, ideas begin to surface about ways of enhancing the brand.

Brand as identity

The concept of brand as identity has attracted the interest of researchers in marketing, organizational behaviour and strategy. Drawing on the review by Hatch and Schultz (2000), brand identity is the distinctive or central idea of a brand and how the brand communicates this idea to its stakeholders. Particularly when the organization brands its offerings with its corporate name, or the brand is strongly endorsed by the corporation, this involves a lot of internal 'soul searching' to understand what the firm stands for and how it can enact the corporate values across all its range. Managers and staff become engrossed in surfacing consensus about who the organization is and what it stands for. For example, Apple believes in increasing people's productivity through challenging inborn resistance to change. Its corporate identity of the bitten apple epitomizes this – the forbidden fruit with the colours of the rainbow in the wrong order. Communication is not directed just at consumers but also at staff, so they can appreciate how they must behave to be the embodiment of the brand.

This perspective of the brand is in sharp contrast to that of the brand as a 'legal instrument' and a 'logo', since the emphasis is on the brand as a holistic entity.

Regarding a brand as a 'logo' or 'legal instrument' leads to almost a checklist mentality regarding the elements necessary to create a brand, whereas an emphasis on the brand's identity encourages more integrated thinking about several component parts, as shown in Figure 2.9.

Central to any brand is its vision, which provides a clear sense of direction about how it is going to bring about a better future. Achieving this stretching future depends on a culture with staff who believe in particular values and managers who have a common mental model about how their market works and therefore how the brand must be developed. The core thinking behind the brand can now be translated into a positioning strategy that manifests the brand's functional values and a personality which brings the brand's emotional values to life. Underpinning all of this is a clear understanding amongst staff about the types of relationships they need to have with each other, with customers and with other stakeholders to enact the brand's values. If there is a unified form of internal behaviour, the organization can be more confident about presenting the brand to stakeholders with a design and promotional support that differentiates the brand in a manner which stakeholders welcome. Figure 2.9 shows the different interactions between the five components of a brand's identity, and the challenge for managers is to find ways of blending these components to gain maximum internal reinforcement.

This interpretation may help managers to reinforce a meaning behind a brand for consumers, and also to communicate the essence of the brand to other stakeholders. The concept of brand identity offers the opportunity to develop the brand's positioning better, and encourages a more strategic approach to brand management. A carefully managed identity system also acts as a protective barrier against competitors.

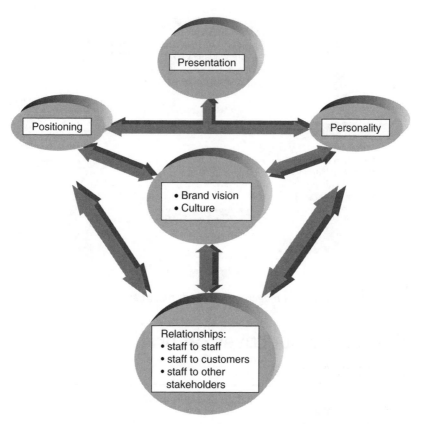

Figure 2.9   *The components of brand identity*

One of the weaknesses of this perspective is that managers focus on the internal aspect of branding, thinking predominantly about the desired positioning. Thought also needs to be given to the way customers perceive the brand, since their perception (brand image) may be different from the intended projection (brand identity). One of the problems with seeking to develop a brand through minimizing the gap between brand identity and brand image is that image refers to a customer's perception at a specific point in time and thus leads to short-term fluctuations. By contrast, reputation relates to perceptions about a brand over time, and as it is a customer-based measure it is more stable. Thus, brands could be managed by developing a brand identity, then regularly fine-tuning the brand identity components to minimize the gap with the brand's reputation amongst stakeholders, as shown in Figure 2.10.

These ideas about minimizing gaps will be developed in further chapters.

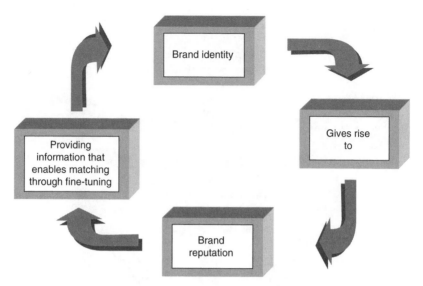

Figure 2.10   *Brand management through minimizing gaps*

Output perspectives on brand interpretations

Brand as image

People do not react to reality but to what they perceive to be reality. This perspective encourages a more consumer-centred approach to brands as the set of associations perceived by an individual, over time, as a result of direct or indirect experience of a brand. These may be associations with functional qualities, or with individual people or events. It is unlikely for two people to have exactly the same image of a brand (since no two people have the same experiences), but their images may have common features. These features constitute, for example, 'the sociable image' of a particular brand of beer.

Adopting an image perspective forces management to face the challenge of consumers' perceptions – i.e. owing to their perceptual processes, the sent message is not necessarily understood as was intended. It therefore necessitates checking consumers' perceptions and taking action to encourage favourable perceptions.

Evaluating a brand's image needs to take into consideration customers' levels of involvement with the category (Poiesz 1989). For those categories where customers are actively involved in spending time and effort seeking out and processing brand information, it has been argued (by, for example, Reynolds and Gutman 1984) that brand image relates to a network of information stored in the memory that helps the customers to define their self. As customers are so involved in the brand selection process, it is appropriate to use an involved procedure when measuring brand image – for example, the laddering technique within means–end theory. In this approach, customers are first asked what they see as being the difference between the brand in question and a couple of competing brands in the category. Having elicited a functional attribute, which acts as the anchor point, customers are asked why such an attribute might be important to them. They are then asked why this reason is important, and through repeatedly probing about why the reason is important a value emerges. While this takes time to administer, it provides a rich insight into the brand's image.

For low involvement categories, where customers habitually buy the brand or undertake minimal information searching, brand image is a holistic impression of the brand's position relative to its perceived competitors. To identify the brand's image a low involvement evaluation procedure would be appropriate – for example, mental mapping. Customers are asked which brands they believe a particular brand competes against. The brand under attention and the other named brands are then written on cards. These are shuffled and given to the customer, who is asked to arrange all the cards on a desk in such a way that those brands perceived to be similar are placed close to each other. After the way the cards are arranged has been photographed, the respondent is asked to explain the map, and from this insight is provided about the brand's image.

Brand as relationship

The interpretation of a brand as a relationship is a logical extension of the idea of a brand's personality: if brands can be personified, then customers can have relationships with them. Research (for example, Fournier 1998; Aggarwal 2004) has shown that relationships are purposive and enable both parties to provide meanings. Customers choose brands in part because they seek to understand their self and to communicate aspects of their self to others. Through engaging in a relationship, albeit briefly, customers are able to resolve ideas about their self and, with the brand metaphorically akin to an active member of a dyad, it helps legitimize the customer's thoughts about themselves. Within this perspective, managers consider how the brand's values should give rise to a particular type of relationship.

Activity 2.3

For a brand that you are familiar with, state its values. For each value, identify the type of relationship that the brand should be seeking to build with its customers.

Discussion

Table 2.2 shows the relationship implications for a brand with four values. Note that when the values reinforce each other, a consistent and coherent type of relationship is likely to emerge. Customers, particularly those with notable experience of the brand, expect consistency over time. However, as Aaker *et al.* (2004) showed, if a relationship of sincerity has emerged and the brand breaks with this, it is highly likely that consumers will break their relationship with the brand.

Table 2.2   *The consequences of values on types of relationships*

Values		Resulting relationship
Innovative	→	Trustworthy, confident
Team working	→	Co-operative, open
Caring	→	Friendly, altruistic
Fun	→	Informal, socially-oriented

The interpretation of brands as relationships enables managers to involve staff more in the branding process. Some people find the concept of brand values difficult to understand, but they feel more confident about the idea of describing relationships. One way of getting employees to consider the implications of their brand's values is to use a variant on the party game, 'in the manner of the word'. Members of a department are brought together and someone is asked to leave the room with their manager. That person chooses one of the brand's values and spends a few moments thinking about what this means in terms of the relationship they should be building with clients to reinforce the brand. They return to the room and in front of their colleagues mime a series of activities. As these are taking place, their colleagues shout out the value they think is being enacted and terms to describe the relationship. A facilitator writes on a flip chart what is being shouted, and the miming continues until the 'actor' feels someone has correctly mentioned both the value and the relationship implications being acted. Besides being a fun activity, it surfaces lots of assumptions about the brand's values and relationships. As staff have used their own phrases and their own scenarios, it enables their manager to build on their frames of reference and help them develop more appropriate relationships in their daily working tasks.

When considering what the relationship implications are from the brand's values, it is important to recognize that relationships come about because of reciprocal exchanges between at least two individuals. While the organization may wish to use its brand to develop a close relationship with its customers, these customers may prefer instead to have a more distant relationship. It is therefore important that once a relationship has been identified, research is undertaken with customers to evaluate their view about the desired relationship. Through understanding what customers want from a relationship and then revising the relationship strategy, there is a greater likelihood of brand success. This process is depicted in Figure 2.11, where a continual process

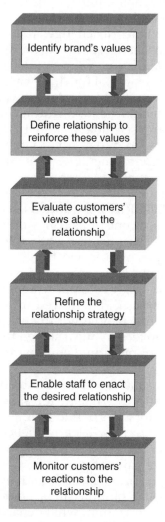

Figure 2.11 *The interactive process to develop a relationship which reinforces the brand's values*

of feedback is used to refine and better develop the brand relationship.

Time perspectives on brand interpretations

Brands are dynamic offerings. They have to evolve to reflect the changing demands of customers as they gain more experience, as well as continually maintaining a position of strength against ever-changing competition (de Chernatony *et al.* 2004). It is rare for a brand's core values to change; rather, it is the brand's peripheral values that change. Drawing the analogy with fashion, a designer-house brand's core values of decency and stylishness remain fixed, and the length of the dress varies over time – never transgressing a minimum length. A core value is one that the organization will remain true to, regardless of external changes. A peripheral value is a secondary value that the organization is not so strongly wedded to, and it serves a purpose within a particular set of external environments. As the environment changes, so the brand needs to make adaptations.

The evolving nature of a brand and the difference between core and peripheral values can be appreciated from HP. The corporate brand HP has, as one of its core values, serving everyone who has a stake in the business with integrity and fairness. Originally its business was in electronic instruments, and an implicit peripheral value arose associated with its core value – i.e. a paternalistic cradle-to-grave employment policy. As the business environment changed, HP moved into the computer market. It needed to recruit people with new competencies and to lose some of its employees. While it stayed true to its core values, the peripheral value of providing employment for life change to a less paternalistic approach.

The challenge for managers within the time-based interpretation of a brand is to be vigilant for signs of environmental change, then to identify ways of fine-tuning the brand. The long-term success of the brand will be influenced by the clarity of thinking inside the organization regarding what the brand's core values and peripheral values are.

There are several models of brand evolution. Goodyear (1996) believes market evolution can be understood in terms of a continuum of consumerization, which characterizes the degree of dialogue between marketers and consumers. Drawing on this she develops a chronological scheme for brands, as shown in

Figure 2.12. Specifically, she sees brands evolving from 'unbranded commodities' to 'references', where the name is used for identification. For example, in centrally planned economies, consumers came to use the factory code numbers on tyres as proxy for brands to identify the tyres produced by better factories. Brands then develop into a 'personality', offering emotional appeal besides product benefits – for example, safety for Volvo. A fourth development stage occurs as the brand acquires 'icon' connotations – for example, Levi jeans. Brands then progress to the fifth stage, where the status is 'brand as company'. Here the focus is on corporate benefits and integrated communication. The ultimate stage, 'brand as policy', stands for social, ethical and political issues relevant to consumers (for example, Virgin and the Body Shop).

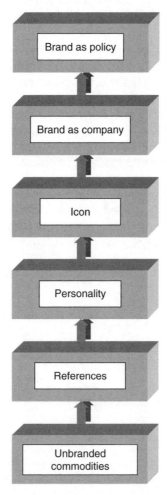

Figure 2.12　*Goodyear's (1996) chronological brand categorization*

Activity 2.4

Think about any brand you are familiar with and consider how it has evolved in this evolutionary process.

Discussion

Goodyear has developed a helpful model. By understanding the degree of market development it is possible to identify what type of brand a firm has, and then to consider possible strategies to defend it or to develop it to the next stage if appropriate. One should not anticipate that every brand has to start at the unbranded commodities phase — if the organization has an established heritage and if consumers already have experience of the product/service, then the brand can be developed to enter at a higher level. For example, when Virgin in the UK entered the financial services market, it took advantage of the iconic status of its founder, Sir Richard Branson, yet again striving, in almost a Robin Hood manner, to make people's lives better by simplifying and taking the risk out of buying pensions.

Another model of brand evolution is that developed by Kunde (2000), founder of the Scandinavian integrated marketing agency Kunde & Co. This model is shown in Figure 2.13. One of the arguments he puts forward is that as the values of a brand become stronger and more relevant to customers, so the brand becomes more involving, and thus managers need to make their brand values more relevant to increase customers' involvement. Within these two dimensions he conceptualizes a five-stage brand evolution process.

The weakest brands are referred to as 'product', which are offerings without any added values. Concept brands have emotional values, which engender greater customer involvement. With stronger values emerge corporate concepts, which are brands

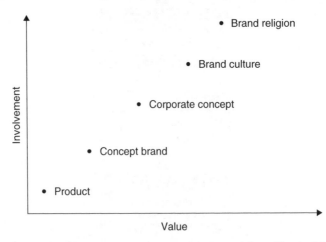

Figure 2.13   *Kunde's brand religion model (adapted from Kunde 2000)*

that fuse so well with the company that they are seen as totally consistent. With even more involvement and stronger value comes brand cultures, which are so strong in customers' eyes that they stand for the function they represent. The ultimate position in this model is the category 'brand religion'. Kunde describes this as 'to the customer they are a must, a belief' (Kunde 2000: 9), and cites Harley-Davidson as exemplifying this category.

Facilitating a company-wide integrated view about the brand

As a result of the backgrounds of all the staff, their experience, seniority and perceptual processes, it is likely that within the organization there are different interpretations of the organization's brands.

Activity 2.5

Using the different brand interpretations shown in Table 2.1, write down which interpretation comes closest to your view about how you conceive one of your company's brands. You may feel more comfortable having a few of these interpretations. Explain the interpretations to a colleague in your department and also to a colleague in a different department, then ask them to let you know which one (or ones) they use. Are there any differences?

Discussion

It is more likely that there would be more similarities between your view and those of your departmental colleague than between you and the colleague in the different department. This is due to the more frequent interactions you have with your departmental colleague, resulting in a greater degree of communication and thus a common understanding. It is not inconceivable that different departments have different cultures, and this can give rise to diverse brand interpretations.

Some differences will occur between all staff in an organization; however, problems occur when there are significant differences between departments. Such differences imply that each department is making different assumptions about their contribution to brand-building. Even though there may be a detailed brand plan about an intended strategy, if these differences are not surfaced the emergent strategy will be less effective as there is a lack of coherence in activities – which at worse may give rise to different departments pulling against each other. By taking time to surface the mental models that each member of the brand's team has about their brand, a more unified approach should emerge. By turning to the knowledge management literature, a process has been devised for the team to understand better each other's views.

To grow, organizations are continually capturing information about new technologies, new processes, changing customer expectations and new competitor initiatives. This information flow is converted into new knowledge and enables managers to make sense of their market through more sophisticated mental models, which helps them to develop more sophisticated brands. For example, with limited experience some managers may make sense of the competing brands of mortgages by categorizing them into a low number of clusters based solely on one attribute. By contrast, more experienced managers are likely to have a more sophisticated perspective, thereby categorizing competing brands according to the extent to which they have several attributes and developing their brand to exceed competitors on several attributes. With little interaction between managers, they are unlikely to share a common mental model about their brand and may be missing branding opportunities.

Knowledge can be categorized into two forms. Explicit (or codified) knowledge refers to knowledge that is transmittable in formal, systematic language. Tacit knowledge is personal, context-specific, and hard to formalize and communicate; it is embedded in personal experiences involving personal beliefs and values. To transform tacit to explicit knowledge, managers need to spend time together to develop and appreciate a mutually comprehensible brand metaphor that reflects the way they think (relating to the rational, functional component of the brand). With only basic branding knowledge and limited time for social interaction, the easiest and most efficient way to conceive the brand is to rely on explicit knowledge. In this case, managers use metaphors of brands as legal devices or logos, enabling both intra- and inter-organizational communication. However, this explicit knowledge represents only the tip of the brand knowledge iceberg, and the full potential of the brand is not being exploited.

Nonaka and Takeuchi (1995) argue that, with greater managerial interaction, more knowledge results from a conversion process passing through the following stages:

1. Tacit to tacit knowledge through socialization
2. Tacit to explicit knowledge through externalization
3. Explicit to explicit knowledge through combination
4. Explicit to tacit knowledge through internalization.

This process is shown in Figure 2.14. Applying this knowledge conversion process enables managers better to understand each other's views about the brand, and presents an opportunity for

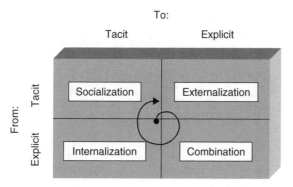

Figure 2.14   *Using knowledge conversion for brand-building (based on Nonaka and Takeuchi 1995)*

brand growth through capitalizing on some of the novel ideas that emerge.

When managers meet as a brand team to debate the future brand strategy and their long-term desires for the brand, their tacit knowledge becomes explicit, using more involved metaphors – for example, someone might say, 'if the brand were to come to life, its personality would be …' Over time, through further discussions, managers combine different facets of the brand – in other words, they convert one form of explicit knowledge to another form of explicit knowledge. This might be apparent from statements such as 'the updated personality from that new advertisement reinforces the race-loving image consumers have of the brand'. Through continuing interaction, managers develop similar mental models about the brand which they all take for granted, i.e. this becomes 'internalized', as explicit knowledge has been processed into tacit knowledge. At this stage of knowledge transformation more sophisticated interpretations of the brand result, enabling the organization to capitalize on its brand's capabilities. In effect, over time managers have the opportunity to go around the knowledge creation 'loop' and each time move up the brand knowledge spiral, as shown in Figure 2.15.

The early stage of this knowledge conversion process (i.e. tacit knowledge held by one person becoming the tacit knowledge of another person) is akin to an apprentice sitting next to the master to understand their thinking and knowledge. All members of the team working on the brand should be involved in this process – in other words, those inside the organization working in different departments, and external agencies advising and implementing brand strategy. Each member of the brand team is asked to 'shadow' another member, who may not necessarily be in the same department. After at least a day of being together the shadower should

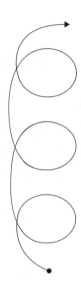

Figure 2.15   *Developing more sophisticated interpretations through managers going around the knowledge creation loop (based on Nonaka and Takeuchi 1995)*

begin to develop ideas about how the associate being shadowed interprets the brand, through actions and conversations. Taking time together, the shadower should explain to the associate how he or she thinks the associate conceives the brand, and a discussion about both their ideas should result in a brief statement of understanding, which is sent to the person co-ordinating this process.

This stage will have encouraged pairs of individuals to better appreciate their brand. It may have led to some degree of consensus, or hardened opposing views, but it will have made each member of the pair aware of the other's views. Having got the individuals to start to think about the problem of diverse interpretations, this can be further surfaced in the second stage. This is concerned with transforming managers' tacit knowledge to explicit knowledge that all the team can understand. Workshops need to be arranged with all members of the brand's team, to get them to surface their tacit knowledge regarding their interpretations of their brand. One way is to encourage them to bring in newspaper articles, radio broadcasts, tapes and CDs, and get them to cut out pictures, advertisements, words and stories that represent their brand. Individuals are then able to find their own brand language and, through discussion facilitated by the co-ordinator, colleagues are able to explore each other's 'story board', thereby enabling their tacit knowledge to become explicit.

One of the objectives for these workshops is for each group to agree upon a metaphor that represents their collective agreement about their brand. The individual tacit knowledge is then becoming explicit, and there is a move towards managers developing a shared mental model.

In the third stage (explicit to explicit knowledge), the views that have emerged from each workshop are combined to narrow the diversity in perceptions about the nature of the brand. One of the ways of doing this is for the summary metaphors from each workshop to be presented to a co-ordinating senior management team. The team then needs to assess:

- the extent to which brand interpretations are similar between groups
- the extent to which groups' brand perceptions converge with the goals set by the organization.

Examining the first of these helps managers recognize the degree to which their perceptions indicate they are pulling together, whilst the second provides insight about the chasm between senior managers' exhortations about the brand and team members' perceptions. A period of soul-searching is then required, to define the brand, to evaluate the extent to which everyone's ideas need changing (both the senior management and the brand's team), and to consider how to align everyone's views.

In stage three, an agreed senior management position regarding the nature of the brand needs to be decided, a metaphor conceived, and this communicated to the co-ordinator who will run the next series of staff workshops.

A new set of workshops then ensues to explore the metaphor for the brand and consider the diversity between this and each group's metaphor. The group has to consider how members' mental models and roles need changing to support the new metaphor. Different types of explicit knowledge are now being combined to develop a more unified approach not only to agreeing the brand interpretation but also to delivering the brand promise.

In the fourth stage (explicit to tacit knowledge), the new explicit knowledge will have been widely communicated and changes made to ensure a more coherent brand implementation process. Through managers continually seeking to congratulate and visibly reinforce new styles of behaviour, the focus is that of getting everyone to internalize their newly gained knowledge. The intention is that over time the new initiatives will become taken for granted and staff will automatically be thinking and acting in the new manner.

While this continual leveraging of knowledge may be regarded by some as a significant cost, it is an investment that is likely to produce healthy returns. By involving as wide a group as possible in debates about the nature of the brand and by getting

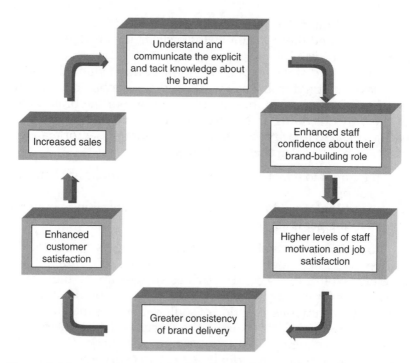

Figure 2.16   *Levering knowledge to build service brands (adapted from Heskett 1987)*

staff to appreciate how they contribute to its success, their commitment and job satisfaction is greater. As the Institute of Work Psychology (1998) has reported, firms with high levels of staff satisfaction show higher levels of profitability. Through the further knowledge they gain in this process, they are able better to deliver high levels of service quality and, as Heskett (1987) argued, this results in higher sales. Advancing the original model that Heskett developed, it can be appreciated from Figure 2.16 how knowledge can be levered to strengthen service brands.

Conclusions

Brands are complex offerings that can be interpreted in a variety of ways. They can be interpreted from an input perspective, as the way managers stress the use of resources to achieve a customer response, or from an output perspective, as the way customers interpret and use brands to enhance their personal existence. A third way of interpreting brands is one that recognizes brands as dynamic entities, evolving to meet changing environmental situations. It would be wrong to interpret a brand solely in terms of one of the eleven input or one of the two output perspectives. Rather, these differing interpretations should be seen as building blocks for a brand, and a balance needs to be struck between the way that some of the input perspectives help customers to achieve greater satisfaction in particular roles. A brand is thus an amalgam of interpretations.

To forge forward with a growth strategy for a brand necessitates a coherent view about the brand amongst all those involved in the adding-value process. Brands are the result of the way explicit and tacit knowledge has been levered. By understanding the transformation of knowledge that produces unique clusters of values, managers' assumptions about their brand can be surfaced and a consensus view reached about a more unified approach to supporting the brand promise.

Brand marketing action checklist

This chapter contains ideas and frameworks that can help organizations to strengthen their brands. To capitalize upon your brand's potential, undertaking some of the following exercises can help you to put these ideas into practice.

1. Table 2.1 shows the different interpretations of a brand, from which we then considered branding implications. The point was made that a brand is an amalgam of these interpretations. Take the eleven input perspectives and write onto the grid below, for those interpretations pertinent to your brand, what the implications are for supporting your brand.

Brand interpretation	Implications for brand strategy
(i) Logo	....
(ii) Legal instrument	....
(iii) Company	....
(iv) Shorthand	....
(v) Risk reducer	....
(vi) Positioning	....
(vii) Personality	....
(viii) Cluster of values	....

(ix) Vision   ....
                             ....
(x) Adding value   ....
                             ....
(xi) Identity   ....
                             ....

Do the actions you have identified on the grid support each other?

Get other colleagues who work on the brand to complete the grid. Collate the replies and identify any new ideas that have emerged. With your colleagues, consider how any of these new ideas might be used to grow your brand.

2. When reviewing the interpretation of brand as company, it was argued that having a naming strategy where the corporation dominates is appropriate when the corporation's values are very similar to those of the products and services that carry the dominating corporate name. There is a danger that over time it is just assumed that any new product or service will automatically carry the corporate name. This may dilute any strength in the corporate name because, by stretching over so many diverse sectors, its credibility could be diminished.

To have a wise brand-naming strategy, regular reviews should be undertaken. The following exercise gives some insight as to how this can be done.

(i) Write down the core values of your organization:

Our core values are:

....
....
....
....
....
....

(ii) For each of your brands that are part of the portfolio with the corporate brand name dominant, write down their values, using the example of the grid below:

Brand 1	Brand 2	Brand 3	Brand 4
Value 1.1	Value 2.1	Value 3.1	Value 4.1
Value 1.2	Value 2.2	Value 3.2	Value 4.2
Value 1.3	Value 2.3	Value 3.3	Value 4.3
Value 1.4		Value 3.4	Value 4.4
Value 1.5		Value 3.5	
		Value 3.6	

In this example there are four brands, with Brand 1 characterized by five values (i.e. Values 1.1 to 1.5), Brand 2 characterized by three values, etc.

(iii) Having collected the data about each of the corporate brand's values, rearrange the data so those values that are similar across brands are on the same line. This might now give the rearranged grid:

Brand 1	Brand 2	Brand 3	Brand 4
Value 1.3	Value 2.2		Value 4.4
Value 1.5		Value 3.4	Value 4.1
Value 1.1	Value 2.3	Value 3.2	
Value 1.4	Value 2.1	Value 3.6	
Value 1.2		Value 3.5	
		Value 3.3	Value 4.2
			Value 4.3
		Value 3.1	

This indicates that, for example looking at the first line, Brands 1, 2 and 4 appear to have similar values (Values 1.3, 2.2 and 4.4). These might all be referring to the general value of courage, with Value 1.3 being resolute, Value 2.2 being bold and Value 4.4 being audacious.

By examining this rearranged grid you can start to identify where there are overlaps between brands in terms of common values. Where there is a notable number of cases of brands sharing common values, this suggests the appropriateness of using an umbrella name that links these together.

(iv) To evaluate this further, each of the core values from (i) need to be assessed against the rearranged grid to see if each of the corporation's core values encompasses the individual brands' values. One way of doing this is to

Core corporate values	Brand 1	Brand 2	Brand 3	Brand 4
Corp. Value 1				
Corp. Value 2	Value 1.3	Value 2.2		Value 4.4
Corp. Value 3				
Corp. Value 4	Value 1.5		Value 3.4	Value 4.1
Corp. Value 5	Value 1.1	Value 2.3	Value 3.2	
Corp. Value 6	Value 1.4	Value 2.1	Value 3.6	
Corp. Value 7	Value 1.2		Value 3.5	
			Value 3.3	Value 4.2
				Value 4.3
			Value 3.1	

produce a grid, with the left column being the core values and then the remainder of the grid showing each brand's values, with the values common to a corporate value being on the same line (see the example above).

In this example of an innovative hotel chain, the corporation has seven corporate values. Corporate Value 6 is sociable, which is shown on the same line as Value 1.4 (sincere), Value 2.1 (hospitable) and Value 3.6 (communicative), since the team thought this corporate value was similar to these values. As Corporate Values 1 and 3 do not embrace any of the values of the four brands, each is on a line by itself. What is interesting in this example is that while Brands 3 and 4 share a common value (Value 3.3 and 4.2), this is not a characteristic of the corporation, nor are Values 4.3 and 3.1 shared with the corporation's values.

By producing this type of grid and evaluating the extent to which the corporation's values comfortably encompass the values of the constituent brands, a view can be taken about the extent to which the corporate brand has (or has not) been overstretched.

3. Find examples of advertisements (press, TV, Internet) that your company uses to communicate its brand benefits. For each advertisement, evaluate how many points are being communicated. Recall from the above section 'Brand as shorthand' that people find it hard to cope with more than seven bits of information. Where there are more than seven points, these should be simplified by thinking about what your customers are really looking for and what is unique about your brand.

4. In the section 'Brand as risk reducer' it was explained that some customers buy brands because they are concerned about aspects of perceived risk. Those brands that are portrayed as being trustworthy on a particular characteristic are more likely to be selected by these customers.

Brand ....

	Little emphasis				Lot of emphasis
Performance risk	1	2	3	4	5
Financial risk	1	2	3	4	5
Time risk	1	2	3	4	5
Social risk	1	2	3	4	5
Psychological risk	1	2	3	4	5

As a brand team, evaluate the extent to which you are promoting your brand to reduce customers' perceived risk on each of the five dimensions above. Circle the numbers between 1 (we put little emphasis on this) to 5 (we put a lot of emphasis on this) that best describe your view.

Now use a similar approach with a group of your customers, asking them to provide information about how concerned they are about reducing their perception of risk on each of the five dimensions.

By comparing the risk profiles for your team (i.e. the risk you are seeking to reduce) and your customers (i.e. the risks they are particularly concerned about minimizing), you have an opportunity better to match the brand with customers' needs.

5. The section 'Brand as personality' explains how the metaphor of a brand as a person facilitates the rapid appreciation of the brand's emotional values. However, this is not inferred just from an advertisement, albeit this is a powerful source; it is also inferred from all the other marketing activity supporting the brand. To ensure a coherent message is being presented about your brand's emotional values, find samples of all the materials and messages customers encounter when selecting your brand – for example, web information, brochures, packaging, in-store displays, pricing information, distribution channel partners, etc. For each of these, consider:

   (i) What inferences you make about the brand's emotional values
   (ii) Whether an integrated approach is being used
   (iii) What inferences customers draw (if no information is available, interviews would be most helpful).

6. To identify new sources of added value for your brand, accompany several customers on their brand selection journeys. As they go through this journey, probe to evaluate:
   - what they like and dislike
   - what is missing
   - what they would change
   - what 'quality' means to them
   - what trade-off they are making between quality and price
   - whether your brand is bundled with another brand (e.g. a soft drink with a confectionery)
   - how time-pressured the customer is, and what opportunities there are for enhancing the brand to save customers' time.

This type of questioning will evoke ideas about functional ways of adding value.

To consider emotional ways of adding value, more subtle procedures should be used when accompanying the customer. Listening to how the customer uses the brand, hearing about the roles the brand plays and inferring ideas about the emotional support the brand provides can start to provoke thoughts about emotionally adding value.

References and further reading

Aaker, J., Fournier, S. and Adam Brasel, S. (2004). When good brands do bad. *Journal of Consumer Research*, **31** (1), 1–16.

Aggarwal, P. (2004). The effect of brand relationship norms on consumer attitudes and behaviour. *Journal of Consumer Research*, **31** (1), 87–101.

Alt, M. and Griggs, S. (1988). Can a brand be cheeky? *Marketing Intelligence and Planning*, **6** (4), 9–26.

Banister, E. and Hogg, M. (2004). Negative symbolic consumption and consumers' drive for self-esteem. *European Journal of Marketing*, **38** (7), 859–68.

Bauer, R. (1960). Consumer behaviour as risk taking. In *Dynamic Marketing for a Changing World* (Hancock, R., ed.). Chicago: American Marketing Association.

Bettman, J. (1979). *An Information Processing Theory of Consumer Choice*. Reading MA: Addison Wesley.

Blackett, T. (1998). *Trademarks*. Basingstoke: Macmillan.

Browne, A. (2005). Customs not able to keep up with rise of fake goods. *The Times*, 9 February.

Clarkson, J. (2003). *The Sunday Times*, 26 October.

Conchar, M., Zinkham, G., Peters, C. and Olavarrieta, S. (2004). An integrated framework for the conceptualization of consumers' perceived risk processing. *Journal of the Academy of Marketing Science*, **32** (4), 418–36.

Davies, G. (1998). Retail brands and the theft of identity. *International Journal of Retail & Distribution Management*, **26** (4), 140–6.

de Chernatony, L. (1993). Categorising brands: evolutionary processes underpinned by two key dimensions. *Journal of Marketing Management*, **9** (2), 173–88.

de Chernatony, L. and Dall'Olmo Riley, F. (1998). Defining a 'brand': beyond the literature with experts' interpretations. *Journal of Marketing Management*, **14** (5), 417–43.

de Chernatony, L., Drury, S. and Segal-Horn, S. (2004). Identifying and sustaining services brands' values. *Journal of Marketing Communications*, **10** (2), 73–93.

de Chernatony, L., Harris, F. and Dall'Olmo Riley, F. (2000). Added value: its nature, roles and sustainability. *European Journal of Marketing*, **34** (1/2), 39–56.

Fombrun, C. (1996). *Reputation: Realizing Value from Corporate Image*. Boston MA: Harvard Business School Press.

Fombrun, C. and van Riel, C. (1997). The reputational landscape. *Corporate Reputation Review*, **1** (1&2), 5–13.

Fournier, S. (1998). Consumers and their brands: developing relationship theory in consumer research. *Journal of Consumer Research*, **25** (4), 343–73.

Goodyear, M. (1993). Reviewing the concept of brands and branding. *Marketing and Research Today*, **21** (2), 75–9.

Goodyear, M. (1996). Divided by a common language. *Journal of the Market Research Society*, **38** (2), 110–22.

Grunert, K. and Grunert, S. (1995). Measuring subjective meaning structures by the laddering method: theoretical considerations and methodological problems. *Journal of Research in Marketing*, **12** (3), 209–85.

Gutman, J. (1982). A means–end chain model based on consumer categorisation processes. *Journal of Research*, **46**, 60–72.

Hatch, M. J. and Schultz, M. (2000). Scaling the tower of Babel. In *The Expressive Organization* (Schultz, M., Hatch, M. J. and Holten Larsen, M., eds). Oxford: Oxford University Press.

Henderson, P. and Cote, J. (1998). Guidelines for selecting or modifying logos. *Journal of Marketing*, **62**, 14–30.

Heskett, J. (1987). Lessons in the service sector. *Harvard Business Review*, **March/April**, 51–61.

Ind, N. (1998). An integrated approach to corporate branding. *Journal of Brand Management*, **5** (5), 323–32.

Institute of Work Psychology (1998). *Happy Workers Yield Higher Returns*. Sheffield: University of Sheffield.

Jacoby, J., Szybillo, G. and Busato-Sehach, J. (1977). Information acquisition behaviour in brand choice situations. *Journal of Consumer Research*, **3**, 209–16.

Kapferer, J.-N. (1995). Stealing brand equity: measuring perceptual confusion between national brands and 'copycat own labels'. *Marketing and Research Today*, **23**, 96–103.

Keller, K. L., Sternthal, B. and Tybout, A. (2002). Three questions you need to ask about your brand. *Harvard Business Review*, **September**, 3–8.

Kotter, J. and Heskett, J. (1992). *Corporate Culture and Performance*. New York: The Free Press.

Kunde, J. (2000). *Corporate Religion*. London: Pearson Education.

Lomax, W., Sherski, E. and Todd, S. (1999). Assessing the risk of consumer confusion: some practical test results. *Journal of Brand Management*, **7** (2), 119–32.

Meadows, R. (1983). They consume advertising too. *Admap*, **July–August**, 408–13.

Miller, G. (1956). The magic number seven, plus or minus two. *The Psychological Review*, **63**, 91–7.

Mitchell, A. (1997). *Brand Strategies in the Information Age*. London: Financial Times Business.

Mitchell, V.-W. and Kearney, I. (2002). A critique of legal measures of brand confusion. *Journal of Product & Brand Management*, **11** (6), 357–79.

Nonaka, I. and Takeuchi, H. (1995). *The Knowledge Creating Company*. Oxford: Oxford University Press.

Poiesz, T. (1989). The image concept: its place in consumer psychology. *Journal of Economic Psychology*, **10**, 457–72.

Reynolds, T. and Gutman, J. (1984). Advertising is image management. *Journal of Advertising Research*, **24**, 27–37.

Ries, A. and Trout, J. (1986). *Positioning: The Battle for Your Mind*. New York: McGraw Hill.

Sherrington, M. (2003). *Added Value*. Basingstoke: Palgrave Macmillan.

Sirgy, M. (1982). Self-concept in consumer behaviour: a critical review. *Journal of Consumer Research*, **9**, 287–300.

Trout, J. and Rivkin, S. (1996). *The New Positioning*. New York: McGraw Hill.
van Riel, C. and Balmer, J. (1997). Corporate identity: the concept, its measure and management. *European Journal of Marketing*, **31** (5/6), 340–55.
Zinkhan, G., Haytko, D. and Ward, A. (1996). Self concept theory. *Journal of Marketing Communications*, **2** (1), 1–19.

Part Two

Planning for Integrated Brands

Chapter 3

A strategic process for building integrated brands

Summary

The aim of this chapter is to make readers aware of the need for an integrated branding programme. It opens by drawing attention to the way that the myriad of brand communicators may be emitting inconsistent messages. Models are presented to evaluate where inconsistencies are arising in branding programmes, and guidance is provided about securing a more integrated approach to services branding. Customers are often attracted to brands' websites through traditional sources, and the need for consistency between off-line and on-line sources is clarified. A model to enhance the coherence of the on-line brand experience is explored.

Staff are motivated by different issues, and unless these give rise to styles of behaviour that support the brand's values, the brand is unlikely to attain its potential. Barrett's model of the seven levels of human consciousness is reviewed as a means of encouraging a suitable profile of motivated staff to support the brand. Finally, the point is made that an integrated branding process is more likely if a planning perspective is adopted and a seven step brand-building model is overviewed.

The importance of integrated branding programmes

Chapter 2 explained that there can be diverse interpretations amongst members of a brand's team about the nature of their brand. To ensure all members of the team are 'pulling in the same direction', the chapter reviewed ways to enable members of a brand's team to reach a consensus about their interpretation of a brand. Through gaining a similar view amongst all the staff working on a brand, there will be a greater likelihood of a unified programme of activities that support a brand. Unfortunately, though, because there are so many different departments working on the brand, there may be a lack of integration between these different departments. When consumers choose a brand they rarely rely on just one source of information, and, through coming into contact with different sources of information, the total brand experience may be perceived as inconsistent.

Strong leadership is one way of minimizing the problem of an inconsistent brand experience. A weak chair, with many problems on his or her mind, might briefly exhort fellow directors to consider ways of halting the decline of a brand at a board meeting, then quickly move on to another item on the agenda. Without coordination amongst the directors, they could be driving change initiatives that cause conflict as managers compete internally against each other for scarce resources.

For example, a telephone-based financial services organization was aware of the problem of an inconsistent brand experience, and the managing director was of the view that if there was inconsistent brand work amongst the board of directors, this was likely to be amplified throughout the corporation. Therefore, when setting the overall corporate objectives he asked the directors to take each of the other directors' objectives and plans, and then to consider what the implications would be on their individual teams for each period throughout the year. This soon surfaced internal conflict and inconsistent brand experiences. For example, one of the objectives for the customer services director was to increase the strength of the corporate brand's relationship with its customers, and this was to be achieved through enhanced training that freed the customer services staff from using scripts and encouraged them to use their database regarding their customers' lifestyles and insurance needs to tailor their individual products better. Around the same time, the marketing director was seeking to launch a new service that would take customer services staff time to promote during each of their telephone conversations. The problem was that the customer services staff were unsure about when to build stronger relationships and when to promote the new service. Only by the directors taking the others' objectives and plans were the most senior team of managers able to identify possible instances of inconsistent brand experiences, and to minimize such problems.

One of the simplest ways of evaluating whether an integrated approach is being followed is for each member of the brand's team to collect any material the organization uses to communicate with external stakeholders (e.g. with suppliers, distributors, consumers, the media, etc.). These are then brought together and displayed on a large table. Against the benchmarks of the brand's values, each of the items is assessed for:

- its contribution towards supporting the brand
- its reinforcement of the other forms of communication
- the ease with which stakeholders can understand the messages.

Regarding the latter point, there can be instances when very creative approaches sometimes cause uncertainty about the nature of the message. For example, there was once a press campaign with the headline 'How UPS shows other parcel carriers a clean pair of heels', beneath which was a can of Kiwi shoe polish and then some detailed text, with the Conqueror brand shown at the bottom of the page. While this is a most creative way of reinforcing the high quality of Conqueror paper, the inclusion of three brands in one advertisement may have detracted some attention from Conqueror as the key brand.

Activity 3.1

Pause for a moment and consider what some of the different types of brand communicators are.

Discussion

There are numerous brand communicators, including:

- web-based updates about the brand
- logos, e.g. the golden arches of McDonald's, the coloured windows of Microsoft
- brand characters, e.g. the Andrex puppy
- strap lines
- jingles or tunes, e.g. the way brands maintain their modernity by using popular musical themes

- celebrities
- packaging that acts as a 'silent' communicator
- sponsorship, e.g. links with football sponsorship
- uniforms, e.g. the pride of Alitalia cabin crew in their Armani-designed uniform
- offices, e.g. the almost village atmosphere of BA's office headquarters at Heathrow
- the relative pricing of the brand
- the distributors being used, e.g. selected grocery brands selling through Harrods rather than Kwik Save
- the staff, with their values, attitudes and behaviour.

By considering how each of these resources interacts with the others to make a positive or negative contribution to the brand's desired values, there is a greater likelihood of a more integrated branding approach. Management in a hotel chain may believe it is reinforcing the brand's welcoming value by having a sign at the breakfast dining area saying 'Please wait here for the next smile'. However, when an overstretched restaurant manager then appears, asks guests for their room number in a cold manner and then quickly marches them to the nearest free table, this detracts from the desired brand promise of being welcoming.

Models to enhance integrated branding

One way the brand's team becomes more focused on integrated brand development programmes is by considering the journeys each of its stakeholders undertakes as they come into contact with the organization. After identifying the key stakeholders, each member of the brand's team is allocated a stakeholder he or she does not normally come into contact with. This type of allocation enables situations to be seen through fresh eyes, unhindered by the baggage of biases formed through years of interactions.

The team members then spend some time with their particular stakeholder, focusing on the sequential array of topics identified in Figure 3.1. After all the members of the team have completed this task, they reconvene and present their findings. This task unearths a rich insight about the cohesion of the brand strategy and enables the team to identify inconsistent activities.

During the debriefing about the findings there is benefit in considering how the organization is facilitating stakeholders' learning processes. In the early stages of interacting with the brand, stakeholders have rather basic mental models and feel challenged using their limited knowledge to form decision rules. Organizations add value by 'teaching the stakeholder how to

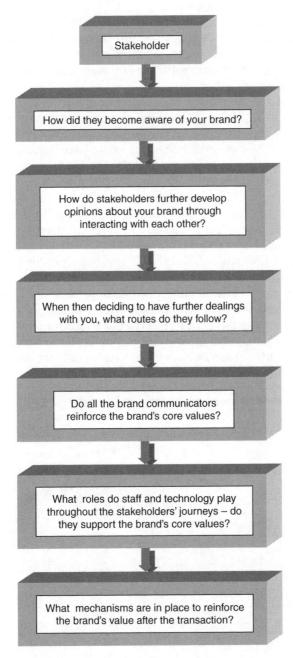

Figure 3.1   *Striving for an integrated brand journey*

learn' about the category but, more to the point, about their particular brands. Understanding the stakeholders' learning processes sometimes leads to the conclusion that some clues about the brand may be better transmitted as relationships start to develop with stakeholders.

One of the problems this exercise unearths is brand over-claims. For example, a chain of hotels, each with conference facilities, had a welcome pack for the workshop leader, typically given at the start of the day. Inside the pack was a proclamation about the hotel taking pride in ensuring that the infrastructure will be perfect for the event and that staff will rapidly respond to requests. Alas, the hotel was not delivering the promised standards. This was partly because of staff not being committed and partly because of the way they outsourced presentation equipment to other suppliers and hadn't explained to them the brand promise.

Hatch and Schultz (2001) have devised a powerful corporate branding toolkit which strengthens corporate brands by seeking better alignment. The starting point is that there are three groups interacting with brands: managers shape corporate brands through the vision they devise, staff reflect the brand through unique organizational cultures, and stakeholders perceive the brand's image. By exploring the gaps between the vision, culture and image, as shown in Figure 3.2, it is possible to surface instances of diversity and to identify ways of better aligning these critical components.

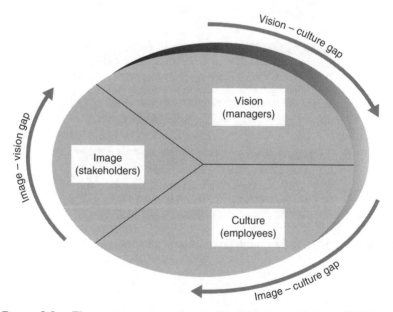

Figure 3.2   *The corporate branding toolkit (Hatch and Schultz 2001)*

The vision–culture gap occurs when staff don't compre-hend, or are not committed to, the vision managers have defined for the brand. While a stretching vision is to be encouraged, hav-ing an overly stretching vision leads to staff cynicism and in turn to a souring of relations between staff and management.

The image–culture gap emerges when consumers are unsure or confused about what the corporate brand stands for. An organ-ization may extol particular aspects about their brand, but then behave in a non-supporting manner. Of particular concern is an ambivalent attitude amongst staff regarding claims the corporation makes about itself.

The image–vision gap is misalignment arising from conflict between the vision and the image stakeholders have of the brand. This arises from factors such as managers not properly under-standing their stakeholders' characteristics and their specific needs from the brand.

Another way to enhance an integrated branding process comes from building on a model developed by Wolff Olins (1995). They argue that a brand's central idea is transmitted through its products/services, staff's behaviour, the environment and commu-nication. The importance of these will vary according to the brand – for example, the high performance of the BMW is rapidly apparent from the aesthetics of their range of cars; the behaviour of the police in public situations says a lot about their beliefs and standards; the splendour of Harrods Food Hall says much about their obsession with superior quality; and the numerous campaigns from Levi leave little doubt about the acceptable face of being a rebel. Adapting this model, as shown in Figure 3.3, provides scope for developing a more integrated branding strategy. This comes about through the team making explicit their brand's values and then, for each of the four key communicators in Figure 3.3, evaluating:

1. The extent to which that communicator reinforces the brand's values
2. The extent to which each of the four brand communicators reinforce each other.

In addition, for each of the four brand communicators managers can benefit by considering:

- what they have been exhorting internally about that specific brand communicator
- to what extent their exhortations have been enacted, not just by the staff but by the managers' own behaviour.

Phoney brands become evident when senior managers urge their staff to adopt particular behavioural styles, yet their own actions do not support such exhortations.

One of the themes regularly recurring when striving for integrated brands relates to the inconsistency of communications. Brand owners seek to project a message, yet, being insufficiently attentive to their stakeholders' backgrounds, experience and context, the message is misinterpreted. Simmons (2003) provides a good example of this:

'How old Cary Grant?'
'Old Cary Grant fine'

He also draws to our attention the way that brevity in apparently insignificant messages draws clear interpretations in consumers' minds. For example, an expanding clothes retailer priding itself on its chic brand may be oblivious to the damage being caused to the brand when recruiting staff through a poster in its window saying 'Sales consultant needed: no experience necessary'.

An indication of the importance of writing in a style that supports the brand is provided by further work from Simmons (2000). In an era when we extol the virtue of living the brand it is

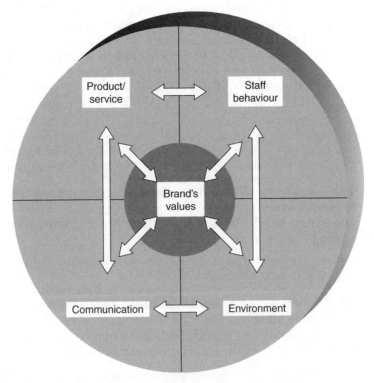

Figure 3.3   *Facilitating an integrated brand through addressing four key brand communicators (adapted from Wolff Olins 1995)*

imperative that the writing style is 'on brand', and this becomes notable when the writer puts some of their personality into the style, reflecting the desired brand personality. Consider how a brand may unwittingly appear aloof by using terms such as 'undertake', 'envisage', 'purchase', 'making provision' and 'upon receipt of'. By contrast, Simmons (2000) gives a wonderful example of the committed, caring and persistent personality of the United States Post Office with one of their (rather long) slogans: 'Neither snow nor rain, nor heat nor gloom of night stays these couriers from the swift completion of their appointed rounds'.

Striving for integrated services brands

Services brands pose particular challenges when evaluating the extent to which a branding strategy is integrated, because of their intangible nature and the numerous staff that co-produce value with consumers. However, to consider solely the intangible component overlooks the full picture, as Figure 3.4 clarifies.

All services brands have a tangible component – for example, the instruction manual accompanying a new brand of software. The intangibles that are inherent in the brand promise relate to the attitudes, beliefs, values and behavioural styles of staff. The supporting system relates to the brand infrastructure that enables staff to communicate both with other employees in the

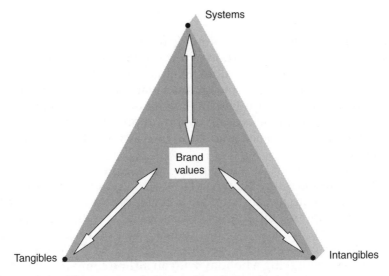

Figure 3.4   *The integrated services brand triangle*

value chain and with databases about specific customers. Each of these three components emits a particular message about a brand's values. By auditing the three components and comparing them against the brand's values, insight is provided about the extent to which they support the desired brand values.

Activity 3.2

Take a familiar services brand and consider how you would use the integrated services brand triangle to evaluate the cohesiveness of that brand.

Discussion

If an airline had been selected, the cohesiveness of its branding strategy could be evaluated through checking its brand values against the three elements:

1. Tangible elements such as staff uniform, check-in facilities, logo, decor inside the aircraft, cleanliness of the aircraft, in-flight magazine, variety and quality of food and drink services
2. Intangible elements such as the tone of voice used by staff greeting customers, the patience of staff, the perceived professionalism of staff, the extent to which conversations are stern or jovial, the concern staff have for pleasing their travellers and the extent to which they are helpful
3. Supporting systems such as the ease with which staff can access computer systems, whether staff away from desks have mobile telephones, whether staff have up-to-date telephone numbers for everyone in the organization, whether supervisors can be rapidly contacted by customer-facing staff, whether there is a back-up computer system if the checking-in computer system fails, and whether the checking-in staff can amend passengers' sudden requests for in-flight meals and rescheduled flights.

It should be noted that if a brand is to be a coherent entity, there is normally a large proportion of the employees whose values are aligned with the brand's values. Evaluating the diversity between employees' values and the brand's values through the value chain can provide helpful insight about departments where staff are less likely to be delivering the brand promise. This point was raised earlier in this book, and will be considered in more depth in later chapters.

Another model that helps to encourage more integrated services brands is that shown in Figure 3.5. An integrated services brand starts with having a unique and welcome promise known to customers and to staff. If the services brand is to thrive, then the delivery system reinforces the promise. For example, brands that offer last-minute holiday bookings depend on IT to speed up processes, yet having a holiday with an airline company that does not issue e-tickets brings into doubt the brand's promise. Finally,

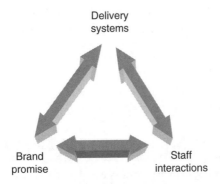

Figure 3.5   *Self-supporting integration in services branding*

the way staff interact with customers says much about the brand's promise. When the frustrated customer trying to book a last-minute holiday is told by a customer services employee that it is only possible to search for hotel availability on a Greek island if the customer can specify towns on the small island, it says much about the lack of 'customer orientation'.

Striving for integrated digital brands

When using the Internet to build or sustain brands, stakeholders develop expectations about the on-line experience from numerous sources. The first point at which a poorly integrated brand raises problems is when the on-line brand experience gives rise to different messages about the brand from those anticipated. On-line, the stakeholder might have taken advantage of electronically ordering the brand, with a guaranteed promise date. If this is not honoured, or if the delivery organization uses old vehicles or has staff who are not particularly customer-oriented, the cracks in the brand become more apparent.

Some organizations have taken time to appreciate the route that people have followed. For example, someone may have used Yahoo! to find out information about a capital city. On screen is an Amazon.com box, and when clicked this doesn't go to Amazon's home page but instead to those few books that are of relevance to the Yahoo! search. Not only does this save the user time but, through integrating these two stepping stones on the brand journey, this reinforces a seamless brand experience.

When working to ensure that the delivery of the on-line brand is integrated, Clarity, an on-line business development consultancy, has evolved a helpful approach. Clarity makes explicit a brand's value and then derives the ideal on-line delivery by considering the website against the attributes:

- content
- functionality
- customer service
- look and feel.

Activity 3.3

If a retailer specializing in mobile phones has impartiality as one of its values, how could this be delivered over the Internet?

Discussion

- Content could be that of comprehensive information, with an unbiased judgement made regarding each mobile phone.
- Functionality could enable the enquirer to check the coverage of different networks around a specific area by typing in the postal address.
- Customer service should ensure there is expert advice via e-mail.
- The look and feel of the site should be straightforward, clean, and give a feeling of being informed.

Developing integrated brands through understanding employees' motivations

Brands, regardless of whether on-line or off-line, start their lives through the work of employees and mature through the ways stakeholders incorporate them into their support systems. Underpinning each brand's competitive advantage is the culture resulting from employees' values and their commitment to delivering the brand's values. Strong leaders strive to encourage unique cultures that attract employees who believe in the firm's brand and who wish to be part of the organizational team delivering the brand promise. Sam Walton, founder of Wal-Mart, exemplified this. In 1984 he proudly danced the hula-hula, dressed as a Hawaiian, down Wall Street. He had promised to do this if Wal-Mart's pre-tax profits for the year reached 8 per cent of sales. The event was videotaped so staff in Wal-Mart stores could see this, and he commented that it helped his goal of 'making our people feel part of a family in which no one is too important or too puffed up to lead a cheer or be the butt of a joke'. Actions like these helped to instil the values of accessibility and looking for the good in other people which still characterize Wal-Mart, even though Sam

Walton is now dead. One of the acid tests of a strong culture is when staff question 'what would our founder do in this situation?'

The challenge is to foster a culture that supports and encourages employees to want to be part of the branding process. When employees are aligned with their brand's values, they are more likely to find their own meaning at work and to tap their creativity to find new ways of enhancing the brand's values. The problem is that each employee has his or her own motivations, and when developing an integrated brand strategy these different staff motivations give rise to potentially conflicting forms of behaviour. To understand the motivations of staff working on a brand, we can draw on Barrett's (1998) model, 'The seven levels of human consciousness', shown in Figure 3.6.

This insightful model provides a helpful way of understanding an individual's motivation for working on the brand. As Barrett lucidly argues, it is possible to identify four broad types of human need, which lead to seven personal motivations, manifest at seven levels of human consciousness. Using a basic example, if a brand's promise is about helping society through environmental concerns (for example, Greenpeace), and if there is a notable number of staff concerned with self security, this mismatch could be detrimental to the brand. From Barrett's model it is possible to audit the personal motivations of staff and evaluate their fit with the brand's values. This can be done by understanding his model.

Some employees' basic needs give rise to a form of behaviour that drives staff to think more about their interests, rather than the

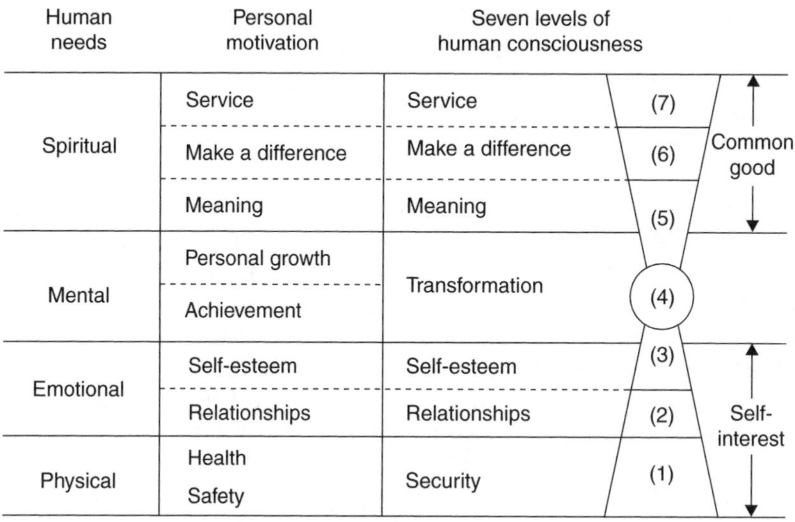

Human needs	Personal motivation	Seven levels of human consciousness		
Spiritual	Service	Service	(7)	Common good
	Make a difference	Make a difference	(6)	
	Meaning	Meaning	(5)	
Mental	Personal growth	Transformation	(4)	
	Achievement			
Emotional	Self-esteem	Self-esteem	(3)	Self-interest
	Relationships	Relationships	(2)	
Physical	Health	Security	(1)	
	Safety			

Figure 3.6   The seven levels of organizational consciousness (Source: Barrett 1998)

common good of their stakeholders. The most basic need of security results in people coming to work primarily for economic purposes, and the concept of a brand as a cluster of values has little appeal for this group. In his turnaround of the UK grocery retail chain Asda, partly contributing to enhancing its attractiveness to Wal-Mart, Archie Norman gradually changed the profile of his workforce, with part-time staff having longer hours in their contracts deliberately to encourage the recruitment of staff who were not just thinking of payment but also of a commitment to serving customers.

The next motivator for some people is the need for friendship and respected relationships. People in this group want to be part of a team, but for fear of upsetting colleagues they do not express their thoughts at meetings. For brands whose values stress innovation and challenging norms, these types of staff are unlikely to help the brand achieve its vision.

The third motivation, moving up the hierarchy, is the employee's drive for self-esteem. These employees are concerned with gaining respect. They are ambitious and competitive, striving to improve their status and salary, constantly testing their actions by checking whether they gain the approval of their peer group. Their lifestyle is rather unbalanced, with them being prepared to sacrifice their family and friends for extra effort at work. Such employees could be described as being 'outer directed'. They are more likely to use cues – for example, overtly branded clothing – to communicate their status. There is, however, a growing proportion of people who could be described as being 'inner directed'. Their primary drive is achieving self-actualization, and they abhor the use of status cues. If the brand's values are targeted at inner-directed stakeholders, as is the case with charities, educational institutions and museums, having a notable proportion of staff concerned with self-esteem is unlikely to bring out the best of the brand.

After working on a brand for some time, individuals start to question why things are done in particular ways and what the purpose of their brand is, beyond making a profit. This transformation state concerns staff thinking about self-actualization and how the brand helps stakeholders to achieve this – for example, questioning the existing positioning of their yoghurt brand as being the best quality and evaluating instead how it enhances a household's dining experience. It is not unusual for organizations to recruit senior marketers who exhibit novel ideas, and brief them to turn around poorly performing brands. Staff who are in this transformation state are likely to be most receptive to new brand initiatives, particularly when they are aware of a clear vision being set and a well-defined cluster of values being widely communicated. Transformation state managers, particularly if they are senior, are more likely to relax their need to control staff and to feel more comfortable trusting them. Brand strategies based on the brand as a risk reducer are likely to succeed with these staff, particularly when the brand moves beyond reducing functional performance risk to reducing social and psychological risks.

At the next level on this motivation hierarchy are those employees who are seeking meaning through their work. They have a strong sense of values, and look forward to working on the brand as this resonates with their values. These employees enjoy the sensation of trust, teamwork and being encouraged to take risks, knowing that failure will not result in blame but, rather, leads to shared learning. Staff in this category welcome opennesses and, regardless of their status, like to have responsibility for changes. A good example of a brand where many staff are at the meaning stage is Harley-Davidson. An internal video for staff includes such comments as:

> *[Our people] have freedom to do what's right – never care what others think of them – just do the best.*
>
> *People who go to work because they want to, people who can't wait to get to work*
>
> *If someone says you can't, we say you can; if someone says good, we say better.*

At the penultimate level are employees driven by the need to make a difference. An example is the Apple PC. When competitors were extolling their brands' productivity benefits, Apple spoke about enhancing individuals' creativity. Steve Jobs was once quoted in an interview as saying:

> *Apple is about people who think 'outside the box', people who want to use computers to help them change the world, to help them make a difference and not just get a job done.*

These individuals recognize that by forming partnerships with other organizations they can reach their audacious goals of making a difference to the lives of many stakeholders. People driven by this motivation shun the 'not invented here' syndrome and relish a 'can do' culture. Intuition and creativity are these individuals' hallmarks. Challenger brands such as Virgin and the UK insurance company More Th>n thrive by having a notable number of employees who are enthused by the notion of making a difference. This type of person thrives in a culture that continually recognizes staff who go beyond the remit of their jobs to achieve customer delight. Frequent hero stories on a firm's intranet encourage pride at work and stimulate a passion to achieve more.

The top level is defined by those staff who wish ultimately to be of service to humanity and society. Their motivations are ethics, justice, human rights, and how the firm's behaviour might influence future generations. Brand decisions are not just taken on economic but also on moral grounds. Brands such as the Body Shop, with its core values of social responsibility, environmental protection and animal protection, depend on staff who wish to be of service to society. They feel pride when sourcing suppliers who can revitalize deprived communities. The Co-operative Bank, with its strategy of undertaking business in a profitable and ethical manner, succeeded because of people who believe strongly in serving the community. A good example of this is the way they polled customers about how they should deliver value in a socially responsible manner. Based on these findings, rather than the views solely of a senior team, they took on board issues such as:

- equal opportunities in the workplace
- screening suppliers along ethical and ecological lines
- supporting charities
- involvement with local communities.

Where brands have prominent philanthropic aims, there needs to be a notable proportion of staff whose motivations lie at the upper end of this spectrum.

Based on Barrett's model, it is possible to evaluate the profile of all the employees working on the brand. By comparing these profiles against the desired brand values, an assessment can be made about the motivation of staff to support the brand. To capitalize on an integrated team of employees working on a brand there needs to be a planned approach to brand-building, as the next section explores.

The stages in building and sustaining brands

The task of ensuring an integrated branding strategy is one that necessitates working with many people across numerous functional specialisms and throughout many levels of seniority. By adopting a planned approach, everyone is more likely to understand the brand objectives and the role they need to play in supporting the brand. In the final part of this chapter, we will review a systematic process for developing and strengthening

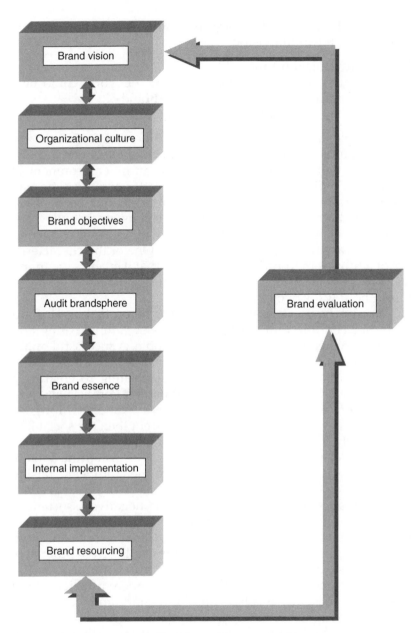

Figure 3.7   *The process of building and sustaining brands*

brands (see Figure 3.7), which will be covered in more detail in the subsequent chapters of this book.

The process commences with the *brand vision* stage. This stage is concerned with putting down markers about the desired future for the brand. There are three inter-related components constituting the brand vision:

1. An envisioned future
2. The purpose for the brand – i.e. how the world could be a better place as a consequence of the brand
3. The values that will underpin the brand.

For example, a clothes designer might differentiate their brand by envisioning a future when there will be only beauty and joy; a software organization may envision a future environment in which a PC will be on every desk. The latter organization may use the argument that software is currently not particularly 'user-friendly', and clearly one of their challenges is to develop software that is so easy to use, people will regard it as second nature always to have their PC close by. One of the characteristics of a future environment statement is that it enables the brand team to start to appreciate likely barriers, and forces them to think about ways of overcoming these.

The purpose of a brand is not just to be profitable. This is a necessary condition for existence, just as breathing, eating and sleeping are necessary conditions for people. A successful brand is one that makes the world a better place. For example, a clothes designer might have its brand purpose relating to creating a pleasurable life for notable people. Collins and Porras (1996) provide a wonderful example of the Federal National Mortgage Association, whose core purpose is 'To strengthen the social fabric of society by continually democratizing home ownership'. As more people are able to own their homes, they feel pride and are likely to want to maintain and enhance their property, raising their sense of self-respect. What is particularly impressive about this purpose is the way it overcomes the negative associations with the term 'mortgage'. Furthermore, it makes homeowners recognize the sacrifice others have made to have a home through a mortgage, and should deter them from stealing from other people's homes.

The values characterize the brand's inherent beliefs about desirable types of behaviour of both staff and consumers. A clothes designer might define itself through values such as opulence and pleasure. Some of the values defining British Airways include safe, responsible, innovative and caring, while the Volvo appeals to drivers concerned about safety.

The *organizational culture* needs appreciating, since this can help or hinder the brand's development. An appropriate organizational culture can help create a competitive advantage for a brand, since it is not so much *what* a customer gets but also *how* they get it. There therefore needs to be an assessment of the artefacts, values and assumptions (i.e. the cause and effect mental models of managers) characterizing the organizational culture. Furthermore, some assessment is needed of the extent to which the subcultures are likely to hinder the desired brand. The hypothetical clothes designer might decide to have its headquarters in Milan, and another artefact might be the flamboyant language of the staff. Some of its values constituting its culture could include creativity and striving for sensual design. One of the mental models might relate to the way that success is underpinned by having iconic designers.

The brand vision then needs translating into stretching, but realistic, *brand objectives*. Ultimately these need to give staff a clear target to aim for, and should provide some idea of what the brand needs to achieve. For example, the clothes designer might have a long-term objective of providing designs representative of a specific lifestyle it wishes to bring about. This should then lead to designs which achieve specific sales targets. Catalytic mechanisms also need considering at this stage, to ensure that appropriate actions take place to achieve the objective and that all actions focus on the target. Thus, if a brand's objective is to offer the customer outstanding service, then having a catalytic mechanism of paying staff a bonus based on customer feedback encourages appropriate behaviour.

However, while visionary leaders may have worked with a brand's team to set stretching objectives, there may have been some barriers identified in the envisioned future environment which cause concern. This is not unusual and, rather than looking at problems on a piecemeal basis, *auditing the brandsphere* encourages managers to audit the five key forces of the corporation, distributors, customers, competitors and the macro-environment (political, economic, social, technological and environmental). The purpose of this stage is to identify the critical forces which may facilitate the brand's route towards its vision, and also where it will be facing its greatest challenges. The result of this audit might force the brand's team to reconsider the brand objectives, or even the brand vision.

Out of this process ideas will begin to emerge about what the core of the brand might be and what statement might summarize the brand For example, the clothes designer might define its brand's essence as being the sheer pleasure of life. At the *brand essence* stage, the management team works to identify the central characteristics that will define the brand. Through a laddering process starting with the distinguishing attributes, the rational benefits, emotional rewards, values and personality traits characterizing the brand can be defined. This should clarify thinking about how the brand is to be positioned and how the metaphor of personality can help people recognize its values.

Internal implementation needs addressing next, to consider how the organization should be structured to deliver the promise inherent in the brand essence. A key issue at this stage is deciding upon the type of delivery system needed to ensure the brand's functional and emotional values. A consideration of mechanistic inputs enables the brand's team to consider the details about the value chain to capitalize on core competencies. Staff input considerations are likely to address employees' values, the degree to which they are empowered and the relationships they build with their stakeholders.

More detailed consideration about implementing the desired brand essence can be addressed at the *brand resourcing* stage. At this point, issues such as the naming of the brand, selecting communication vehicles, the use of staff to engender a specific relationship with stakeholders, and quality need clarifying.

On a regular basis, *brand evaluation* needs to take place to monitor brand performance against key criteria. Depending on whether the monitored results are favourable or unfavourable, this feedback provides guidance about future action.

Even though this flow process has been described from the perspective of developing a new brand, it is also suitable for sustaining existing brands. With existing brands the challenge is to keep them refreshed and relevant for a changing environment. Therefore, on a regular basis (typically annually) brand reviews need undertaking to assess the brand against each of the boxes in the flowchart shown in Figure 3.7, and to consider the need for new strategies.

Conclusions

Brands do not die just because of customer dissatisfaction, but also because staff from different departments in the same firm are pulling against each other. With numerous people inside an organization working on a brand, in addition to external consultants, it is not difficult to overlook the need to evaluate how all the branding jigsaw pieces are fitting together. Without effective co-ordination, different departments may be communicating inconsistent and conflicting messages about the brand.

One way of appreciating the extent to which a branding programme is integrated is to pull together all the brand communicators and assess the extent to which they are self-supporting. By also considering these communicators against the journeys the different stakeholder groups follow as they get closer to the brand, the brand's team can better gauge whether a homogeneous organizational approach is evident.

The intangible nature of services brands presents more of a challenge when striving for an integrated branding programme. This can be surmounted by considering the extent to which the three components (i.e. tangible aspects, the interactions with staff and the systems infrastructures) reinforce the brand's values.

In the world of e-commerce, customers form views about brands from traditional sources plus on-line experiences. Like birds building a nest, customers build their brand impressions from diverse sources, and unless the expectations raised from off-line sources match the experiences achieved on-line the brand may falter. Due to the way customers are more involved with the brand in cyberspace, they are likely to be more aware of branding messages and thus more critical of the organization that doesn't support their expectations of service and rapid communication after leaving the brand's website.

Staff are motivated at different levels, and unless their motivations lead to styles of behaviour supporting the brand's values, the long-term future of the brand is questionable. Through the concept of Barrett's seven levels of human consciousness it is possible to obtain a profile of the motivational states of the brand's team, and by comparing this against the desired brand character the suitability of staff can be assessed.

Developing an integrated brand necessitates a united pan-company approach. While several techniques have been identified to strengthen the brand's coherence, a planning perspective can help stimulate a more consistent series of activities. A sequential brand planning process has been identified, to help build and strengthen brands, which integrates different departments' activities. Each of the stages will be addressed in more detail in subsequent chapters.

Brand marketing action checklist

This chapter has presented ideas and frameworks that can help organizations to strengthen the integrated nature of their brands. Undertaking some of the following exercises could help the enactment of these principles.

1. Take one of your brand's values and then pull together all those communicators that you consider to be important transmitters of the brand's value. Approach a colleague in a different department, present him or her with the material you have assembled and ask the colleague:

    (i) What brand value does the material communicate?

(ii) Are there any brand communicators they regard as transmitting values different to those in (i)?

(iii) Do they perceive any inconsistencies between the messages being emitted by the communicators?

Having recorded this colleague's comments, explain your views and explore why there might be differences in your perspectives. This exercise will have surfaced possible sources of inconsistency. It may be beneficial to broaden your discussions with other colleagues not only to understand conflicting communicators but also then to consider ways of minimizing such problems.

2. Figure 3.1 presents an overview of a stakeholder-based journey to enhance the integrated nature of a brand. Allocate stakeholder groups to team members in such a way that members have a stakeholder group that they do not normally focus on in their daily jobs. Each person should then approach a representative of their stakeholder and, through discussions, elicit replies to each of the boxes in Figure 3.1. A senior member of the brand's team then needs to convene a workshop at which the findings about each stakeholder group are presented and ideas are generated to reduce inconsistencies.

3. The model in Figure 3.3 shows four ways in which a brand's values are expressed. Take one of your brand's values and, using the scoring system below, evaluate for each of the four media the extent to which that particular medium reinforces the brand's value, then circle the appropriate number.

Value ....

	Very weak reinforcement of the value				Very strong reinforcement of the value
Product/service	1	2	3	4	5
Staff behaviour	1	2	3	4	5
Environment	1	2	3	4	5
Communication	1	2	3	4	5

Ideally, you will be looking at a set of scores of between four and five for a well-integrated brand. Lower numbers indicate the need for corrective action.

Repeating the exercise for the other values should provide ideas about ways of presenting a more coherent brand.

4. All brands have a service element, and brands traditionally considered as services brands are more intangible. Figure 3.4 shows how an integrated brand results in its values being resonated through three components – tangible, intangible and supporting systems. For your brand, make explicit the details of these three components.

Tangibles _____

    _____

    _____

    _____

Intangibles _____

    _____

    _____

    _____

Supporting systems _____

    _____

    _____

    _____

Now focus on one of the brand's values and evaluate the extent to which each of the three components supports that value, presenting your results on the table below.

	Very weak reinforcement of the value			Very strong reinforcement of the value
Tangibles	1	2	3	4	5
Intangibles	1	2	3	4	5
Supporting system	1	2	3	4	5

Ideally you will see scores of 4–5 on all three components for an integrated brand; lower numbers indicate areas for attention. By repeating this exercise for each of the brand's values, areas needing corrective action can be identified.

5. By talking with some of your customers, explore their expectations about the on-line experience with your brand. Enabling them to access your website, encourage them to explain the extent to which their expectations about the on-line experience were exceeded, met or not achieved. Ask them to talk you through any differences between their expectations and perceptions for the brand characteristics they consider to be important. Finally, get them to clarify

their views about the brand experiences once they came off-line, to identify whether the delivery of the brand, supporting services and communication were satisfactory. Summarize your finding using the table shown below.

Brand   _____
Expectations about   _____
the on-line brand   _____
experience   _____

How did the on-line   _____   Exceeded expectations
brand experience   _____   Met expectations
compare with   _____   Below expectations
expectations

Where there were variances   _____

between expectations and   _____
experiences, on which   _____
characteristics did these occur?   _____

When then off-line, how satisfied were customers with the following:

	Very dissatisfied				Very satisfied
Brand delivery	1	2	3	4	5
Supporting services	1	2	3	4	5
Communication	1	2	3	4	5

Through considering these results,   _____
what are the branding implications?   _____

6. Below are statements that provide clarification about the motivators relating to Barrett's seven levels of organizational consciousness. Use these in discussions with members of the brand's team to elicit their key motivators, by asking them to select the statement which best describes them.
    (i) Coming to work is about ensuring a good level of income so I (and my family) can enjoy life to its full. I get irritated when meetings don't finish close to the end of the working day and when I have to start work earlier than normal (cf. security).
    (ii) Being at work is a good social experience and I think it is important that people should be nice to each other all the time. I don't like being asked to give my opinions about an issue in a meeting before other people

state their opinions. I find it hard to accept that people can become so dogmatic in meetings about their views (cf. relationship).

(iii) I think it is important to succeed in your career and I relish taking on work to show how capable I am, even though it means I'm going to have to put in long hours and this will eat into my social life. If I continue to put all this work in, I'll keep on going up the salary bands at my annual appraisal and will become more senior. I'll be able to change my car more regularly and will keep going for more prestigious cars. I think it is important to gain the respect of colleagues and I often check out their views (cf. self-esteem).

(iv) I don't see why we should keep on doing the same things in the same ways. I'm always curious about how else we could do things. If I can see a way of doing something differently I enjoy trying the new approach. I find it particularly stimulating talking with customers, because this gives me ideas about looking at my job in a different way and encourages me to change. I like to work for people who want to bring about change (cf. transformation).

(v) When you go for a new job, it's important to find out what the people believe in and what the culture is like. I'd not feel comfortable working in an organization that has beliefs contrary to those I hold. I'd even work for a organization paying slightly less if they are involved in something that I believe is important. Working with like-minded people in teams, where you don't need a lot of supervision because you all believe in the same cause, enthuses me. I think it's important that my manager is very open with me (cf. meaning).

(vi) I want to come to work to achieve something. When I think about my market, I'm aware of where things need doing to make a real difference and I really enjoy bringing about improvements to others' lives. While it is often daunting facing these challenges, I ignore those who keep saying 'you can't' and I enjoy working out new ways of achieving things. It's so good when you get letters of thanks from customers – these really make my day (cf. make a difference).

(vii) I think it's very important that we spend time working out our corporate philosophy and being clear about our soul. Yes, we need to make profits, but this should not be our only goal. I think we need to look at each project in terms of how we are helping our stakeholders and the environment, and whether we are making the world a better place. Being a good corporate citizen is important, even though it's going to reduce our profitability. I'm always conscious that value is not defined by us, but by our stakeholders. I encourage people to get involved with the local communities (cf. service).

Through asking your colleagues to comment about which one of these statements best describes them, you should be able to gauge their motivational level. By undertaking this exercise for the team, you can obtain some insight about their motivation profile. The appropriateness of these motivation profiles can be assessed through considering the brand's values and identifying an 'ideal' motivation state. It may help if, on an individual basis, you feed back your view about the person's motivations and discuss his or her views about how well these fit with the brand's values. As a consequence of this discussion, you may be able to identify any changes that might be helpful for specific individuals.

If you wish to delve deeper into this subject, you may find it useful to read Barrett's (1998) book.

References and further reading

Barrett, R. (1998). *Liberating the Corporate Soul*. Oxford: Butterworth-Heinemann.

Collins, J. (1999). Turning goals into results: the power of catalytic mechanisms. *Harvard Business Review*, **July/August**, 70–82.

Collins, J. and Porras, J. (1996). *Built to Last*. London: Century.

de Chernatony, L. and Daniels, K. (1994). Developing a more effective brand positioning. *Journal of Brand Management*, **1** (6), 373–9.

Duncan, T. and Moriarty, S. (1997). *Driving Brand Value*. New York: McGraw Hill.

Hatch, M. J. and Schultz, M. (2001). Are the strategic stars aligned for your corporate brand? *Harvard Business Review*, **February**, 128–35.

Keller, K. (1998). *Strategic Brand Management*. Upper Saddle River NJ: Prentice Hall.

Keller, K. (2000). The brand report card. *Harvard Business Review*, **January/February**, 147–57.

Shrimp, T. (1997). *Advertising, Promotion and Supplemental Aspects of Integrated Marketing Communications*. Forth Worth TX: Dryden Press.

Simmons, J. (2000). *We, Me, Them & It*. London: Texere Publishing.

Simmons, J. (2003). *The Invisible Grail*. London: Texere Publishing.

Smythe, J., Dorward, C. and Roback, J. (1992). *Corporate Reputation*. London: Century Business.

Wolff Olins (1995). *The New Guide to Identity*. Aldershot: Gower.

Part Three

Employing the Brand-building Process

Chapter 4

Brand visioning

Summary

This chapter focuses on the brand vision block of the process for building and sustaining brands (see Figure 4.1). The purpose of the chapter is to clarify the importance of brand visioning, as the first stage of the brand-building process, and to provide insight about the three components of a powerful brand vision. The chapter opens by explaining the directional benefit that a brand vision can provide. It then looks at the first component, the envisioned future, and considers how to set about identifying an envisioned future. The second component, the brand purpose, is then reviewed and ways to elicit this are explored. The third component, brand values, is then addressed. The rationale for having a clear set of values is reviewed, the difference between category values and brand values is clarified, and the need to understand actual rather than espoused values is explained. Ways to identify brand values are discussed and the need to differentiate between core and peripheral values is considered. It is not inconceivable for some employees' values to be at odds with the brand's values, and because this may lead them to behave in a way which does not support the brand, the issue of aligning staff and brand values is discussed.

The brand's vision

Brand visioning is about considering how a brand could benefit its stakeholders over a long time horizon. It is about being brave, putting a marker on a timeline about a changed environment, then motivating staff to become enthused to bring about change.

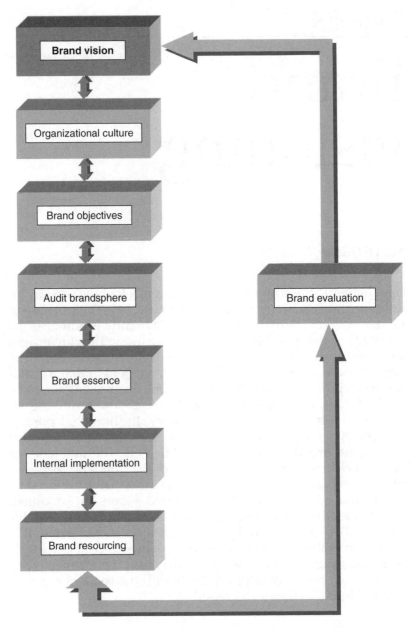

Figure 4.1   *Brand vision in the process of building and sustaining brands*

Some of you might have visited the Eden Project in Cornwall (www.edenproject.com). At first glance this might be regarded as a botanically themed park where a series of greenhouses display an exceptionally broad variety of vegetation. Yet, as Tim Smit,

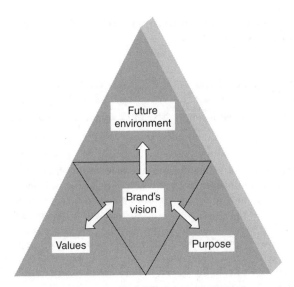

Figure 4.2   *The three components of a brand's vision*

the founder, states in one of the guides, this is not the case. This brand emerged because of a vision. To quote Tim Smit:

> But if this place becomes no more than an upmarket theme park it will all have been the most gigantic waste of money. We have intended to create something that not only encourages us to understand and to celebrate the world we live in, but also inspires us to action. Eden isn't so much a destination as a place in the heart. It is not just a marvellous piece of science-related architecture; it is also a statement of our passionate belief in an optimistic future for mankind.

A characteristic of successful brands is having a strong leader who has a clear vision for the brand. Bill Gates and Sam Walton are but two visionaries who helped to establish Microsoft and Wal-Mart respectively. It is dangerous for a brand to drift with an implied strategy of 'any road taking it anywhere' – if nothing else because when a new leader wishes to provide a clear sense of direction an internal audit may reveal the status of 'I wouldn't like to be going there from here'! Furthermore, if their strong leader makes staff aware of the cause they are crusading (e.g. Virgin being the equivalent of Robin Hood, trying to improve the consumer experience in categories where they are poorly serviced), it encourages commitment and pride.

As Figure 4.2 indicates, a brand vision consists of three components.

These three components – the desired future environment, the purpose for the brand (how the world will be a better place as a consequence of the brand) and the brand's values – are interlinked and self-supporting.

Activity 4.1

Is there a particular order in which these three components should be devised?

Discussion

When managers undertake brand visioning, while they might focus on one of the components at a time, as they do so they will be rapidly considering in their minds the implications of that component on the other two. For example, when two entrepreneurs start out together, they do so because they share a belief in a common set of values they consider to be important. At the back of their minds is the challenge of how these values can inspire their employees to work on a brand which should bring about a better world. Arriving at the three components of a brand vision is akin to entering a circle – entry can be gained from any point, but the trajectory will encounter all three components

---

This chapter will address the three components by first considering the need to envision a desired future, secondly identifying the brand's purpose and thirdly making explicit the brand's values.

The case study describing the launch of the Orange mobile phone helps to provide an overview of this topic.

Orange: A brand with a clear vision

In April 1994 Hutchinson launched its new mobile phone, Orange, aided by WCRS. The two key competitors, Cellnet and Vodaphone, had the advantage of ten years' presence, full national coverage and millions of subscribers. They had both sought to sustain their positions by developing low-user tariffs to block new entrants in the consumer market, and developed their digital (GSM) networks to strengthen their positions in the business market. At its launch Orange had only 50 per cent network coverage.

Extensive qualitative research was undertaken. This showed that mobile telephony had a significant appeal, but the day-to-day reality of confusion, distrust, complicated tariff deals and price claims took that excitement away. To identify how to develop the brand, a notable amount of time was then spent visioning, and eventually a view emerged as to the envisioned future for the brand, summarized as:

> There will come a time when all people will have their own personal number that goes with them wherever they are so there are no barriers to communication.
> A wirefree future in which you can call people, not places, and where everyone will benefit from the advances of technology.

The first component of the brand vision had been clarified.

> The two key competitors had built their category around a technology theme. Orange decided not to join this category and not to have to play by the established rules. Its brand purpose was to liberate people from the technology of communication and give them the freedom to communicate. This purpose led to a brand strategy which necessitated the opening of a new category, i.e. wirefree communication. In fact the advertising proposition for WCRS as a consequence of such a brand purpose was simply:
>
> *The future is wirefree and it's Orange.*
>
> With the brand vision becoming clearer, the brand values needed to reflect forward thinking, dynamism and accessibility.

While Orange's early success was in part influenced by its vision, the brand has seen other competitors with refreshing ideas. For example, O$_2$ was relaunched in April 2002 with the objective of becoming the most 'enabling' brand in this market. To achieve this it sought to provide more ways for consumers to work, play and communicate (Maunder *et al.* 2005). Such challengers should provoke a rethink of the brand's vision to enable the brand to lead consumers with exciting new ideas.

Activity 4.2

Put yourself in the position of a company producing a small four-seater car. It enables consumers to personalize the car by getting onto its web page and choosing the body colour, interior colour, wheels and size of engine. It also plans to encourage owners to form 'clubs' in their particular area, so they can meet on a regular basis and enjoy the beauty of their area by travelling in a convoy, following a route devised by their area secretary. To differentiate their brand better, they need to devise a brand vision. What might the three components of this be?

Discussion

1. Envisioned future: let's strive to have bigger national parks of outstanding beauty and smaller parking places
2. Purpose: by respecting each other and smiling more, roads and the world they connect will be more enjoyable
3. Values: escapism, individuality, excitement and energy.

Note how the term 'car' and technological facets do not appear. Such thinking does not constrain the organization as it extends the brand, and builds on the fact that consumers prefer benefits and not products.

Developing a brand vision can engender more committed employees if they have been involved in some of the brand-visioning workshops. Brand visioning is typically a team-based activity that involves a process of amending drafts through a combination of analytical thinking and dreaming. It should result in a statement that is simple to understand and can be easily communicated (Kotter 1996). One of the challenges the senior team has to face when involving staff is that it is raising expectations that staff's views will be incorporated in the final decision. For some cultures, particularly those that are bureaucratic or autocratic, engaging staff in the process may cause senior managers to feel uncomfortable, since they are not used to having their ideas questioned. Some relaxation of control could help these types of organizations to capitalize on staff participation.

There are distinct advantages in involving a broad cross-section of staff in the brand-visioning process, for example:

- it provides a much richer array of ideas
- it makes staff more aware of the challenges and opportunities for the future
- it helps all employees better to understand the resulting vision
- it encourages staff commitment if their ideas are seen to be taken seriously
- it provides a stronger cultural bond.

In an era of greater brand similarity, having a company-wide approach to brand visioning may provide a stronger competitive advantage from staff who are committed to delivering the brand.

By adopting a shared approach to visioning, rather than limiting this to the top management team, the perspective amongst staff about the brand changes from 'theirs' (i.e. management's responsibility) to 'ours'. If the visioning is solely left to the senior team, this fails to test the viability of ideas amongst those who are going to implement the new thrust and it may not awaken the necessary energy and commitment. It may take longer to embrace the views and ideas of employees throughout the firm, but by engaging them in the visioning process the employees' involvement is likely to shift from compliance to commitment. By being ignored and having a vision imposed on them, there may be a significant proportion who grudgingly accept the vision or, worse still, are apathetic about brand initiatives to achieve the vision.

Brand visioning is an important task, as it seals the future for the brand. The process is time-consuming and through company debate is likely to surface conflicting views. Through encouraging debate, helping to connect people throughout the firm, being enthusiastic and continually stressing clarity and openness, the process should be fruitful.

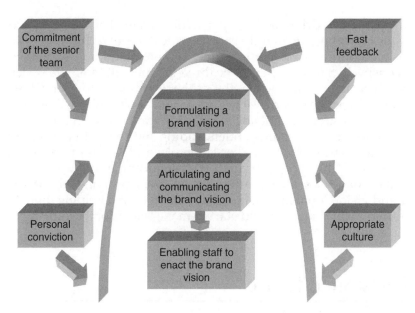

Figure 4.3 *Factors enhancing the process of brand visioning (adapted from Kakabadse* et al. *2005)*

Kakabadse *et al.* (2005) argue that there are four factors that positively influence the three-step process of visioning, as shown in Figure 4.3. Devising a brand vision is a challenging task that can attract much criticism. Personal conviction and tenacity are essential if ideas are to be conceived and refined in light of the ongoing debate. A powerful leader will form a senior team to spark off each member and harness their collective competence and experience to create and nurture a brand vision. However, the team's effectiveness depends on each individual's commitment and enthusiasm. Brand-visioning meetings should not be regarded as options in diaries. As soon as ideas emerge, they need to be exposed to staff and rapid responses sought. Only by welcoming fast feedback from employees can the viability of ideas be gauged. Related to this is the need for a culture that embraces constructive criticism and where the visibility of the senior team flags the importance of a collective approach to formulating a vision.

If these four factors are heeded, the process should drive more challenging and appealing brand visions. It should be appreciated that the first stage of the process, i.e. formulating a vision, is but the start of a journey. At this stage an interactive process of idea generation and fast feedback from employees should help engender the evolution of the brand vision statement.

To ensure this drives actions, the second stage of articulating and communicating the brand vision is critical. A powerful vision can only be appreciated if it is widely disseminated and expressed in crisp, clear terms – hence the three-component template which is advocated. At this stage, the senior team need to spend time evangelizing the brand vision. This will no doubt involve time talking, demonstrating, replying to questions and, through numerous internal events, spreading understanding and commitment behind the brand vision. Once this has taken place, all levels of staff need to be given the necessary support systems and empowerment to make changes which are concerned with bringing about the brand vision. Enabling staff to make changes and helping them to overcome problems should start to make the vision become more realizable.

Envisioned future

If a brand is to thrive, it is helpful for the team to have a stretching vision about the future environment they would like to bring about 'ten years ahead'. Saying 'ten years ahead' discourages incremental projections and encourages a more challenging, lateral view about the future. The notion of ten years is that it is a sufficiently long period to stop incremental thinking. It should not be a dogmatic ten-year horizon, but rather the time period should reflect the dynamics of the market. In a stable market ten years is appropriate, but in a rapidly changing market this may need to be reconsidered (e.g. five years). Not only should this stretch staff to deliver the enhanced benefits, but it should also be an enjoyable working experience. As James Dean once said, 'Dream as if you'll live for ever, live as if you'll die today.'

To be appreciated, a brand should bring about *welcomed* change, and by thinking a long way into the future managers should not consider themselves to be shackled by the current constraints under which they operate. If we doubt, recall Sir Winston Churchill's comment, 'History will be kind to me for I intend to write it.' Specifying a long-term horizon encourages managers to think about discontinuities that will result in step changes in the market. For example, an office removal company might envision a future environment in which far more people work from home, offices become smaller and the frequency of office moves diminishes. While such a negative scenario may worry some, for others it presents an opportunity to consider how to embrace the opportunities of more people needing to set up offices at home.

To stimulate ideas and hopefully arrive at an informed vision, a review is needed of any factors that could affect the brand in the future – e.g. changing birth rate, new distribution channels, changing advertising rates. These factors should be categorized on a matrix whose dimensions are the likelihood of the factor coming about (low vs high probability) and the impact of the factor on the brand (favourable vs unfavourable). By focusing on those factors that are likely to occur and should have a favourable impact on the brand, ideas can be considered about possible future environments and how the brand must change to bring these about and capitalize on them.

While some advocate the advantage of circulating summaries from external sources about the future (e.g. Ritchie 1999), such documents may 'lead' people down a particular line of thought. An alternative approach is to use a hybrid Delphi technique–consensus workshop. Those who are envisioning the brand's future environment are individually sent a postal questionnaire. On this are examples of the future environments envisioned for another sector, to help them appreciate the task, along with a request for their views about the environment they would like to see at least ten years ahead for their brand. Once the questionnaires have been returned to the facilitator, the participants are sent a brief set of notes summarizing any of the forecasts from external sources about the future macro-environment (political, economic, social, technological and environmental) and their views sought, yet again, about the envisioned environment at least ten years ahead.

The facilitator then works through the replies to identify common themes across the respondents, without and with any external stimulus. The themes are categorized, with numbers to indicate their frequency of occurrence, but with no indication as to who said what. These themes are then circulated to all the participants and, several days later, a workshop is convened. At the workshop the facilitator helps the team to arrive at a shared view of the future – and one that does not look as if it is based on incremental projections. The workshop should start to explore some of the challenges the brand is likely to face and possible strategies that might help bring such a future about.

The benefit of envisioning a distant future is that it enables managers to consider what role the brand needs to play to bring about this future. In this exercise the managers become aware of the challenges the brand faces, and this encourages them to think creatively about how to circumvent such challenges. For example, when Canon envisaged a future where all senior secretaries would have a photocopier in their offices, they had to counter the dominance of Xerox and the might of its service infrastructure (Hamel and Prahalad 1994). Their response was to reinvent the photo-copier, eliminating the need for servicing through incorporating the optical system into a disposable cartridge, with a design that significantly reduced costs.

Some organizations might regard this need for envisioning a new future as being less pressing, since they have already completed some work. To these organizations are commended three questions adapted from Hamel and Prahalad (1994):

1. Has this work on an envisioned future been based predominantly on issues external rather than internal to the organization?
2. When looking ahead, has the time been spent considering how the world could be different in five to ten years, rather than thinking about incremental projections based on a variety of contracts or changes to pricing policy?
3. How much work has been undertaken within the management team, whereby they have developed a shared view of the future that they are all comfortable with, rather than maintaining their personal views?

If these do not stimulate action, it may help to consider the case of Boeing. Managers feel comfortable anticipating the future by considering the past. Boeing challenged this and brought about a sense of urgency to think about the future by simulating a crisis. A video was commissioned, creating a future news programme that reviewed the demise of Boeing. This was widely distributed, and awoke the need for a rethink about the future.

The core to envisioning a new future is to move the focus away from re-engineering and restructuring the organization to reinventing markets and acting in a different manner. New brand strategies are required which are not about better returns on investment through cutting costs, nor about better returns through efficiencies gained by re-engineering value adding processes. Rather, they are about superior returns through thinking differently and reinventing markets.

Part of the problem of thinking differently is managerial mindsets. We all have mental models that enable us to explain and predict how markets operate (Schwenk 1988). Having like-minded people together reinforces the common mental model amongst a management team, and makes it difficult for a new model to be accepted (Huff 1990). Being aware of this resistance to mental change is part of the process of accepting new ideas of the future, and involves forgetting the old ideas about the dynamics of the market. Another way of engendering new views is to leave the comfort zone of the organization's offices and work on the brand visioning in a different environment, where the artefacts no longer reinforce the original model (Schein 1984). Having an external moderator responsible for directing the process enables new ideas to be debated, rather than being rapidly rejected. Having participants who think differently also encourages the likelihood of challenging ideas emerging.

Hamel (1996) has proposed several routes that managers can follow when reinventing their markets for a different future. These could act as a stimulus by considering analogies from other markets. Drawing on this, the team could consider whether there might be a different future brought about by:

1. Reconceiving the product or service through
   - radically improving the value equation, as HP has done in computer printers
   - separating function and form, for example reinventing credit cards to open hotel doors and act as international passports
   - achieving joy in use, as exemplified by the Forum shops in Las Vegas where everything in the shopping mall is themed around an ancient Roman marketplace.
2. Redefining market space through
   - increasing accessibility, for example 24-hour banking over the Internet
   - striving for individuality, for example Levi's 'Personal Pair' system providing individually tailored jeans.
3. Redrawing industry boundaries through
   - driving convergence, for example grocery stores offering financial services.

Another route to stimulating ideas about the future is through considering how an organization's competencies can be combined to open up new ideas about the future. For example, Canon considered how it was able to combine its competencies in precision mechanics, optics and micro-electronics to envision moves into the camera, printer and fax markets. Sometimes just considering the organization's competencies may be restrictive, since these can be broadened through strategic alliances.

A further stimulus to help envision a different future is to consider undertaking interviews with users and non-users of the product/service category. The lack of experience of non-users allows them to approach the situation with few preconceptions. After they have been allowed to try the existing brands in the category, their critical views are sought about what they disliked, what is missing and what they would like to change. Users of the category are asked to consider how they would adjust their lives without the category.

Brand purpose

The second component of a powerful brand vision is the brand's purpose. This is more than just increasing shareholder wealth, or making a profit. To make a profit is akin to breathing air – it's an essential prerequisite, but is a taken-for-granted essential. As Anita Roddick (quoted in Bainbridge 2000), founder of the Body Shop, pertinently observed:

> Profit is not the objective of my business. It is providing a product and a service that's good enough that people give you a profit for providing it.

Likewise, an advertising executive recalled an interview with David Plastow, when Chief Executive of Vickers:

> Profit is a by-product of our business and when we make our tanks, incubators and Rolls Royce cars to a very high standard and promote them the best we can, then profit is a by-product that flows into the company ... But, if we ever get the impression that profit is a product of our company, that our Rolls Royce's, tanks and incubators are the by-product, then we will be 5 years from extinction.

A motivating brand purpose is concerned with answering the question, 'how is the world going to be a better place as a consequence of the brand, and will this inspire and guide staff?' This can be appreciated from the powerful brand purpose of Federal National Mortgage Company:

> To strengthen the social fabric by continually democratizing home ownership.

Broadening the profile of people who own their homes, gives a nation pride and makes civil rioting and looting less likely.

Several organizations have made it explicit why their brand must have a purpose. For example, Henry Ford once stated (quoted in Collins and Porras 1996a):

> Business must be run at a profit ... else it will die. But when anyone tries to run a business solely for profit ... then also the business must die for it no longer has a reason for existence.

Lee Clow, Chairman of TBWA Worldwide (quoted in Clifton and Maughan 2000), remarked:

> The Body Shop and Ben & Jerry's are good examples of brands that say 'we're not just here to make money. We're here because we think there's something we can contribute to the world by doing our business the way we do it.'

One of the ways that Ben & Jerry's helps society is through its policy of giving 7.5 per cent of pre-tax profit to the community.

Deriving a brand purpose of increasing shareholder wealth does not provide inspiration and guidance for staff. Collins and Porras (1996a) provide some helpful examples of motivating brand purposes, for example:

- Johnson & Johnson – to alleviate pain and disease
- Marriott – to make people away from home feel that they are among friends and are really wanted.

Activity 4.4

In view of what you've just read and your perceptions of different brands, what do you believe to be the purpose of the brands Walt Disney and Nike, respectively?

Discussion

The purpose of the brands, according to Collins and Porras (1996b), is as follows:

- Walt Disney – to make people happy
- Nike – to experience the emotion of competing, winning and crushing competitors.

To this list of examples could be added the BBC, with its purpose to educate, inform and entertain. So committed to this purpose is the BBC that a temple to programme-making was built, BBC Broadcasting House, and everything from microphones to its vehicles is branded.

The primary reason for the brand purpose is not to differentiate the brand, although this is an important contributor to brand differentiation. Through focusing on making the world a better place, it seeks to guide and inspire staff over the long term. From a more negative perspective, it is akin to the response to the question, 'Why don't we sell this brand off?' Again, Anita Roddick provides helpful insight into how a brand purpose can provide guidance. As she commented (quoted in Bainbridge 2000):

> The area that really worries me in the Body Shop is language. I don't want words like 'nourishing' when it comes to shampoo because it doesn't nourish, it cleans your hair. ... Out there [gesturing to her colleagues in a meeting] there's a big discussion on the word beauty. It's not about being Caucasian, not about having balanced features ... the industry is missing out on the reverence for women and the love of women and their passion.

Likewise, Amazon's purpose is less to do with books, but rather with customer fulfilment. The brand has been developed to stand for excellence in delivery, enabling its progression from its core business of books to adopting a view that it is not tied to any product category.

Identifying a brand's purpose

There is an assumption that all brands have a clearly articulated purpose. However, this is not necessarily the case, as Oechsle and Henderson (2000) explained regarding Shell. In 1991, US Shell awoke to the fact that it earned $26bn yet made virtually no profit. This stimulated the need for a new CEO who, amongst other things, encouraged the organization to question what the purpose of the Shell brand is. The brand had been around for 100 years, yet had no explicit brand purpose. Thirty-two workshops were undertaken, in many countries, amongst staff to elicit their views about the brand's purpose. Out of this exercise emerged the purpose of the Shell brand, i.e. helping people build a better world. The intent was to achieve this 'by creating communities of people who relentlessly pursue challenge with an unwavering commitment to be the best' (Oechsle and Henderson 2000: 76). The route forward became clearer as a result of this exercise. First, the internal programme 'Count on Shell' was launched to get employees to recognize the need to be able to count on each other because, without a team approach, the future would be uncertain. The initiative was strengthened by linking individual and team performance to support behaviours consistent with the brand's purpose. A communication programme was then devised, which in the first phase was directed at specific publics to inform them of the new campaign. A national campaign was then launched to provoke dialogue on key issues.

This case illustrates the way that the process involves a broad cross-section of employees to surface views about the brand purpose. One way of stimulating staff to make explicit their views about the brand's purpose is the 'five whys' method proposed by Collins and Porras (1996b). Employees are brought together in a workshop and the facilitator encourages debate around the question 'We are all involved in producing and delivering this brand. Why is it important?' As each reply is received and discussed, the facilitator continues to probe 'why is it important?' After around five rounds of probing, some indication of the brand's purpose should become clear. For example, a market research agency that has devised a proprietary statistical analysis technique may argue initially that their brand is important because it provides the best data available. After several rounds of further probing, the purpose of the brand starts to emerge as contributing to customers' success by helping them to understand their markets better.

Activity 4.5

Taking the example of an organization that originally defined its purpose as 'we make gravel and asphalt products', use the 'five whys' method to identify a more motivating purpose.

Discussion

You may have ended up with something along the lines of 'we make people's lives better by improving the quality of man-made structures'.

The 'five whys' method is a helpful stimulus for new brands, as well as existing brands, when seeking ideas about motivating purposes. For existing brands, the critical episodes technique may prove helpful in unearthing the brand's purpose. A team is brought together and set the task of delving into the brand's history to understand critical episodes. These are periods when significant events took place and the brand faced new opportunities or new challenges. Having established a thorough understanding of these critical episodes, the findings are presented to the brand's team in a workshop. Against each of the critical episodes the team is then asked to consider what inferences can be drawn about the brand's purpose. This debate may generate a variety of points, which are then categorized into a few themes. Amongst a broader group of staff, the themes can then be presented and used to open a company-wide debate about what the brand's purpose is.

Such approaches can help to generate views about the brand's purpose, which can then be tested through questioning:

- Will this purpose make a real change and bring about a better world?
- Does this excite staff?

- Does it provide a clear sense of direction for staff?
- If staff won a major lottery, would they retire rich or would they continue to work to bring about the brand purpose?

Brand values

The third component of the brand vision is the brand's values. These need to reinforce the brand purpose. Thus, if the purpose of an antidepressant brand is improving the quality of life for patients and their support group, brand values such as dignity, respect and restoring self-confidence will be appropriate.

Earlier in this book it was shown that brands are based on clusters of values, and thus making explicit what the values are to be is an important part of brand visioning. A particularly clear definition has been advanced by Rokeach (1973):

A value is an enduring belief that a specific mode of conduct or end-state of existence is personally or socially preferable to an opposite or converse mode of conduct or end-state of existence.

Values are important in brands for several reasons. First, values drive behaviour and, from an internal perspective, a particular cluster of values results in specific behaviours. For example, Red Cross and Red Crescent have three core values – humanity, unity and independence – and these drive its staff to go into disaster-stricken areas to help others. Secondly, values relate to particular personality traits, and thus customers choose brands with values that reflect the actual or desired personality of the user.

Activity 4.6

From an internal and an external perspective, why else do you think values are an important ingredient of a brand?

Discussion

The importance of values driving behaviour cannot be overstated. For example, when a man who has honesty as one of his cherished values passes a house with a door left unlocked, he is unlikely to attempt to steal. Identifying a set of values that is to characterize a brand helps staff to understand how they should behave, and customers better to appreciate the brand promise. Particularly in the case of service brands, where staff *are* the brand, by understanding their brand's values the staff have a better feel for the types of behaviour they should adopt to reinforce the brand. For example, Virgin Atlantic has as its values fun, value for money, sense of challenge, innovation and quality. By contrast, British Airways' values encompass safety and security, responsibility and honesty, innovation and team spirit, and finally a global and caring outlook. One has only to think of the different styles of behaviour of the cabin crew in these two brands of airlines to recognize how different clusters of brand values result in different types of staff behaviour. Therefore, brand values offer an opportunity for brand differentiation and attract people whose values match those being projected by their chosen brand. The people attracted by these values are employees who are proud to align themselves with these values, as well as consumers. A brand with a clear set of values is particularly welcomed by some groups of consumers because it enables them to make symbolic, non-verbal statements about themselves. For example, having an account with the Co-operative Bank, which has a policy of ethical banking, enables customers to portray something about themselves (Antonides and van Raaij 1998). Thus, as will be clarified further in this section, values are critically important in brand-building.

Identifying the core values for the brand enables an organization to be very clear about why it is different. While there are many brands of trainers and sportswear, Nike differentiates itself through its brand values:

- authenticity – being real in the eyes of athletes
- inspirational – through emotion and passion for sports
- courage – conviction to stand by beliefs
- innovation.

Having a clear set of values provides guidelines about how to develop a brand for the benefit of its customers. Sir Richard Branson publicly stated (in Macrae 1996: 232) that:

> We give top priority to the interests of our staff; second priority to those of our customers; third to our shareholders.

His argument is simply that if staff are committed to the values of the brand then their enthusiasm and behaviour should delight the target market, and in the long term this should enhance shareholders' wealth. Branson also declared that one of the benefits of having a clear set of values is that these enable his organization to evaluate the appropriateness of stretching the Virgin brand into new markets. His rule is that at least four of the five Virgin values must be applicable for any new market under investigation. Interestingly, Virgin never goes into a new market just for money – its purpose can be appreciated from the edict that there must be a passionate belief within the organization about being able to turn the market on its head to better satisfy customers.

Three of the Body Shop's values – social responsibility, environmental protection and animal protection – provide a clear sense of direction and inspiration for its business activities. When sourcing products, it seeks to revitalize deprived areas through its Community Trade Programme. For example, it switched the sourcing of wooden foot rollers from a factory in Germany to a village in India, where it paid the same prices and educated orphaned children.

Activity 4.7

Choose a brand you are familiar with and write down its values.

Discussion

There are many DIY retailers, but B&Q successfully differentiates itself through its values of:

- down-to-earth approach
- respect for people
- being customer driven
- being positive
- striving to do better

People buy brands whose values concur with their own, and potential employees are attracted to organizations that have similar values to theirs – in other words, the brand's values have an impact on both consumers and staff. As Rokeach (1973) explained, personal values are enduring. Initially they are taught by a child's parents and subsequently are learnt from the person's peer group. People's values are ordered in importance, and our behaviour is the result of the relative importance of competing values. A value is a belief that cognitively enables a person to know the correct way to behave, thus a particular value leads to a specific form of behaviour. As such, it is more important for individuals to know who they are rather than where they are going, since where they are going will change as the world changes, and to ensure a clear sense of direction there needs to be a particular constellation of values.

One of the principles of effective branding is that there should be a low number of values underpinning the brand – typically no more than five. As the number of values rises, it becomes more difficult for staff to recall all the values and the task of devising and sustaining a clear unique promise becomes more complex. A further advantage of majoring on a low number of values is that, as they encourage specific types of staff behaviour, there is less scope for internal confusion and thus there is a greater likelihood of behavioural consistency amongst staff. This is particularly significant for organizations that operate across many countries and can capitalize on the brand's values as the glue that unites staff's behaviour.

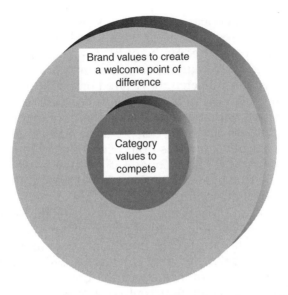

Figure 4.4   *The brand as an amalgam of category values and its own unique values*

One of the issues when conceiving a brand's values is to ensure they are unique and are not the generic values of the category within which the brand competes. It is not inconceivable to encounter a mature market with discerning customers who take for granted the category values of:

- delighting customers
- quality and excellence in all interactions with staff
- innovation.

The brand must have these values, as an 'entry price' to compete in the market, but in addition to these it needs its unique brand values, rather than just the generic category values (see Figure 4.4).

It is possible to find markets where a consideration of press advertisements indicates that different organizations are placing notable emphasis on promoting category values, with a small emphasis on values unique to their brand. For example, a review of financial services advertisements revealed several organizations majoring on performance, convenience and flexibility rather than unique values.

Some organizations seek to develop a more coherent approach to brand-building by placing their brand values at the heart of everything they do. For example, when the Midland Bank (as it was then) set up a team to develop a new approach to banking, i.e. telephone banking through First Direct, one of the team's early actions was to define the brand's unique values. These were: respect, openness, energy, thinking and getting it right. When they then recruited their telephone bank representatives, they were less concerned with applicants' banking skills (which they argued could be taught) and put emphasis on whether the applicants' values reflected the desired brand values.

By being clear about the core values of the brand, managers in a 'green field' situation can design their organization around processes that are tuned to deliver these values. For example, when Daewoo developed its brand strategy to launch its range of cars in the UK, it had as one of its values 'hassle-free' inter-actions. Being true to this value, it recruited sales staff and trained them not to put customers under pressure to buy; it advertised the fact that its car prices are fixed, and installed interactive in-store terminals to enable customers to find out more about their cars at their own pace. Interestingly, this organization adopted a novel launch strategy when it entered the UK. It addressed the initial problem of ignorance about the brand through an intri-guing advertising campaign centred around 'Daewho?' In an attempt to overcome apathy, it then advertised for 200 people to act as guinea pigs who would be loaned a car in order to provide feedback. In addition to creating over 200000 volunteers, this stimulated further interest in the brand. However, while it is laudable to see such adherence to a core value, it is imperative that the rest of the business model is wisely conceived and enacted. After entering the UK market in 1995 with its direct sales strategy, Daewoo announced in 2001, while awaiting a takeover by General Motors, that it was recruiting dealers to sell its cars. One reason for this is that Daewoo and its partner Halfords did not have a competence selling second-hand cars. Daewoo has subsequently been taken over by General Motors.

One of the problems when defining a brand's values is that managers announce what the brand's values should be – i.e. the espoused values – but fail to gain the commitment of staff to enact these, and thus the actual values differ from the espoused. For established brands, by auditing staff throughout the firm, managers can evaluate what staff think are the values of the brand and thus identify gaps between the espoused and per-ceived values. To identify differences, the senior management team can draw on the work of Martin (1992) and question:

- Are they communicating the desired values to staff?
- Is there action inconsistency? For example, a director may continually talk about the importance of customers, yet when presented with a recommendation to change the brand to reduce consumer complaints rejects this due to the cost of production retooling.

- Is there symbolic inconsistency? For example, staff may continually hear about 'striving to achieve the highest quality', yet the carpet in the offices looks worn out.
- Is there ideological inconsistency? For example, a financial institution may proclaim its policy of ethical investments, yet accept an invitation from a tobacco company to assist in its pension planning.

By working together to surface why gaps have occurred between the espoused and perceived values, organizations are in a much stronger position to take pan-company actions to ensure greater consistency in delivering the brand promise.

Thus there are core values, which are the timeless definition of the brand's beliefs. There are category values that all brands must hold if they are to compete in a category. There are espoused (or aspirational) values that managers typically talk about in an organization but are rarely enacted when delivering the brand. There are also accidental values that the brand acquires through a poorly conceived staff recruitment policy, when new employees work with the brand but have values outside the desired cluster.

In summary, values play an important role in building and sustaining brands. Benefits include the following:

1. Staff know what the brand stands for and should therefore better appreciate their roles to support this
2. Values present an opportunity for motivating and aligning staff
3. Staff and consumers are better able to appreciate the points of difference of the brand
4. People who believe in a brand's values are attracted to working for a particular organization
5. Consumers are better able to appreciate the promise being made by the brand
6. Marketing activities to support the brand, such as communication, pricing and dealership networks, become easier to identify from the values.

Identifying a brand's values

There are several ways for organizations to surface their brand values. One approach is the 'Mars group method' recommended by Collins and Porras (1996b). For this, the management team is asked to imagine that it is able to recreate the very best of the brand on planet Mars, where space technology has advanced sufficiently for civilization to be supported. There are, however only five seats on the rocket, and the first stage is for the team to identify who should be sent. The aim is to get the team to identify the few people who really have good intuition, understand the brand's values and are seen as being credible and competent. In effect, these people are exemplars of the brand's values and are very good at articulating its values.

With a facilitator, this small group is brought together and asked to consider a series of questions such as:

- What are the values of your brand?
- What values do you personally bring to work? (i.e. are your values so central to you that you would hold them regardless of being rewarded?)
- What are the values that you would tell your children you hold at work, and hope they will hold when working?
- If you were to start a firm tomorrow, what values would you put in place?

While this procedure will produce insight about brand values, it might be enhanced by another workshop session. From Schein's (1984) work, the values of a brand are manifest through artefacts such as its advertising, pricing, the type of people working on the brand, the offices and brochures, and the language used by staff. In advance of the workshop, the facilitator should explore the visible manifestations of the brand and formulate hypotheses about what values are common across these artefacts. In the workshop, examples of such material (e.g. photos, brochures, etc.) should be presented and members of the 'Mars group' encouraged to talk about their inferences as to their brand's values. Another part of this workshop could relate to 'critical episodes' for the brand, as described earlier in this chapter. The participants should be asked to think about the history of their brand and to identify critical episodes where the brand faced new opportunities and threats – for example, for an existing brand, points in its history when a competitor launched a new brand. By identifying these critical episodes and considering what actions their firm took, they can draw inferences about their brand's values.

A further way of surfacing a brand's core values is to use the laddering technique developed by Reynolds and Gutman (1988), which is based on Gutman's (1982) means–end theory. In essence, the theory states that the attributes that define a brand (the 'means') have consequences for the person, and these reinforce that individual's personal values (the 'ends'). As such, a facilitator works on an individual basis with members of the brand team to identify their views about the key attributes of the brand, what the consequences of these attributes are and thus what personal values are being reinforced.

The detail of the technique is as follows. The process starts with an individual manager stating the most important unique attribute of the brand, along with the second, third and, if they exist, fourth and fifth important unique attributes. For the most important brand attribute, the manager is then asked 'why is that important?' The reason is recorded, and for this new reason the question 'why is that important?' is again asked, repeating this procedure until the laddering reaches a point where the respondent has given a value. The second most important brand attribute is then selected and this procedure followed, and then subsequently the remaining attributes.

An example of the application of the laddering technique is the way that Federal Express developed an advertising campaign for its overnight delivery service (Wilkie 1994). One of the key markets is executives' secretaries. By undertaking the laddering technique amongst them, a summary hierarchy value map was elicited, as shown in Figure 4.5. Through identifying important key attributes of this brand, then repeatedly asking why these are important, the consequences and then the values were identified from these. As a result of the value 'peace of mind' and the consequence of

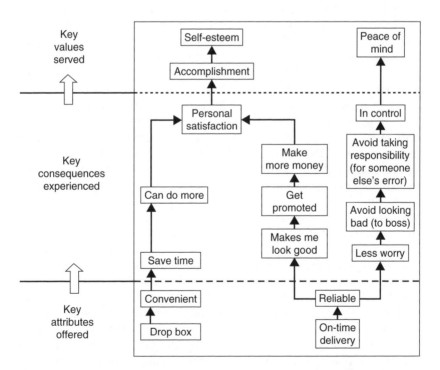

Figure 4.5   *Federal Express summary hierarchy value map (from Wilkie 1994)*

'wishing to stay in control', a humorous campaign was developed. This centred on a secretary trying to find how close a package was to delivery. In the campaign, a guide takes the secretary to view the Federal Express satellite communication system and the secretary realizes the dependability of this service.

Unlike the Mars group method, this can be a tiring technique for each respondent. It does, however, surface each manager's views about the brand. It provides a basis for identifying what the team perceives to be the most important unique attributes of the brand, and for team members to recognize the variety of values they hold. The challenge then becomes identifying which are the few core values, as we consider next.

Core vs peripheral values

A distinction can be drawn between core and peripheral values. A brand's core values are those values that the brand will always uphold, regardless of environmental change, and which will always be a central characteristic of the brand. By contrast, peripheral values are secondary values that are less important to the brand and which can be deleted or augmented according to environmental conditions. These less-central values can be better appreciated through the analogy of fashion – thus while a lady holds the value of fashion, she buys dresses with different lengths according to the prevailing fashion of the time.

HP is a good example of an organization that found itself having to be clear about its brand's core, timeless values (Kotter and Heskett 1992). In its early days of competing in the instruments market, the values of the HP brand were made explicit. These included providing customers with technically superior products and services of the greatest value, being genuinely interested in finding effective solutions to customer problems, and sharing success with its staff. As the market changed so HP developed a new strategy, resulting in its move into the computer market. However, to stay true to one of its core values of providing customers with technically superior products of the greatest value, staff became concerned when they saw a recruitment process taking place to bring in new managers. This was seen as contrary to the expected action of promoting staff internally, which would reflect the value of sharing success with staff. It was at this stage that the value 'providing customers with technically superior products of the greatest value' became a notable core value. To be true to this core value, HP had to have people who knew the computing business. Its audit showed a weakness here, so it recruited new staff. In effect, it realized that some of its values must always be key characteristics of its brand, but other less-central values must be allowed to adapt, to reflect changing market conditions.

Another example where a brand has been true to its core value but allowed its peripheral values to change is the retailer Wal-Mart. Its core value of exceeding customer expectations has continually been emphasized by each generation of management, yet one of its peripheral values, welcoming customers, was relaxed as customer expectations changed, resulting in foregoing the customer greeters.

Activity 4.8

How could you evaluate which of your brand's values are core and which are peripheral?

Discussion

Building on some of the points raised by Collins and Porras (1996b), the following questions could prove insightful:

- Would the team want to be true to these values for the next 100 years, regardless of environmental change?
- If the environment were to change to the extent that the organization felt it was penalized for a value, would that value still be kept?
- Does this value provide a clear guide for behaviour, and has it proved helpful in the past?
- Does this value set the brand apart from competitors?
- Is the logic for this value still appropriate?
- Is this value still credible, consistently achievable, and resulting in an outcome welcomed by customers?

Aligning brand and staff values

In view of the considerable importance of values in brands, staff are critically important resources. As John Seely Brown at Xerox Park was quoted as saying (Macrae 1999: 11):

> When it comes to attracting, keeping and making teams out of talented people, money alone won't do it. Talented people want to be part of something that they can believe in, something that confers meaning on their work and lives – something that involves a mission. And they don't want that mission to turn into the kind of predictable 'mission statement' that plasters many a corporate-boardroom wall. Rather they want spiritual goals that energize an organization by resonating with the personal values of the peoples who work there.

In view of the importance of values, it is inappropriate to think that the challenge is to identify values, then to leave the HR team to put these into practice. Just as searching for brand values is an important task, so it is necessary to recognize that a significant amount of work needs to be done on a pan-company basis to get the brand values enacted. The brand, representing a cluster of values, is ideally placed symbiotically to give meaning to employees and customers, to give staff a common cause, to provide them with a meaning for coming to work, to enthuse them, to make their brand superior and to gain their commitment. As Steve Jobs, Apple's CEO, once stated:

> Apple is about people who think 'outside the box', people who want to use computers to help them change the world, to help them make a difference and not just get a job done.

Clearly, the more the values of the staff and consumers concur with the brand's values, the more likely the brand is to succeed. However, these two quotations indicate the need for brand-building as an activity directed at customers and also at staff. If firms are to capitalize on the opportunity of brand-building through staff, this leads to the need to ensure that staff's values are aligned with the desired brand values. Otherwise, the brand's claimed promise will quickly be seen through when the experience of interacting with staff shows a marked disconnection.

It is not uncommon for staff in the same organization to have different views about the values of their brand, and a consequence of this is that the organization is, in effect, pulling against itself.

Activity 4.9

How could you go about assessing the extent to which staff in your organization are aligned with your brand?

Discussion

One approach (de Chernatony and Harris 2000) is to take the organization's marketing documents and from these identify the organization's values. These values are inserted on a questionnaire, which has some general values, and postal questionnaires are sent to staff nominated by the senior marketer. On the questionnaire, staff are asked to circle a code from 1 to 5 to signify for each value the extent to which this describes their brand (1 = a little, 5 = a lot). On a separate question, later in the questionnaire, staff are asked to assess the same list of values, again on a 5-point scale, but this time in terms of the importance of the value to them. By comparing the scores on each of the values for the brand question and the later staff question, the alignment of each individual with the brand can be evaluated.

Through providing feedback to individuals who have participated, the staff are able to consider how their values' profile compares with that of their brand and therefore where they need to think more about their commitment to the brand.

Another way of assessing staff's alignment with their brand is that of Thomson *et al.* (1999). The central argument behind this is that staff's 'buy-in' can be considered in terms of two underlying dimensions. The first is intellectual buy-in, which assesses the extent to which people are aware of and aligned with their firm's strategy and whether they understand how they can contribute to this. The second dimension is emotional buy-in, evaluating commitment to achieving the firm's goals. Through a series of questions which measure these two dimensions, a matrix is produced showing the extent to which each member of staff has bought in intellectually and emotionally to the firm's brand, as Figure 4.6 shows.

The matrix identifies four categories of staff, according to their buy-in. The 'champions' are behind the firm and are its ambassadors. The 'bystanders' know what they need to do, but emotionally do not feel committed. By appreciating why members of this group do not feel committed (for example, they may disagree with some of the plans), corrective action can be taken. The 'loose cannons' are emotionally committed, but do not understand the goals or how to achieve them. With this group, time needs to be spent rationally explaining the firm's intent. The worrying group is the 'weak links', who have neither the emotional commitment to nor understanding of the firm's goal. Too high a proportion of staff in this quadrant can signal serious problems for the organization.

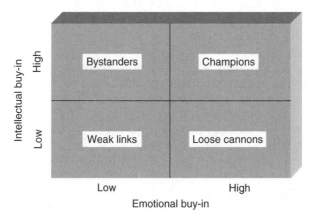

Figure 4.6   *A matrix to evaluate staff buy-in (adapted from MCA)*

Activity 4.10

If you have commissioned an audit to assess the extent to which staff in your organization are aligned with your brand, and the report reveals diverse views about the
brand's values, how might you set about aligning staff?

Discussion

If your report has identified a lack of understanding among staff, this may indicate a
need for an internal brand values communication programme. However, there is a
view that by just communicating with staff, the staff feel passive recipients of information which they do not internalize and soon forget. By showing staff the implications of misaligned brand values within their department, they can start to
understand this more. By involving them in a programme whereby they play a more
active role in identifying, they are more likely to be committed.

To encourage greater integration between a brand's values and
staff's values, it is not only important to recruit staff whose values concur with the brand's values; there also needs to be a continual reinforcement of the brand's values. This can occur during
the induction process, the performance assessment process, and
training, and in rewards and activities. For example, at the
American department store Nordstrom, renowned for its customer service value, staff are regularly reminded of instances
where individual initiatives left customers with a 'wow' sensation. Not only do they frequently hear about customers' praise
for outstanding service, but they are also alerted to customers'
comments about poor service.

It is not enough solely to communicate to customers the
brand's values; staff also need to appreciate what the values mean
in terms of their behaviour. For example, amongst the legal team
in a financial services consultancy, the brand value of professionalism could be interpreted as always being well informed, never
issuing any advice or response until it has been thoroughly
assessed, and documenting everything. By contrast, amongst the
business development team this could be interpreted as rapidly
responding to potential clients' requests with well-conceived pro-
posals. The problem is that owing to the different interpretations
between these two teams, there may be conflict. By discussing
amongst the teams how they interpret the values, instances
where there may be conflicting behaviour can be minimized.

When getting employees to consider what the brand values
mean in terms of their job, it may be helpful to use some
prompts. For example, once staff identify a change in behaviour
it could help to get them to consider 'how does this new behaviour make the brand different?' This will doubtless generate many

comments but, to drive the point home, it could help to get them to then consider, 'why does this matter to a customer?'

Just telling staff that there is a need to recognize and become committed to the brand values is not the most effective way of encouraging change. Ogbonna and Harris (1998) provide an interesting case study of Westco, a grocery retailer that had to respond to an increasingly competitive market.

Westco: the need to stress new values

Westco, a grocery retailer, faced the challenge of an increasingly competitive market. One aspect of its new strategy was to reposition its brand as being customer focused. To support this emphasis on a new value, staff had to recognize this value and change their in-store behaviour to enact this. Employees went on a one-day workshop to appreciate the need for change and why the firm was restructuring, and to reflect. A typical workshop encouraged groups of employees to describe previous and current working practices. They were then encouraged to criticize past attitudes and behaviour, while praising the newly espoused values. The day ended with a senior manager condemning the old-style behaviour and exhorting the desired new approach. There was some scepticism amongst staff about this, and as the programme developed so the researchers found opposing views between staff and management as to why change was needed. Partly because of management not being sufficiently attentive to this scepticism, and also because of the way staff were told rather than being involved in the process, four types of value changes were identified.

First were those who rejected the new values and left. Secondly, there emerged the 'reinvention' group, who recycled existing values and presented them as aligned with the newly espoused values. In essence, they were camouflaging their existing values behind a veneer of the company's espoused values. The 'reinterpretation' group translated some of the newly espoused values to accept them partially, albeit with elements of the existing values. Finally, there were those who appreciated the style of behaviour the firm wished them to adopt, and who unquestioningly adopted the new values.

Adopting a more participative approach, which has a greater involvement of staff, can help staff better to understand the values desired for their brand, and then to become more committed to enacting these. Gatley and Clutterbuck (1998) provide a case study of Superdrug, which had a far more involving approach with their staff. The executive team had identified the essence of their vision for this health and beauty retailer. To gain staff alignment, their views were cascaded to all employees through team briefings, and a competition was set to find the best crisp statement encapsulating these points. A cash prize was awarded, then staff were all invited to consider how these aspirations should result in different in-store behaviour. Again working in small teams, staff identified new styles of in-store behaviour to reinforce their brand's values, and it was not uncommon to see, on the staff room walls, contracts staff had drawn up showing how they would 'walk the talk' in their stores.

Activity 4.11

Ballantines, a dominant Scottish whisky marketed globally by Allied Domecq, has as one of its core values 'inspiring'. If you were told that resources would be made available to you to help you align the 80 marketers globally behind this brand, how would you go about achieving this?

Discussion

In an 'involve them' rather than 'tell them' tactic, Elmwood Design adopted a very creative approach. Not only was Elmwood Design concerned about aligning staff's values behind the brand, it also sought to encourage them to enact the brand's values and think more creatively about how they could market Ballantines. The process started with everyone receiving a metallic silver pack inviting them to work through the material enclosed and analyse their 'selves'. This device got them to think about who they were, what inspired them and what they wanted to do. It was the first stage on the new journey to developing a stronger personal bond with the brand. After gaining a better understanding of staff's views, marketers were sent an invitation to 'The Gathering', a two-day programme in Vienna to reinforce the marketing team's understanding – and to unlock more innovative thinking. As the Head of the International Brand Group explained (Gowar 1997: 44–8), everyone was then given a 'Daily Companion' which is a diary planner-cum-inspirational mentor to act as a daily reminder of personal brand vision, striving to integrate personal and brand objectives.

Thus, to thrive brands need to have a clearly defined set of core values, which staff should understand and be committed to, and which should appeal to the target market. It is advantageous to ensure that everyone inside the organization is behind the brand, otherwise internal tensions can damage it. As a cartoon once commented:

> If two people are in a boat heading towards a rapid, they should not be arguing about how they got there, but row together.

Conclusions

Without a clear sense of direction a brand will flounder. A well-conceived brand vision enables employees better to appreciate the journey they are undertaking. Through focusing on the first component, the envisioned future, there is an opportunity to consider what environment the firm wants to bring about ten years ahead. This is best done in groups, recognizing that managers are going to have to challenge their current short-term views and be receptive to novel ideas.

The second component, the brand purpose, needs to consider how the brand can bring about a better world. Statements such as 'maximize profits' don't motivate staff and are stating the taken-for-granted requirement of any business, rather than the unique contributions the brand can make to society. A corporate crisis acts as a stimulus for organizations that have never made their implicit purpose explicit.

Values provide guidance about desired styles of behaviour and are the third component of a brand vision. They differentiate brands, provided a unique cluster of values have been defined and enacted, rather than majoring on the 'entry point' category values necessary to compete. When every department takes each of the brand values and questions what this means for them, there is a greater likelihood of a more consistent pan-company approach being followed in support of the brand. Furthermore, there is likely to be greater commitment to a brand when the management team espouses values that conform with managers' behaviour.

A variety of methods is available to stimulate ideas about the desired values. By looking back in time, the organization is able to identify the low number of core values that it has continually upheld, and which will be the backbone of its future. As environments have changed, so secondary values will have played a short-term supporting role.

If staff are committed to delivering the brand's promise, their values are likely to concur with the brand's values. By recruiting staff whose values align with the brand's desired values, it becomes easier for them to deliver the brand through a genuine commitment, rather than acting out a scripted role that customers regard as being phoney. Audits to surface discrepancies between employees' and brands' values can help to provide ideas for correcting discrepancies and encouraging a more coherent brand experience amongst different stakeholders.

Brand marketing action checklist

Several ideas and frameworks have been developed in this chapter. To capitalize upon your brand's potential, undertaking some of the following exercises may beneficially help you to put these ideas into practice.

1. If you have not envisioned a future for your brand ten years ahead, the following exercise could help you and your colleagues to arrive at a possible scenario.

Select a well-known market and either undertake an on-line search to identify any forecasts as to how this market will undergo change over the next ten years, or devise some hypothetical scenarios. Circulate a copy of these scenarios to all members of the brand's team. Explain that just as they now have examples about another market's future, so they should send you a few written paragraphs about how they hope their brand's environment will look ten years ahead. Specifically ask them to consider issues such as:

- What changes do they anticipate the brand making (e.g. performance, quality, supporting technology, packaging, features, size, format, etc.)?
- What benefits might customers expect?
- How will customers gain access to the brand?
- How will customers know about the brand and its benefits?
- What might the nature of competitors be?

After receiving these replies, undertake another on-line search to identify what forecasters are anticipating regarding political, economic, environmental, social and technological forces ten years ahead. Summarize these on a few sheets of paper, but do not average any differences in opinions: instead, present differing views. Circulate these sheets to the brand's team at least two weeks after the first set of replies were received (deliberately to let them forget their first replies), and ask them again to send you a few written paragraphs about how they hope their brand environment will look ten years ahead. Ask them to structure their replies using the same categories as in the first round of questioning.

When the replies to both rounds of questioning are returned, analyse these by the categories:

- brand changes
- expected benefits
- customer access to brand
- customer communication
- nature of competition.

Within each of these categories summarize the themes, indicating the frequency with which they were mentioned, but do not show who made the comment. Present the results so the envisioned futures are shown first, without knowledge of the experts' views about the environmental forces, then secondly with knowledge of these forces. An example of how a table might look is shown below:

	Themes about the envisioned future	
	No forecasts supplied	Experts' forecasts supplied
Brand changes	Theme 1 (frequency)	Revised Theme 1 (frequency)
	Theme 2 (frequency) etc.	Revised Theme 2 (frequency) etc.
Expected benefits	Theme 1 (frequency)	Revised Theme 1 (frequency)
	Theme 2 (frequency) etc.	Revised Theme 2 (frequency) etc.

Circulate these results to all members of the brand's team and, once they have had time to consider these, convene a workshop. The aims of this workshop should be:

- to communicate the diverse views amongst the brand's team
- to arrive at a consensus view about a future ten years ahead.

Since the workshop is going to challenge views, it would be wise to use an external facilitator and to run it in an environment away from the office. The external facilitator will not have the preconceptions and biases each manager has, nor a position to defend. The facilitator can also recognize when managers are reticent about leaving the comfort of incremental projections for the uncertainty of quantum change. A good facilitator should be able to use the results from the internal questionnaires to provoke discussion, as well as engender ideas about a desired brand future.

2. If you are seeking to develop a future brand environment ten years ahead and do not have the budget to employ an external facilitator, the following may help you to arrive at a consensus view about a desired brand future.

    Having collected and analysed the data as specified in the first exercise, convene a day's workshop at a location you and your brand team have never used before. The day should open by having a crisp presentation summarizing the findings from both rounds of questioning from the first exercise. While this reveals a starting point, it may be subject to incremental thinking and might not have covered a sufficiently broad range of issues. To enrich ideas about the desired future environment, a series of group exercises can be undertaken.

    In the first exercise, groups are asked to think about the ten-year desired environment by focusing on the following questions:

- What radical changes could be made to the brand that would bring significant changes to the benefits customers receive, and at the same time reduce customers' costs, yet result in strengthened brand profitability?

- What new channels could be used to deliver the brand to customers, and how must the brand be modified to capitalize on these new channels?
- How can excitement be added as one of the brand's benefits for customers at both the brand selection stage and throughout their continued usage of the brand? Recognize that greater customer experience leads to a feeling of boredom with continued use of the same brand.
- How can the brand be tailored to meet the needs of much smaller groups of customers, but still remain profitable?

A plenary session following this syndicate exercise may provide interesting insights about future possibilities.

Having made participants aware of the need to challenge their ideas about the brand, a second exercise can add further novel perspectives. In this exercise, syndicates are asked to specify their organization's competencies – i.e. the low number of skills they have nurtured over the years for which they have a strong reputation. Having identified each of these competencies, the syndicates are then asked to consider how these can be combined in such a way that new clusters of benefits can be provided. In the subsequent plenary session, the strengths of each of the new ideas can be explored.

In order to undertake the third exercise, non-users of the brand (who have been recruited prior to the workshop) are invited to try the brand and their comments are video-recorded, covering what they dislike and how they would like the brand to change. Likewise, users of the brand are video-recorded prior to the workshop as they discuss how they would cope without the brand category, were it to be deleted. The workshop participants should be shown the videos and then, using these as a stimulus, syndicate groups asked to consider how the brand needs to be changed to delight a far more sceptical and experienced customers base ten years ahead.

Through undertaking these workshop activities, a richer insight may emerge about the desired future brand environment.

3. Having an envisioned brand future not only enables the brand team to check how stretching this is, but also encourages them to consider the route forward. Test your envisioned brand future and consider the implications for brand strategy by considering:

    - Has your statement about the envisioned future made it explicit in which domain your brand seeks to lead?

- How will the envisioned future stretch your organization, and where are internal changes needed to bring out the new future?
- As a result of your stretching envisioned future, what must your organization do differently with each group of stakeholders to help achieve this?
- How must internal ideas change to bring about the envisioned future?
- How can you communicate the envisioned future to your staff so this motivates them?
- Is the envisioned future being masterminded and promoted by just one or two people? If so more needs to be done to promulgate the envisioned future amongst the senior team to ensure all members play a notable role in communicating this to staff and encouraging ways of bringing this about.

4. If you have not made explicit your brand's purpose, consider using the company's intranet to seek employees' views about this by asking, 'how is our brand seeking to make the world a better place?' This should provide a rich array of ideas which should be categorized and the frequencies recorded against each theme. After analysing these results, the brand's team should be invited to a workshop where the results should be presented and debate encouraged to explore which of the themes might provide the most motivating brand purpose.

Having narrowed down the variety of potential themes, the brand's team should then start to question, 'why do we produce and market this brand?' Through repeated questioning, the team can further explore potential brand purposes.

To then identify the most suitable brand purpose, the team should score each potential purpose against the questions:

	A little				A lot
	1	2	3	4	5
(a) To what extent will this purpose make a real change and bring about a better world?	❑	❑	❑	❑	❑
(b) To what extent does this purpose excite staff?	❑	❑	❑	❑	❑
(c) To what extent does this purpose provide a clear sense of direction for staff?	❑	❑	❑	❑	❑
(d) Given this brand purpose, if your staff won the lottery tomorrow, how likely would they be to stay working with you?	❑	❑	❑	❑	❑

Recognizing that the maximum score for a brand purpose is 20, this series of questions allows the purposes to be ranked in order of attractiveness.

5. From your internal documents, or those held by your agencies, focus on your brand's values. Against each of these values, state their implications in terms of actions the brand should be following. Now evaluate the recent marketing activities for the brand to identify how true the brand's behaviour is to its espoused values. Where differences are noted, discuss with your colleagues whether any of the espoused values have continually been ignored and therefore are no longer suitable.

6. If your organization has extended any of its brands into new markets, evaluate the extent to which the parent brand has been used. For the parent brand and for each of the extended brands carrying the parent's name, list the brand values under each brand, using a table akin to that shown below:

Parent brand	Brand extension A	Brand extension B	Brand extension C
Value 1			
Value 2			
Value 3			
Value 4			

For each of the brand extensions, where their values are similar to any of the parent brand values record these on the line relating to the specific parent value. Examination of the resulting table provides insight about the extent to which the extension strategy has diluted the parent brand (seen when for each of the extensions there are only a low number of the parent's values used) or has strengthened the parent brand (through extensions whose values frequently draw on the parent's values).

7. For your brand, consider the cluster of values which characterize it. How many values define your brand? If there are more than about five values this may indicate that the brand may be diffuse, staff may not remember all of these values and consumers may not recognize what is particularly impressive about the brand. Where there is a notable number of values listed, consider whether several of these values are similar and what value might encapsulate some of the similar values. If you are unable to reduce the number of values through grouping, rank the values in order of importance and, as a brand's team, explore why you cannot characterize the brand solely by the top five values. It is important to realize

that when customers choose between competing brands they frequently use a very limited amount of information. Presenting more than five messages about the brand is not particularly helpful.

8. Focusing on the market in which one of your brands competes, collect copies of competitors' advertising. As a brand's team, infer the values of each of these brands. Now produce a matrix using the template below:

Your Brand	Competitor 1	Competitor 2	Competitor 3 etc.
Value 1			
Value 2			
Value 3			
Value 4			

Where the same value is common across many of the brands, this is indicative of a category value – i.e. a characteristic that customers automatically expect all brands to have and which is not used to discriminate between brands.

From this matrix, consider which values are unique to your brand and then assess the importance of these values as (i) motivators and (ii) discriminators when customers make their buying decisions.

9. Focusing on the brand your team supports, take the team away from their work for a workshop concerned with values enactment. Prepare a brief presentation showing your brand's values, then, dividing your team into syndicate groups, ask them to consider what one of these values means in terms of the roles they need to play on a daily basis. Against each of these roles, ask the syndicate groups candidly to consider whether they are following the implied behaviour. During the plenary sessions, encourage participants to consider how their roles need to change to support the brand.

10. To capitalize fully on the opportunities offered by having an explicit cluster of brand values, work with your colleagues and consider the following:
    - How widely are the brand's values communicated amongst staff and external stakeholders?
    - Against each of the brand's values, assess the extent to which the actions your organization has followed have been aligned with the expectations arising from these values.
    - Audit your factories, offices and distribution channels to evaluate whether the physical cues associated with your brand reinforce the espoused values.

- Evaluate the major ethical challenges your brand has faced, identify the responses taken, then consider how appropriate these have been in terms of the espoused values.

11. Check how appropriate the brand's values are by using the 'Mars group method'. Bring together the five people in your organization who epitomize all that the brand stands for. In a workshop, encourage them to explore the following:
    - What do they see as being the brand's values?
    - What values do they bring to work which they regard as being common to their brand?
    - If they had to explain to their children the values they hold at work, and would like their children to adhere to, what would they be?
    - If their organization had been destroyed by a fire and they were part of a team planning to rebuild the organization that supports the brand, what values would they put in place?

    Compare the values from this exercise against the espoused values in your brand documents to assess any differences.

12. Some staff may not share the same values as those of the brand they work on, and thus may not be totally committed to delivering the brand promise. To gauge where there are differences between employees' values and the brand's values, the following exercise may provide insightful. Prepare a questionnaire in which one of the questions asks staff to evaluate the extent to which they believe a series of statements describes their brand. The statements should cover the values of your brand plus the values of your competitors' brands, for example:

    Below is a list of statements. For each of these please state how much you feel they describe your brand.

	Describes our brand a little			Describes our brand a lot	
Value statement 1	1	2	3	4	5
Value statement 2	1	2	3	4	5
Value statement 3 etc.	1	2	3	4	5

You may wish to assess employees' views about other aspects of your brand, which should appear on subsequent questions. After these questions, repeat the first question, only this time show it as:

Below is a list of statements. For each of these, please state how important that statement is personally to you.

	Not important to me			Very important to me	
Value statement 1	1	2	3	4	5
Value statement 2	1	2	3	4	5
Value statement 3 etc.	1	2	3	4	5

Focusing on those statements that describe your brand's values, for each employee calculate the differences on the five-point scales between their rating of the statement describing the brand and their assessment of its importance to them. Sending each employee a copy of these differences scores will help them to appreciate where they are at odds with the brand.

References and further reading

Antonides, G. and van Raaij, F. (1998). *Consumer Behaviour*. Chichester: John Wiley.

Bainbridge, J. (2000). Body and soul. *Marketing*, **24 February**, 32.

Clifton, R. and Maughan, E. (eds) (2000). *The Future of Brands*. Basingstoke: Macmillan.

Collins, J. and Porras, J. (1996a). *Built to Last*. London: Century.

Collins, J. and Porras, J. (1996b). Building your company's vision. *Harvard Business Review*, **September/October**, 65–77.

de Chernatony, L. and Harris, F. (2000) The challenge of financial services branding: majoring on category or brand values? Paper presented at the European Marketing Academy Conference, Erasmus University, Rotterdam.

Gatley, L. and Clutterbuck, D. (1998). Superdrug crafts a mission statement – with the help of 12,000 employees. *International Journal of Retail & Distribution Management*, **26** (10), 394–5.

Gowar, R. (1997). Ballentines. In *Advantivity: Building a Competitive Advantage Through Creative Cultures*. Leeds: Elmwood Design.

Gutman, J. (1982). A means–end chain model based on consumer categorization processes. *Journal of Marketing*, **46**, 60–72.

Hamel, G. (1996). Strategy as revolution. *Harvard Business Review*, **July/August**, 69–82.

Hamel, G. and Prahalad, C. K. (1994). *Competing for the Future*. Boston MA: Harvard Business School Press.

Huff, A. (1990). *Mapping Strategic Thought*. New York: Wiley.

Kakabadse, N., Kakabadse, A. and Lee-Davies, L. (2005). Visioning the pathway: a leadership process model. *European Management Journal*, **32** (2), 237–46.

Kendall, N. (ed.) (1999). *Advertising Works 10*. Henley-on-Thames: NTC Publications.

Kotter, J. (1996). *Leading Change*. Boston MA: Harvard Business School Press.

Kotter, J. and Heskett, J. (1992). *Corporate Culture and Performance*. New York: The Free Press.

Macrae, C. (1996). An invitation from MELNET 96 to contribute to the brand learning organization. *Journal of Brand Management*, **3** (4), 226–40.

Macrae, C. (1999). Branding reality editorial. *Journal of Marketing Management*, **15** (1–3), 1–24

Martin, J. (1992) *Cultures in Organizations: Three Perspectives*. Oxford: Oxford University Press.

Maunder, S., Harris, A., Bamford, J. *et al.* (2005). O$_2$. It only works, if it all works. In Hoad, A. (ed.), *Advertising Works* (13). Henley-on-Thames: World Advertising Research Center.

Oechsle, S. and Henderson, T. (2000). Identity: an exploration into purpose and principles at Shell. *Corporate Reputation Review*, **3** (1), 75–7.

Ogbonna, E. and Harris, L. (1998). Organizational culture: it's not what you think. *Journal of General Management*, **23** (2), 35–48.

Pine, J. and Gilmore, J. (1998). Welcome to the experience economy. *Harvard Business Review*, **July/August**, 97–105.

Reynolds, T. and Gutman, J. (1988). Laddering theory, method, analysis and interpretation. *Journal of Advertising Research*, **28**, 11–31.

Ritchie, J. (1999). Crafting a value-driven vision for a national treasure. *Tourism Marketing*, **20** (3), 273–82.

Rokeach, M. (1973). *The Nature of Human Values*. New York: The Free Press.

Rosier, B. (2000). Amazon leads race to expand web services. *Marketing*, **24 February**, 19.

Schein, E. (1984). Coming to a new awareness of organizational culture. *Sloan Management Review*, **Winter**, 3–16.

Schwenk, C. (1988). *The Essence of Strategic Decision Making*. Lexington MD: Lexington Books.

Thomson, K., de Chernatony, L., Arganbright, L. and Khan, S. (1999). The buy-in benchmark: how staff understanding and commitment impact brand and business performance. *Journal of Marketing Management*, **15** (8), 819–35.

Wilkie, W. (1994). *Consumer Behavior*. New York: John Wiley.

Chapter 5

The importance of organizational culture in brands

Summary

This chapter focuses on the organizational culture block of the process for building and sustaining brands (see Figure 5.1). The purpose of this chapter is to explore the importance of organizational culture in branding. It considers the way a brand can achieve a competitive advantage through a particular type of staff behaviour, related to the values characterizing the organization's culture. The concept of an organization having a unique culture (integration paradigm) or several cultures (differentiation paradigm) is discussed. Schein's thorough definition of culture is addressed, from which the three levels for its measurement are clarified. The extent to which the organizational culture supports or impedes the brand's vision is discussed. The need to understand the diverse nature of an organization's culture is explored and the challenges of brand management after the merger of two different organizations' cultures is reviewed. A process for strengthening a brand

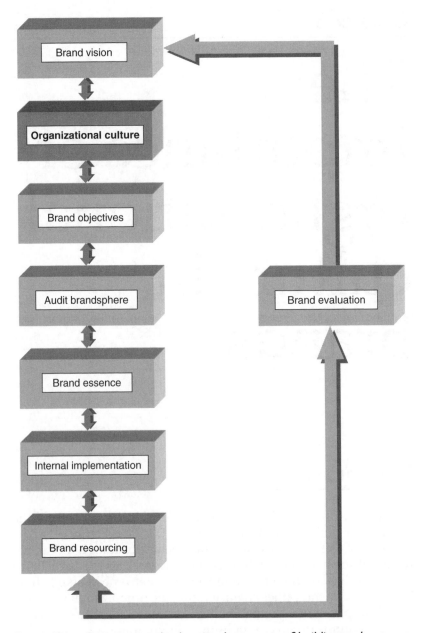

Figure 5.1 *Organizational culture in the process of building and sustaining brands*

through enhancing the alignment of staff with the desired organization's culture is presented. Finally, the chapter considers the culture characteristics likely to encourage higher levels of brand performance.

The link between organizational culture and branding

As the previous chapter explored, the starting point for developing and sustaining a brand is its brand vision. One of the components of a powerful vision is the brand's values, and these are recognized as being part of the organization's culture. By understanding an organization's culture there is a better appreciation of the organization's values and therefore insight about how the brand's values might be linked to those of the organization. Particularly for corporate brands that draw heavily on the corporation's name, organizational culture provides a strong indicator about the values that characterize the brand.

A clearly understood organizational culture provides a basis for differentiating a brand in a way that is often welcomed by customers. Earlier in this book it was clarified that a brand can be considered as being a cluster of functional and emotional values. With competitors being able to emulate functional values, a more sustainable route to brand-building is through emotional values. In other words, it's not so much *what* customers receive, but rather *how* they receive it. When two organizations provide similar functional brand benefits – for example, Burger King and McDonald's – the discriminator that may influence customers is the way the service is delivered. Organizational cultures are unique, and provide a stimulus for staff behaving in ways unique to the organization.

Organizational culture can act as a 'glue', uniting staff in disparate locations to act in a similar manner. It can motivate staff and, through coherence of employees' behaviour, help to engender a feeling of consistency about a brand. Ultimately, a strong organizational culture can increase the level of trust stakeholders have in a brand and thereby enhance performance levels, as shown in Figure 5.2.

Perspectives on organizational culture

Until interest started to grow in corporate identity and reputation, organizational culture did not attract much attention in the marketing literature (Deshpande and Webster 1989). In part this may be due to this concept's complex nature, which has given rise to over 160 definitions (Kroeber and Kluckhohn 1952).

Interpretations of organizational culture can be categorized into two main groups (Smirchich 1983), as shown in Figure 5.3.

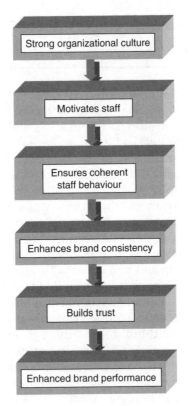

Figure 5.2   *How a strong culture contributes towards brand well-being*

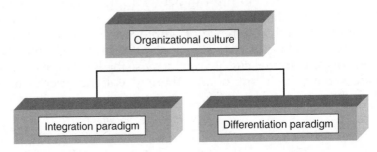

Figure 5.3   *Categorizing interpretations of organizational culture*

The first group of writers conceptualized it as something an organization 'has', and are referred to as those in the integration paradigm. Deshpande and Webster's (1989: 5) definition is a good example:

Culture is a set of shared assumptions and understandings about organizational functioning.

Plate 1   *In this advertisement, Allinson emphasizes the reputation for quality that it has maintained over the years (reproduced by kind permission from Allied Bakery)*

Patricia   Missy

As well as an operation, she needed love

" The Blue Cross gave my cat Missy the expert veterinary attention
she needed, but nobody can love her like I do. That's why they always
do everything possible to keep pets and loving owners together.
If you're passionate about the happiness of pets and want to make
a difference, visit **www.bluecross.org.uk** today. "

THE BLUE CROSS
Britain's pet charity

SINCE 1897

ANIMAL HOSPITALS I REHOMING PETS AND HORSES I PROMOTING RESPONSIBLE PET OWNERSHIP

The Blue Cross, Shilton Road, Burford, OXON OX18 4PF. Registered Charity No: 224392.

Plate 2   *People often give to particular charities because they strongly
believe in the values of that charity (reproduced by kind permission from
The Blue Cross)*

Plate 3   *The key functional value emphasized in this advertisement for Bosch refrigerators is accessibility (created by The Design Group, London, for BSH Domestic Appliances and reproduced with kind permission)*

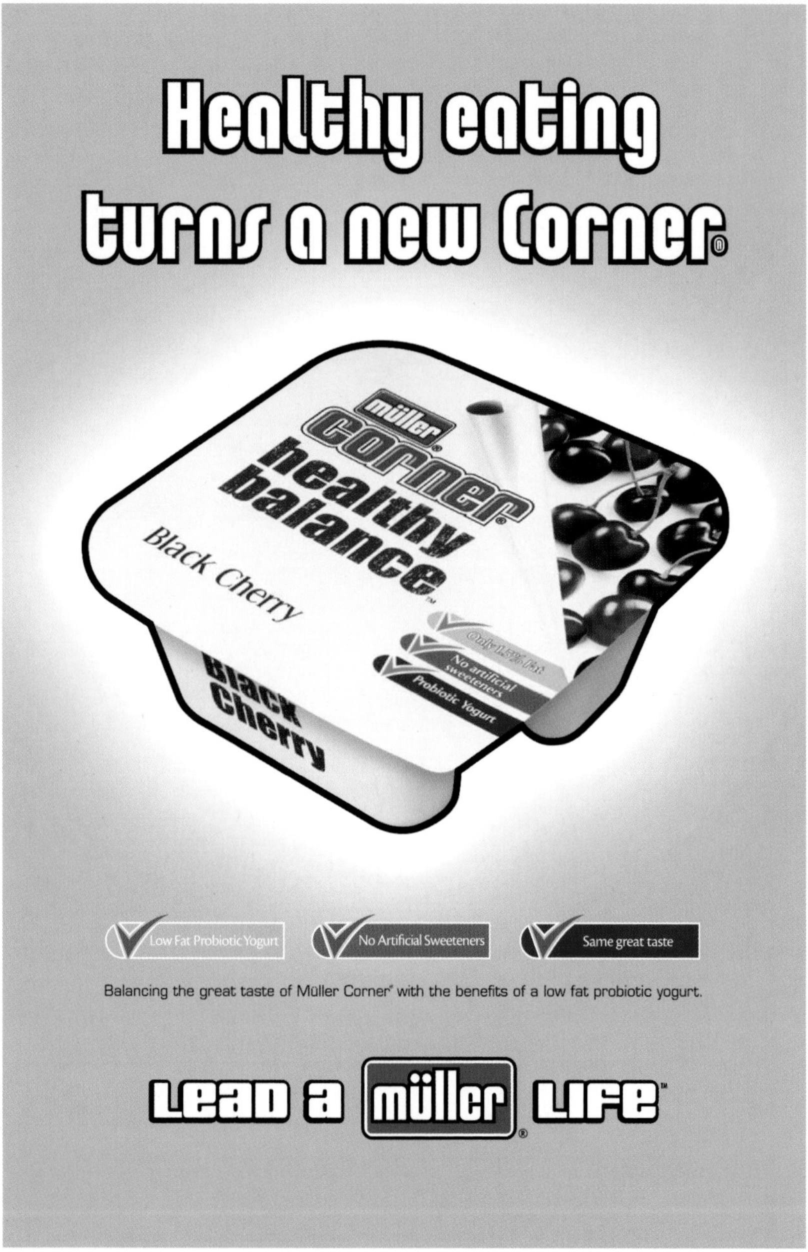

Plate 4   *Muller's Healthy Balance Corners emphasize the functional value of healthy eating (reproduced by kind permission from Muller Dairy UK Ltd)*

Our Production Manager

Up to 22 different butterfly species have been spotted giving our farms the once over, thanks to the farming techniques we use to encourage the return of wildlife. We believe that great tasting food comes from working closely with nature. Find out more at www.jordanscereals.co.uk

Jordans. Back to nature.

Plate 5   *The emotional value of caring for the environment is expressed in this advertisement for Jordans Country Crisp (Photographer: Nadege Meriau; Agent: Wyatt-Clarke; reproduced by kind permission from W. Jordan Cereals Ltd)*

Sample the true taste of Ireland

Irish food isn't just about potatoes. The South West of Ireland boasts award winning restaurants and produce including the famous seafood of Kenmare and Kinsale, which are gourmet hotspots. This is Ireland's most popular touring region with Killarney, the birthplace of Irish tourism celebrating 250 years of welcoming visitors in 2005.

For old times sake

Just like a good whiskey the whole area has matured with age and there are over one hundred heritage sites scattered around the beautiful countryside. You can visit the Jameson's Distillery in Midleton,

Co.Cork and a drive around the breathtaking Ring of Kerry gives you a taste of real beauty. There is plenty of contemporary action going on too. Cork city is the European Capital of Culture for 2005 and it annually hosts world renowned jazz and film festivals.

Seventh heaven

Whether your idea of paradise is taking on a world famous links golf course, relaxing at a luxury spa or indulging in a gourmet dinner, you'll find it here. It's easy to drift into another world and you'll leave feeling so revitalised and relaxed that you'll certainly want to return soon.

Call now on 0800 952 2005 or visit www.tourismireland.com

Ireland

Air routes

To Cork from Birmingham, Bristol, Cardiff, Durham Tees Valley, East Midlands Nottingham, Edinburgh, Glasgow, Leeds Bradford, Liverpool, London Gatwick, London Heathrow, London Stansted, Manchester, Plymouth, Southampton.
To Kerry from London Stansted, Manchester.
To Shannon from Birmingham, Coventry, East Midlands Nottingham, Glasgow Prestwick, Liverpool, London Gatwick, London Heathrow, London Stansted, Manchester, Kent International Manston, London Luton.

Ferry routes

To Cork from Swansea.
To Rosslare from Fishguard, Pembroke.
To Dun Laoghaire from Holyhead.
To Dublin from Holyhead, Isle of Man, Liverpool, Liverpool (Birkenhead).

All routes at 15th February 2005.

Now you know some of the great things to do in the South West of Ireland. Look out for other Ireland holiday highlights over the coming weeks. Win an amazing trip around Ireland by entering our new 'Taxi' promotion. Visit www.tourismireland.com/taxi for more details.

Some come in search
of the legend of Odysseus.
Others come to find the sun god.

Being shipwrecked probably isn't the ideal introduction to a new land.
Unfortunately though, for Odysseus, that's how he first stumbled upon the golden sands of Gozo.
In Homer's famous poem the Odyssey, he battled single-handedly against a raging storm before
his crippled ship eventually found refuge in Ramla Bay. There, his luck changed in the form
of the beautiful Calypso, Queen of Ogygia. She implored him to stay, showering him
with gifts and affection. But Odysseus desperately missed his family and, after
seven years, the gods intervened and he was free to leave. While for Calypso
the story didn't quite have a fairytale ending, for the hundreds of couples
who visit Malta and Gozo every year, it's really just the beginning. It seems
the opportunity to visit the land where Calypso seduced Odysseus
proves irresistible to young lovers and mythologists alike.
That and the chance to worship the ever-present sun.

visitmalta.com/uk or call 020 8877 6990   AIR MALTA

MALTA
MALTA GOZO COMINO
Discover the heart of the Mediterranean.

Plate 7   *Malta is strengthened as a brand in this advertisement which emphasizes the legends and literature in which it features (reproduced by kind permission of Malta Tourist Office)*

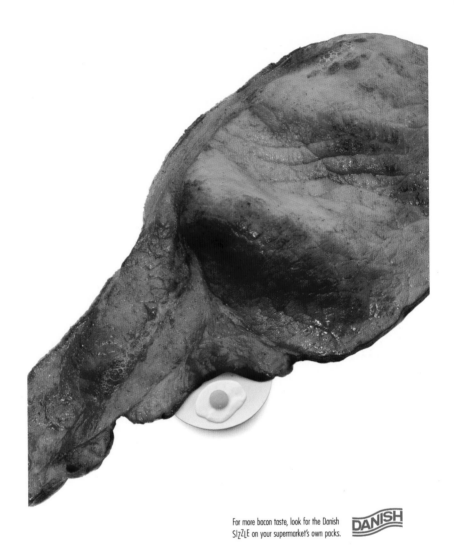

For more bacon taste, look for the Danish
SIZZLE on your supermarket's own packs.

DANISH

Plate 8   *Due to consistent advertising and promotional support, the wavy Danish bacon logo is widely recognized (reproduced by kind permission of Danish Bacon and Meat Council)*

Plate 9   *Birds Eye engender consumers' trust in their products by emphasizing the lack of added ingredients (reproduced by kind permission from Unilever UK)*

Plate 10 *Tesco pursue a strong corporate branding strategy, allowing the brand to easily extent into new areas (reproduced by kind permission from Tesco PLC)*

Plate 11 *Consumers may be attracted to Miele's Navitronic based upon this advertisement if values portrayed are congruent with their 'desired self' (reproduced by kind permission from Miele Company Ltd)*

Plate 12 *Soups from the New Covent Garden Food Co. are packaged in cartons because the consumer associates food in cartons (e.g. milk) as being fresh, in keeping with the brand's values (reproduced by kind permission from New Covent Garden Food Co.)*

Plate 13   *In this advertisement for the smart forfour BRABUS, the use of text messaging to secure a test drive is consistent with the brand's modern and innovative approach (reproduced by kind permission from Daimler-ChryslerUK Ltd)*

SHELF
STACKER
REQUIRED
38K p.a.

THE TIMES
TOP 100
GRADUATE EMPLOYERS

At Aldi, we believe that if you don't make a great shelf stacker, you'll never make a great Director. Because understanding everyone else's role in store gives you the best chance of motivating them.

Those are the guiding principles behind the Aldi Area Management Programme. To be considered for the programme, you'll need a strong set of A-Level grades or equivalent and a good degree. Qualifications aren't a measure of character though.

We're looking for candidates with a never-say-die gene, who have initiated and achieved things outside the academic arena. You'll need an abundance of personal qualities; motivational skills, drive, ambition.

But you'll also have to be sensitive to the needs of those around you and mature enough to know that you've still got plenty to learn. The programme runs for approximately a year and it will be one of the most intensive working periods of your life. You'll start in store and it's hands on from day one as you quickly gain a grass roots appreciation of retail management. Within weeks, we'll have you managing a store. Even during your initial training, the levels of authority, empowerment and personal responsibility on offer are well beyond those you're likely to find with other employers.

Area Management Programme Trainee

38K
+ Audi A4

Area Manager in charge of six stores

54½K
+ Audi A4

Over the coming months, you'll tackle the broader issues of Area Management; from store operations and trading to administration; from logistics to property management. We'll give you enough support and freedom to confidently apply your leadership skills, commercial awareness, technical and management ability.

As soon as you're ready, you'll take on total responsibility for four to six stores. Effectively, you'll be running your own multi-million pound business. What can you expect for all your hard work? £38K plus an Audi A4 from your first day rising through annual increments to £54½K after three years and includes a pension, private healthcare, life assurance and five weeks' holiday. There are also opportunities for Area Managers to spend two years on secondment in Europe or further afield. Within five years there's every chance of a directorship. Not bad going for a shelf stacker.

Opportunity for directorship within 5 years

Apply online: www.aldi-stores.co.uk or send CV and recent photograph, together with a letter illustrating your leadership potential, quoting reference BVSS to: Aldi Stores Ltd, Area Management Recruitment, Wellington Road, South Marston Park, Swindon, Wiltshire SN3 4FN.

Plate 14 *Trainee managers at Aldi get a thorough grounding in the organization's culture during their training programme (reproduced by kind permission from Aldi Stores Ltd)*

"The world is flat and the moon is made of cheese"

Graduate Opportunities – Autumn 2006

Cambridge, Gatwick, Milton Keynes, Norwich, Reading, Southampton, St Albans, Uxbridge

A lot of things you're led to believe don't turn out to be entirely true. For example, you may think 'a career with one of the world's leading professional services firms' is simply a euphemism for 'desk-job'. But with PricewaterhouseCoopers (PwC), nothing could be further from the truth.

There's a whole lot more to our work than simply number-crunching all day. Whether we're auditing a company's financial results, identifying the commercial risks they face, helping with tax planning or assessing the implications of strategic business decisions, it's all about getting beneath the skin of other organisations.

Wherever in the South East you join us, you'll be dealing directly with clients from the start, learning on the job, while working towards any number of different professional qualifications. And since the challenges we face span virtually every industry sector, the depth and breadth of experience you'll gain will set you up for an exciting career.

Perhaps the biggest myth, however, is that you need a business or finance degree to join us. You don't. Yes, you've got to be good with numbers and you must have a strong academic record. But the subject of your degree is less important than your willingness to work hard and your eagerness to learn.

To separate the facts from the fiction, and to find out how to apply, visit our website.

www.pwc.com/uk/careers/

PRICEWATERHOUSE COOPERS

Plate 15   *PriceWaterhouseCoopers challenge graduates' perceptions of their organizational culture in this recruitment advertisement (reproduced by kind permission from PriceWaterhouseCoopers LLP)*

Hello. Can we tell you something?

We're innocent and we make smoothies. You might have seen our drinks before; if not, the picture above might help you to recognise them next time you're down the shops. Anyway, it's all pretty simple. We just get hold of loads of fruit and squash it into our bottles and cartons. For example, the carton in the picture contains 27 strawberries , 10 apples , 2½ bananas and a dash of fresh orange juice . That means there are 8 portions of fruit in every carton, and no rubbish like concentrates, preservatives or additives. Good news for everyone, unless you prefer drinking strong, cheap cider. We don't make that.

Plates 16 (*above*) and 17 (*right*)   *One of the points of differentiation for the innocent Drinks Company is humour, as reflected in these two advertisements (reproduced by kind permission from innocent ltd)*

knitted by Lynne from Hornsey

This season's
must-have headgear

Our smoothies are wearing home-knitted bobble hats for a couple of reasons:

1. To raise money to help keep older people warm this winter (50p from each bottle sold).

2. Cardigans are so last year.

Find out more at www.innocentdrinks.co.uk/supergran

  **innocent** little tasty drinks

Plate 17

If you think it looks different, wait until you hear it.

The Bose® ACOUSTIC WAVE® music system.

A sound difference.

Touch a single button on this acclaimed, all-in-one music system. You'll hear "big, bold sound" that places it "at the forefront of compact music systems," according to the *Chicago Tribune*.

In fact, the sound is so rich and lifelike that people compare it to much larger, more expensive component systems. No matter what kind of music you enjoy, the ACOUSTIC WAVE® music system brings

Enriched sound from our seven-foot waveguide folded inside.

it alive the way it was *meant* to be heard. The key to this room filling sound is our award-winning patented waveguide speaker technology.

This system is so compact and light, measuring just 27 x 45.7 x 18.7 cm, you can enjoy its big system sound wherever you like - around the house, the office, even in your garden. And with a choice of colours - Platinum White or Graphite Grey - it fits any décor.

Easy-to-use features.

The system is technologically advanced, yet remarkably easy to use. The CD player, AM/FM tuner and three speakers are all built in, so you will have no wires or external speakers to hook up. Simply plug it in and press play. There is even a handy credit card-style remote.

ACOUSTIC WAVE® music system with 5-CD Changer

SAVE £185 when you order the 5-CD Changer together with the ACOUSTIC WAVE® music system.

If you want to enjoy hours of uninterrupted music, the ACOUSTIC WAVE® music system with our 5-CD Changer may be perfect for you. Simply load up to five of your favourite CDs, press play and enjoy.

The CD Changer can also connect your ACOUSTIC WAVE® system to audio sources like a TV, VCR and DVD player so you can enjoy Bose quality sound with everything you listen to or watch.

Try it – risk-free.

Call FREE now on 0800 022 044 to take advantage of our **easy interest-free payment plans** which let you make 4 equal payments over a period of up to 10 months with no interest charges from Bose.* And, with our **risk-free 30-day trial**, you can listen to the system in your home, satisfaction guaranteed. Call FREE today and hear just how different a stereo this small can sound.

☎ Call FREE on
0800 022 044

for further information quoting
reference XXXX

Or ✉ Text 'XXXX' to 84118

Or visit:
www.bose.co.uk/XXXX

BOSE®
Better sound through research®

Plate 18   *Bose provides consumers with extensive information about their products, reflecting that stereo systems are often a high-involvement purchase (reproduced with kind permission from Bose Ltd)*

ACQUIRE TASTE

It's a taste experience like no other: intensely dark chocolate with generous pieces of delicious crystallised ginger. It's not for everyone, and once you've tried it, it won't be for anyone else at all.

GREEN&BLACK'S │ It deserves a little respect

www.greenandblacks.com

Plate 19 *In this advertisement, Green & Black's chocolate is positioned to appeal to consumers' self-esteem needs, by associating the product with luxury and exclusivity (reproduced by kind permission from Green & Black's Ltd)*

Plate 20   *Honda is seeking to add value to its consumers (reproduced by kind permission of Honda UK)*

This school regards culture as an independent variable – for example, imported into a firm when staff join, or as a by-product of the firm's production. It emphasizes the homogeneity of beliefs from a unified, collective consensus of the organization, with senior managers instrumental in defining their organization's culture and directing staff to accept and adhere to it (Legge 1995). One of the best-known writers on culture is Schein (1984), and he is a key proponent of this school of thought. His definition will shortly be considered.

Activity 5.1

What do you consider to be the attractions and limitations of the integration perspective in organizational culture?

Discussion

The integration paradigm is conceptually appealing, since having a shared set of values and basic assumptions about cause and effect relationships reflects employees' needs for order and consistency in their work. When presented with a challenging situation, staff sometimes reflect on their perceptions of their culture to decide how to respond. For example, Wilkins and Ouchi (1983) describe the case study of two executives forced to take a difficult decision when away from their firm. The executives reflect on the way they perceive their organizational culture and how this has historically influenced the decisions of the Board of Directors. Confident in their thoughts about their culture, they return to the problem and make a decision based on the implications they draw from their culture. However, this paradigm implies a culture split between corporate level and departmental level in the same firm.

There is evidence that organizations are characterized by several cultures (Hofstede 1998), raising questions about whether shared values and assumptions should be considered more in terms of frequency, similarity or intensity (Gordon and DiTomaso 1992). This second school of thought, the differentiation paradigm, considers culture as a root metaphor for the organization – i.e. a metaphor for organizational knowledge, or shared symbols and meanings, or the unconscious mind. Culture exists in and through social interactions of staff, negotiating and sharing symbols and meaning. The integration paradigm regards culture as something an organization 'has', while the differentiation paradigm perspective sees culture as something a group of people 'are'. The artefacts are no longer the visible layer of culture, rather the means of its transmission and negotiation (Morgan 1986). This interpretation recognizes that all firms have subcultures, which individually share similar values and assumptions, but the extent to which these conform to the culture of senior management will vary.

Within the differentiation paradigm (Meyerson and Martin 1987), culture is not a mechanism for management to change staff's values, assumptions and behaviour but rather a factor managers need to be attentive to. Some corporate brands have historically performed poorly (for example, some of the corporate brands in the retail financial services sector) as the culture espoused by senior managers ran contrary to employees' views and was not internalized within the diverse units. The implications for corporate brand management are that the subcultures need understanding and the diversity in values need explaining to the senior team and all staff. In the section 'Brand values' in Chapter 4, we earlier identified this problem and showed how it can be appraised by drawing on Martin (1992) and evaluating action inconsistency, symbolic inconsistency and ideological inconsistency. Employees' working patterns may also impede management's goal of greater consistency of values and assumptions. For example, the high dependence on part-time staff in retailing, or the outsourcing of call centres, can result in a fragmented culture as staff feel no commitment to their firm. Some organizations, such as Asda, addressed this problem by employing staff with contracts offering longer hours.

Other organizations are breaking down the boundaries of subcultures. Taking employees out of their daily roles and showing them how their work relates to others in the organization encourages them to reconsider their assumptions and values. It also helps them to appreciate the corporation's intentions and recognize their importance in contributing to customer satisfaction – even if they are distant from customers.

An early example of this is the case of BUPA (Mistry 1998). Faced with the challenge of a more competitive market, BUPA recognized that a way to move forward was to capitalize on its staff as brand-builders. It identified a series of objectives:

- to enable staff to understand the rationale for customer orientation
- to help staff recognize their influence on satisfying and retaining customers
- to make staff feel valued, inspired and motivated
- to help staff understand their brand and their roles in delivering the brand promise
- to make staff feel committed to a programme of change.

To achieve these objectives, managers were first briefed at a national roadshow about the new strategy. All members of staff then attended a one-day event composed of people from different

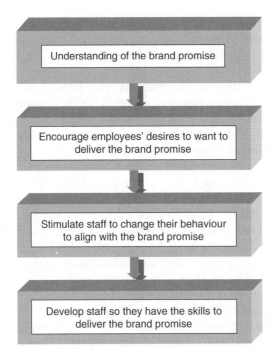

Figure 5.4   *The Hilton International process to encourage staff to deliver the brand promise*

functional backgrounds and levels of seniority. This mix of people was deliberately chosen to break down internal barriers. The day encompassed presentations then break-out activities with the theme 'one purpose, one promise, one chance, one difference and one me'. Just as other organizations, such as British Airways, had sought to enable everyone to recognize the importance of team spirit, so this programme enabled staff to appreciate their importance in brand-building and the way that, through satisfying their internal clients, they were satisfying their customers.

It is becoming increasingly common to focus marketing activity on building a culture that reinforces the desired brand values. For example, Hilton International has a brand promise of putting back a little of what life takes out – i.e. seeking to restore equilibrium in its guests' lives. It defined some of the brand's values as being professional and innovative, and to engender an appropriate culture it then embarked on a four stage process, as shown in Figure 5.4.

The first part of the process was an educational programme concerned with increasing employees' understanding of the brand promise and clarifying why some should change their behaviour to support the brand. The second stage recognized that it is not just a case of communicating the desired brand promise, but rather of motivating staff to want to accept the brand message and to want to change their behaviour. The danger is that without guidelines for the new style of behaviour, staff can erroneously enact inappropriate styles of behaviour. Thus the third stage concentrated on showing employees what they could do in their improved ways of supporting the brand. However, some employees may not have had the right sort of skills sets, and the fourth stage sought to strengthen their abilities to deliver the brand promise.

Another way of working towards a culture that supports the brand's values is through recruitment. Retail banks have an image of being dependable but risk-averse. From a recruitment perspective, Lloyds TSB wanted to give undergraduates a better understanding of career paths and to show that a career with them could be challenging and exciting. In September 2003 it ran a marketing campaign at specific universities, without stating its name or showing the Black Horse logo. This involved unbranded posters on campuses, followed a few days later by horseshoe prints on pavements and life-sized effigies of a black horse. On the posters was the web address: adarkhorse.com. Accessing the web led to a spoof psychometric test and a riddle about the brand. Success on the web gave access to the main graduate site with details about careers in Lloyds TSB. This promotion helped improvements over two successive years in terms of graduate applications. However, there is a potential problem in communicating traditional service-oriented values to current employees and consumers, yet talking about challenging and exciting prospects to new employees.

Defining and measuring organizational culture

In view of the fact that Schein's (1984) definition of culture is one of the best known (Buchanan and Huczynski, 2004), it will be explored in more detail. Schein (1984: 3) defines culture as:

> *The pattern of basic assumptions that a given group has invented, discovered or developed in learning to cope with the problems of external adaptation and internal integration and have worked well enough to be considered valid, and therefore to be taught to new members as the correct way to perceive, think and feel in relation to those problems.*

Although not one of the shortest definitions, this has the virtue of being a thorough statement, as will be explored.

Organizational culture can, argues Schein, be analysed at three levels, as shown in Figure 5.5. The most visible level is to look at the artefacts that reflect an organization's culture. This would include the car parking (just think of the number of firms who proclaim being customer-oriented, yet visitors have problems parking), office layout, manner of dress, the way people talk, any documentation, the firm's technology, etc. While these data are relatively easy to collect, it proves challenging to draw inferences from the artefacts about why a group behaves in a particular way. Seeing an open-plan office layout may indicate the firm's belief in open access to information, but it may also suggest a concern about cutting costs.

A better appreciation of why employees behave in a unique manner comes through understanding values. However, as discussed in Chapter 4, people can publicly exhort *espoused* values, yet behave in a manner that indicates an additional set of core values. In order better to understand the concealed reasons for behaviour, there is a need to dig even deeper into the basic assumptions people hold. Individuals have mental maps, or schema (Schwenk 1988; Huff 1997), which are the rules they have formed to make sense of their environment and to predict outcomes, given certain factors. For example, some managers might have as their basic assumption 'increasing advertising leads to higher levels of awareness and therefore greater sales'. By contrast, other managers might have as their basic assumption 'advertising works by building a reservoir of goodwill and all that is needed is just to have a continual trickle of expenditure to keep the pressure head of goodwill above a critical level'.

People like to be with and work with people who share similar patterns of thought and behaviour. Reflecting people's need

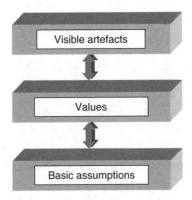

Figure 5.5   *The three levels of culture (from Schein 1984)*

for order and consistency, assumptions become interwoven in such a way that a pattern of assumptions enables a coherent set of beliefs to reflect how an organization thinks and behaves. While this definition strives for an integrated perspective on culture, it needs to be appreciated that some employees' assumptions may be inconsistent and, through the way that people become attracted to like-minded individuals, subcultures can emerge.

Culture reflects particular groups. Where a firm has a set of employees who have been together long enough to face and overcome problems, they will be influential in characterizing the nature of the culture. When new staff are inducted by this group, they will perpetuate the culture. It is not unusual to read about organizations hiring and firing senior marketers over short periods of time. In view of the notable influence these senior people have on culture, it indicates that aspects of the organization's culture may vary over time. To ensure that the brand is a stable entity, some firms are clear about what their timeless core values are, and recruit staff on the basis that while they will have idiosyncratic values, they are committed to the brand's core values. When people therefore leave, the social structure of the organization should stay intact and thus the brand's delivery remain stable.

Auditing organizational culture

The previous definition provides a helpful basis for auditing an organization's culture. Within the perspective of building and sustaining brands, one of the reasons for doing this is to assess the fit between the brand vision and the organizational culture to appreciate where changes may be needed.

From Figure 5.5, the most visible manifestation of organizational culture is through its artefacts.

Activity 5.2

If you were to audit an organization's culture by focusing on artefacts, what artefacts would you consider, and how might these reflect aspects of culture?

Discussion

There are numerous artefacts that could be investigated, including the following.

1. *Material objects*. The logo an organization uses provides clues about its culture. The Apple computer traces its history to being a challenger, refusing to accept

industry rules and competing with a different set of assumptions to the established players. The use of the bitten apple drew on the biblical analogy of the forbidden fruit that should not be eaten. Its use of the colours of the rainbow in the wrong order further reinforced its culture of not accepting established rules and of being a challenger (Rijkens 1992).

2. *Architecture and office location.* An organization's building gives a clue about organizational culture. When British Airways moved during the 1990s to a modern, light building with a lot of glass, it did so because it wanted to signal its change to valuing staff, teamwork and the importance of frequent interaction. The location of an organization's head office give clues about the importance of heritage and, particularly for an exclusive address, its market positioning. Locating the Open University in the 1960s in the new town of Milton Keynes signalled a break with traditional university teaching. Just as Milton Keynes was being built around the new grid system (in England) of roads, so the Open University embraced new ways of teaching using radio, TV, CDs and the Internet. Likewise, when the Midland Bank (now encompassed within HSBC) opened First Direct it deliberately wanted a new culture and chose its headquarters in Leeds, several hours' drive north of London where banks traditionally have their head offices.

3. *Language.* The language the staff and the corporation use provides insight about its culture. Dunhill is proud of its positioning of providing gentlemen's luxury items, and reinforces this through its brand personality of exclusive Englishness. The language in its corporate communication is a good example of how this artefact reflects a culture which deliberately strengthens the brand. For example, one of its corporate videos opens by saying:

> *The most enduring and exacting of tasks is the attainment of true value –*
> *unique, lasting, excellent. The object of value is at once recognized. Its*
> *qualities are innate, strong and understated. It is the perfect balance of*
> *design and craftsmanship, the realization of clear cited principles.*

    The use of this type of vocabulary is perfect for such a prestigious brand, whose target market will equate with these uncommon terms.

4. *Dress style.* It is not uncommon for advertising agency staff to dress informally, since this reflects their creativity. By contrast, airlines place considerable emphasis on uniforms, hierarchically portraying seniority, to reflect the seriousness with which they address their business and their attention to detail.

5. *Stories.* Organizations such as American Express and the Marriott Hotel use hero stories to convey their belief in customer service. Staff talk to each other about corporate events, not just to communicate but also to help understand what their organization stands for. When they see hero stories used in external advertisements, this helps them better appreciate their culture. For example, a press advertisement showing an American Express Service Agent travelling slowly on a motorbike through water in a storm, with the caption 'don't worry about it sir, I'll get those travellers cheques and passport to you come hell or high water', is a helpful reminder of the organization's values. The story is often told of Fred Smith, founder of Federal Express, who in the very early days was refused a loan by the bank to keep his new firm going. About to catch a flight after meeting his bank, he saw a sign for Las Vegas, jumped onto

a new flight, gambled at the casinos and used the winnings to pay his staff. His concern for employees' well-being was soon appreciated. At HP, employees used to be told the story of the garage where the founders set up the business. By using the story, interlaced with expressions such as 'always keep the toolbox open' and 'share tools', employees could start not only to understand the brand but also to then interpret this to help them in their roles.

6. *Ceremonies, rites and rituals.* Ceremonies are celebrations of organizational culture. A firm's annual sales conferences in a variety of exotic locations are not just to inform the sales force about the future year's marketing plans, but also to reward performance. A poor year's sales may well result in a less exotic conference location. Rites and rituals are planned activities that communicate the culture through planned events. A culture that respects staff loyalty can be recognized from the emphasis placed on the ritual of retirement dinners.

7. *Styles of behaviour.* There are norms of behaviour about which new employees soon become aware. For example, the value of industriousness would be reflected in employees being in work early, or staying beyond the standard finishing time.

These are but some of the myriad visible manifestations of an organization's culture. While these characteristics can be relatively easily unearthed, the challenge is drawing inferences about culture.

The second level of culture is that of an organization's values. As Chapter 4 explained, this can be assessed through the 'Mars group' method or the laddering technique.

Particularly for the Mars group method, it was earlier argued that care needs to be taken to select people who are exemplars of all that is good about the brand. This helps to surface the desired, positive values. However, in view of the way that some people are particularly influential in shaping an organization's culture – for example, those who facilitate new employees' integration into the organization – including these individuals in any values research can provide useful insights about the organization's values.

Surfacing people's assumptions can be undertaken using the card sort technique (de Chernatony *et al.* 1994). Here, individuals are interviewed alone in an office. They are first asked who they perceive as being their competitor, and each time a competitor is named it is written on a card. Once the employee has given a list of competitors, the firm's name is written on a card and all the cards are shuffled. The cards are then given to the respondent, who is asked to arrange them on the table in such a way that those organizations that are competitively similar are placed close to each other. Having surfaced perceptual categorizations (Assael 1998), a photograph is taken of the display to record the individual's map. The respondent is then asked to explain why the cards were arranged in this manner, and the comments given provide insights about that individual's assumptions. After respondents have exhausted any reasons for their mental maps, the exercise is repeated, asking respondents if they could arrange the cards in a different manner. Subsequent to taking a photograph, they are again invited to explain why they categorized the brands in the revised structure.

For example, if respondents are focusing on retail financial services brands, they might use comments such as 'This group of brands concentrates on offering the best interest rates. They have large financial resources and are always the first to give the best rates. This group, of which we are one, tries to be customer centric. They always look at their communication to make sure that technical terms are not used and continually try to develop new products which best reflect the time pressured world customers live in.' From the interview, it could be inferred that part of the manager's mental model is the need to be market-driven.

Activity 5.3

What do you regard as being the strengths and weaknesses of this procedure to surface assumptions?

Discussion

One of the strengths of this procedure is that it elicits competitive sets which are totally relevant to each individual. It does not impose any interviewer preconceptions, and it enables a respondent's assumptions to be explored in considerable detail. It is, however, a time-consuming activity, both to undertake the interviews and then to analyse the transcriptions from the tape-recorded interviews.

By following these suggestions, a rich array of information is provided about an organization's culture in terms of its artefacts, values and basic assumptions. The appropriateness of the culture can then be assessed.

Appropriateness of the organizational culture

Writers such as Collins and Porras (1996) have argued that visionary companies share generic cultural characteristics. One way, therefore, of assessing the organization's culture is to consider:

- whether there is a strongly held ideology of which all employees are aware
- whether there is a good induction programme for all new employees
- whether staff feel they belong to something special that gives them an elitist pride
- whether there is ongoing training
- how effective the job socialization by their peers is
- whether staff are exposed to the hero stories
- whether there is a tight values-based screening process at the recruitment stage
- whether incentives and career advancement criteria are linked to the organization's aspired culture
- whether there are public celebrations for particularly successful staff
- to what extent the office layout reinforces the desired values.

These generic characteristics provide a useful starting point to assess the appropriateness of the organization's culture. A further way is to revisit the brand vision and assess the force field of Figure 5.6.

1. To address the appropriateness of the organizational culture for the *brand's envisioned future* it is worth checking the assumptions that were surfaced. As was discussed in Chapter 4, people do not like having their mental models challenged, yet managers are encouraged to go beyond their comfort zones and envision a brand future ten years ahead. They prefer incremental, rather than quantum leaps. By considering the more prevalent assumptions, it is possible to assess the extent to which the envisioned future will be accepted.

   As Bettis and Prahalad (1995) argued, managers have a 'dominant logic', or shared mental model (cf. assumptions). This directs their searching and acceptance of information through focusing their attention on particular issues. Helpful though this is in enabling them to cope with the vast array of information they regularly encounter, the filtering and self-reinforcing behaviour from being in regular contact with like-minded managers denies the need to accept new ideas. As Figure 5.7 shows, a self-perpetuating cycle of organizational learning directs the need for particular types of organizational intelligence that abhor revolutionary suggestions.

Figure 5.6 *Force field analysis of brand vision and culture*

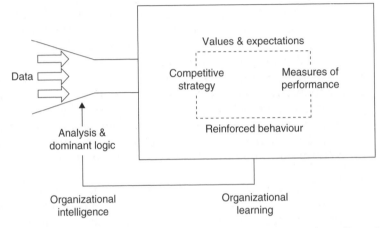

Figure 5.7 *The self-perpetuating cycle from the dominant logic (based on Bettis and Prahalad 1995)*

If the dominant logic indicates that the envisioned future is incompatible, a period of 'unlearning' is suggested by Bettis and Prahalad (1995). This is best undertaken in a location away from the organization, to minimize the artefacts reinforcing the outdated assumptions, with an external consultant committed to surfacing a new set of assumptions. For example, one consultancy took its client away from the office by first collecting everyone in a bus. It then drove to another town, where it had erected a marquee on a roundabout. Inside were deckchairs on which were laptops. They argued that away from the reinforcing artefacts, management were more receptive to having new, challenging ideas. Consultants need to be tactful, as they indicate the weaknesses of the current set of assumptions. The task of encouraging new thinking can be enhanced when one-to-one sessions are run, since the manager cannot fall back on the support of other managers when experiencing cognitive dissonance resulting from the external challenger.

Another way of getting managers to accept the need for a new set of assumptions is when they commission their competitor to undertake a survey for them. A case in point is that of Nicholson McBridge, which devises and supervises culture change programmes (Nicholson 1997: 26–37). On an annual basis, they commission a competitor to undertake a client survey for them.

2. The appropriateness of the organizational culture in helping the brand to achieve its *purpose* can be assessed by considering each of the three components of the culture. From the inherent assumptions, the question needs to be asked whether these block or free managers' minds to think about the role their brand must play in bringing about the brave new world. If managers' assumptions relate to uncertainty and concerns about their firm's ability just to survive, never mind grow, this can act as a block on planning a new role for the brand. Without having a category value of being innovative and recognizing the need for continual change, there is likely to be reticence in amending the brand strategy to realize its purpose.

To bring home the realization that a challenging brand purpose should be the guiding star for everyone there may be a need to consider the relevance of the current artefacts. Do the office decor, layout, equipment, and even employees' terminology about the market represent old thinking about what the brand's purpose is? Hearing staff refer to customers as 'punters' for a brand whose purpose is about increasing customers' confidence raises the need for a staff development workshop. Changing some of the artefacts can both signal and reinforce a new way of thinking about the brand's purpose, and therefore how staff need to behave differently.

At its most basic, the overt communication aspects of the artefacts would benefit from attention in order to assess whether employees understand the purpose. Thus a staff notice board cluttered with notices may be part of the value of information openness, but stifle interest in daily initiatives to achieve the brand's purpose. By contrast, a brand's team which takes time regularly to visit different departments in the organization to provide frequent updates about progress to achieve the brand purpose is more likely to engender acceptance of change.

3. Evaluating whether the *values* of the corporation are going to align with the desired values of the brand can be assessed by first undertaking a survey of customer-facing staff. As this group is particularly influential in transmitting the

brand's values, if the members do have values that conflict with those of the brand, changes amongst the group would have a noticeable impact on consumers. A battery of statements would need to be prepared and staff then sent a questionnaire. They would be asked to read each of the value statements, then rate each one in terms of their importance to them (from not very important through to very important). If the organizational culture is one that supports the brand's values, analysis of each employees' replies should result in high-importance scores being assigned to the values characterizing the brand. Consideration of the differences between the brand's desired values and those values staff rate as being personally important provides insight about the appropriateness of the organizational culture for the brand's values. Knowing where there are divergences between employees' values and the brand's values enables staff to consider whether they are able to amend their views to support the brand, or whether they would find it easier working on another of the firm's brands.

One or several organizational cultures?

It is rare to find an organization where there is one homogeneous culture. Rather, it is more appropriate to talk about the strength of the culture – i.e. the extent to which similar organizational values are reflected amongst a firm's staff. Brown (1995) cites research that categorizes organizational cultures into three categories:

1. *Enhancing subcultures*. In these situations, employees adhere to the values of the dominant culture more notably than in the rest of the organization. These pockets of adherence are critically important for brands, since staff working in enhancing subcultures will, particularly when the culture is appropriate for the brand, act in a manner which ideally projects the desired brand. If the customer-facing staff, i.e. those directly in contact with customers, are part of the enhancing subculture, the external promises being made by the advertising are more likely to be delivered through these brand-committed staff.
2. *Orthogonal subcultures*. These are characterized by individuals who are aligned with the dominant culture, but they also accept a separate, albeit non-conflicting, set of values. Particularly for dispersed organizations – for example, those with international brands – staff in each country will adhere

to the core values of their corporation and at the same time have another set of values that reflect their country values. Brand-owners in these situations are best served by regularly bringing together the disparate groups to strengthen the coherence of values and encourage a commitment to delivering the brand promise. Unlike the enhancing subcultures, there is more likelihood that some groups of employees may feel a stronger bond to their local team rather than the organization, and as such there may be forms of behaviour that do not fully support the brand plan.

3.   *Counter-cultures.* In this category of subculture, there exists a cohort of employees who have some important values that militate against the desired organizational culture. Shortly after a merger, or when a new senior appointment has been made, opposing camps emerge either supporting or disagreeing with the leadership. Not only does this cause uncertainty amongst other staff, it can also result in the brand being pulled apart. A speedy response is required to minimize this infighting. In some organizations this results in those members of the team who find it hard to support the desired approach being replaced. Counter-cultures are damaging for brands since internal morale falls, variable service delivery levels result and customer satisfaction falls. A strong leader is required who is not only attentive to pockets of conflicting cultures but also has the analytical skills and courage to pull the damaging individuals away from the brand.

For a brand to thrive, it needs to be rooted in an organization where there is a unified organizational culture and where the senior team are attentive to pockets of internal cultural diversity. Some diversity is inevitable, but without tracking the homogeneity of its culture, there is a danger of the brand underperforming due to counter-cultures pulling different departments in opposing directions. Appropriate artefacts can help to perpetuate appropriate cultures, which can be reinforced by recruiting staff whose values concur with those of the desired culture.

Striving for a merged unified culture

Takeovers and corporate mergers are often hailed as opportunities for strengthening brands, yet the attempted marriage of the two cultures can be difficult to achieve and this can have an adverse effect on staff morale, adversely affecting brand performance. In fact, KPMG reported that while £209bn was spent on hostile takeovers in Europe in 1999, only 17 per cent of mergers added to shareholder value (Mazur 2000). Many merger decisions are taken based predominantly on rational business models, with less consideration of organizational cultures. Consideration about the compatibility of the partners' cultures and the route for integrating these to achieve the brand's vision often takes place after, rather than before, the merger. When the Daimler Chrysler merger occurred in 1998, there were reports of a marriage of equals being able to exploit managerial talents to capitalize on the strengths of both organizations. The new brand name was devised to signify an equal partnership. Yet the cultures clashed and after a short period the management structure was changed, with the German team adopting the dominant position.

The merger of Lloyds Bank with TSB in June 1999 provides insight about how two cultures were combined into the Lloyds TSB brand. The planned merger was announced in 1995 as being a logical fit of brand network coverage and a shared vision about the future of the retail financial services industry that should produce annual savings of £400m by 1999. The separate brands were investigated and found to be distinct. Lloyds Bank was seen as:

- being middle class
- being a premier-league bank with a slightly impersonal touch
- having a green identity.

TSB, by contrast, was seen as:

- having a younger customer base
- having a friendly image
- being portrayed through a blue identity.

A decision was taken that some of the characteristics of the new brand needed to:

- be personal
- be fresh
- retain the brand identifiers of the Lloyds Black Horse with both green and blue colours.

A vision for the brand was defined as:

> *to be the first choice for our customers by better understanding and meeting their individual needs*

and reinforced through the brand's promise:

> *we always remember it's your life and your money and it's our aim to help you make the most of both.*

This was to be achieved through the CARE brand values, i.e.:

- **C**ustomer understanding
- **A**ccessibility
- **R**esponsibility
- **E**xpertise.

Staff were continually being informed about the benefits of the new vision and the new brand, and their commitment was important in achieving this. However, rather than just relying on communication, job swaps were arranged and 7000 staff spent time working in one another's heritages to break down cultural barriers. Closer to the merger, 5000 staff went to the 'Your Life, Your Bank' event at the NEC Birmingham. The purpose was to involve these staff in appreciating the vision and the new brand in order to enable them to be 'pathfinders' who could return to their colleagues and explain the vision in terms that their colleagues could best appreciate. This example provides a snapshot of the integration process, since for any brand to thrive there needs to be a continual process of reinforcing a brand-supporting culture.

Strengthening a brand through organizational culture

When an organization has its different departments aligned with a desired culture, there is a more unified identity presented to different stakeholders and a greater likelihood that staff will act in a more consistent manner, reducing the need for supervision. Particularly when an organization is dispersed throughout many countries and thrives as a result of the considerable intellectual value of its knowledge workers, the challenges in unifying the organizational culture are immense. KPMG faced this challenge when, in 1997, Colin Sharman took over as International Chairman of this top-five accounting and consulting firm. A consideration of this case study (Thornbury 1999) provides some informative insights about strengthening a brand through aligning staff with an organization's culture.

An objective was set: to turn KPMG into a truly global brand. Part of the strategy to achieve this was based on unifying the organizational culture. KPMG recognized that it is easier to change artefacts than values, and that developing a set of KPMG values to align staff would be a demanding task. However, this difficult challenge of developing a set of values to align staff globally was embraced.

Activity 5.4

If the values are to be motivating values, what characteristics should they possess?

Discussion

If the values are to be motivating, they should:

- stand the test of time
- be relevant in all zones of the world
- catch the interest and commitment of everyone
- be suitable for all levels of employees.

The three-stage process by which KPMG set about this task is shown in Figure 5.8.

Involving many members of staff in this process gives a greater degree of commitment. Engaging many employees enables a wider collection of ideas and is more likely to result in a strategy that should be universally acceptable. As a global

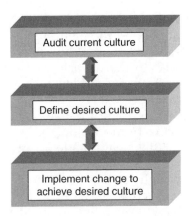

Figure 5.8   *The process of changing organizational culture (adapted from Thornbury 1999)*

player, KPMG regularly ran a series of conferences for its senior managers and partners, and these were thought to be ideal events to involve staff in the process. A further reason for ensuring full staff involvement was the need to keep responsibility and ownership of the culture change at the local level.

Prior to the launch of this change process, research to understand the current culture was undertaken. Interviews were undertaken with staff, who were given the scenario of having to explain to a close friend how to succeed in KPMG. They were asked to clarify:

- what someone must do
- what they can get away with not doing
- what they must never do.

Respondents were asked to justify these forms of behaviour, using the laddering technique reviewed in Chapter 4, to identify the underlying values.

The launch of the change process was at the May 1997 International Council Workshop. At this supervisory board, containing around forty of the top leaders, the results of the culture research were tested and the group's involvement in the process gained. Using a similar procedure, five members of this group surfaced their perceptions about KPMG's values, which concurred with those from previous research. The pre-change core values were clarified as being:

- serving the client comes first
- individualism
- technical excellence and high professional standards
- integrity.

While these values are admirable, some of them result in negative behaviours that needed to be curtailed. For example, individualism encourages autonomy, but may be detrimental to teamwork. Debate led to the need to revise the mission statement, which provided further guidance about the development of the new values.

The next stage in defining the new values involved senior managers and partners from around the world, who attended KPMG conferences. After being made aware of the current culture, small group exercises enabled views to be surfaced about the desired culture. Through feeding back the views of the groups, further discussions ensued and themes for the desired values and implications for behaviour resulted. A long list emerged, and this was narrowed by delegates at a subsequent conference who prioritized the values. These themes were presented to KPMG's

International Board for final formulation of the values. The agreed statement of the three core values are:

- KPMG is passionate about working with clients to deliver exceptional value
- KPMG people flourish and realize their full potential
- KPMG continuously extends the frontiers of its shared knowledge.

For each value, a clear set of behavioural implications was also derived.

Activity 5.5

From the first value, what implications would you anticipate for consultants' behaviour?

Discussion

The stated implications are:

- being passionate about client service
- robust, lasting relationships
- being committed to adding value.

Bearing in mind the need to keep responsibility and ownership for the change process at the local level, a facilitative approach to implementation was adopted. To enable people to develop their culture change programmes, a toolkit was designed. This consisted of a board game to help staff to understand and enact the new values, plus a boxed set of the implementation guide with tools and techniques for implementation. The board game was like Monopoly, based on KPMG, and was to be played with clients, people and knowledge. In the game, winning resulted from the high scores obtained by acting in the manner prescribed by the new values.

Five items in the boxed set facilitated the key activities in the culture change process:

1. Building commitment amongst leaders to enable them to become effective role models
2. Personal and team development material to help people receive feedback and work on changing their behaviour
3. Facilitating internal communications
4. Guidance on how to carry out the different activities
5. An explanation of the values, theoretical background and details of different parts of the programme.

Having focused on the values component of the new culture, this was then backed through artefacts. Examples of these include changing systems, rewards, power structures and internal communication which reinforces the desired values.

The impact of organizational culture on brand performance

Hofstede (1980) was one of the early writers to argue the association between strong cultures – i.e. those that are unified – and high performance. This was followed by others, for example the case studies of Peters and Waterman (1982), and the writings of Kanter (1989) and of Denison (1990). The rationale is that in strong corporate cultures there are consistent values, and thus similar styles of behaviour into which new staff are inducted, which outlive changes in senior management. Furthermore, this should facilitate agreement about key objectives.

In a strong culture, the shared values engender greater motivation. As staff feel proud to be associated with the organization's brands, they are more likely to become committed and to remain as loyal employees. Understanding and conforming to the behavioural expectations from the shared values results in less supervision, not only saving money but also motivating employees who prefer to be empowered. Organizations with strong cultures are better able to capitalize on learning from the past, integrating successful practices into rituals and well-known stories that enable staff to adopt these.

A further appeal of the strong culture–performance theory is that a firm's culture provides the basis for a sustainable competitive advantage. It's not so much *what* is being delivered, but rather *how* it is being delivered. Through working to develop a strategically appropriate culture, corporate brands are underpinned by intangible assets that competitors find hard to emulate.

Questions have been raised about the strong culture–performance theory. Wilkins and Ouchi (1983) take the view that rather than relying on a single unified culture, organizations can manage themselves more efficiently by having 'clans'. Through the socialization process from induction to being part of a team, employees become integrated into clans, doing what is best for the organization by drawing on a shared set of assumptions that the clan holds. Another problem is the differing interpretations of 'strength of culture' amongst writers. For example, Schein (1984) regarded this as stability and intensity, Deal and Kennedy (1982) talked about coherence, while Gordon and DiTomaso (1992) interpreted it as consistency. The literature about the strong culture–performance relationship is notably anecdotal, with few empirical studies.

Kotter and Heskett (1992) undertook a significant piece of work to evaluate empirically the strong culture–performance relationship. One of the problems in this type of research is getting a large enough sample of organizations who will allow their culture to be audited. They got round this problem by sending questionnaires to competitors and analysts asking them to evaluate the cultures of firms known to them. Ideally, interviews should have been completed inside the specified organizations. Performance measures between 1977 and 1988 were based on:

- average yearly increases in net income
- average yearly return on investment
- average yearly increases in share price.

Kotter and Heskett were critical of the strong culture–performance theory. While everyone in a firm may be adhering to the same values, these may be inappropriate and everyone in the firm would then be following the same path to oblivion. They reported correlations between culture strength and measures of long-term economic performance of between 0.26 and 0.46. While this shows a positive, albeit modest, relationship, it is too much to claim that strong cultures create excellent performance.

Kotter and Heskett (1992) argued that if a firm has a strong culture, it is only a valuable asset if it is appropriate for its environment. An organization may have a strong bureaucratic culture, but if the market is one that is characterized by rapid innovation then the culture–environment fit will be poor and the firm unlikely to be achieving high performance levels. Jackson (1997) conceptualized this argument neatly in the matrix shown in Figure 5.9.

The leading brands are more likely to emanate from organizations that have strong cultures that are appropriate for the environments in which they operate. Kotter and Heskett (1992) argued that better performance levels can be expected from corporate brands from organizations with strong cultures which:

- are appropriate for their environment
- adapt as the environment changes
- respect leadership at all levels
- are attentive to satisfying the needs of staff, customers and shareholders.

To thrive by taking heed of organizational culture, managers need to anticipate environmental changes and then consider what the implications are for their organization, adapting their peripheral values yet staying true to their core values. Strong brands depend on strong leaders who have gained respect throughout the organization. Another implication for managing corporate brands is that the shared culture needs to recognize that any brand decisions must balance the needs of customers with staff and shareholders. This concurs with Doyle's (1992) finding

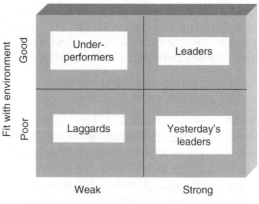

Figure 5.9   *Matching strength of culture with the environment (Jackson 1997)*

that the long-term success of organizations depends on satisfying a coalition of stakeholders, not just one party.

Conclusions

In a competitive environment, where organizations leapfrog each other's functional advantages, sustainable competitive advantage can be gained through the way the brand promise is delivered by staff. An organizational culture enables staff to infer the values of their firm and provides them with guidelines about how they should behave. As such, organizational culture acts as a link for strengthening a brand's performance. However, rather than talking about an organizational culture it is more appropriate to talk about the culture generally characterizing the organization, since it is likely that there will be variants which conform to the norm. The characteristics of an organization's culture can be assessed through auditing the organization's artefacts, its values and the assumptions held about how the market competes.

Brands are more likely to thrive when they emanate from organizational cultures that support the brand's vision. Force field analysis of the vision for the brand and the prevailing organizational culture enables managers to assess the extent to which elements of the culture either enhance or impede the realization of the brand's vision.

In view of the need for all departments of an organization to work together delivering a coherent brand, the brand's team will benefit from evaluating whether each department has an enhancing, an orthogonal or a counter-culture. It is critically important that the culture of the customer-facing department reflects an enhancing subculture, since these staff provide the first point of contact with customers and they need to deliver the brand promise portrayed in promotional campaigns. Some degree of orthogonal subcultures can be accepted. However, it is helpful to have profiles of these subcultures, since this can forewarn the brand's team about resistance to new brand ideas from those departments that may be particularly conservative. Counter-cultures can be more problematic. Those departments exhibiting such contrary ideals should be confronted and encouraged to change, otherwise they may act in a manner that could damage the brand.

Involving all staff in a change programme to achieve the ideal organizational culture presents an opportunity to enhance brand performance. Such activities are best undertaken within an overall plan that is backed by very senior management and which recognizes that the journey will take some time. Without a firm commitment to communicating developments to everyone, the programme may flounder.

Ideally, the brand's team should monitor how appropriate the organizational culture is for the changing environment. Team members should be prepared to evaluate how they can bring about a fine-tuning process to keep the organizational culture synchronized with the market, to help the brand best meet customers' needs. A continual programme reminding employees of the importance of their internal clients, the external customers and shareholders should enhance the likelihood of better brand performance.

Brand marketing action checklist

Undertaking some of the following exercises may help you further to develop your brands by applying some of the concepts in this chapter.

1. To thrive, everyone inside the organization needs to appreciate how their roles help their colleagues ahead of them in the internal value production process. Get your colleagues to identify who their internal client is, and ask them to summarize how their work contributes to building the brand's values. Internal clients should then be given this document and asked to consider whether (i) they agree that these tasks build the brand's values and (ii) any of the tasks could be amended, so between the two of them they identify a more efficient shared approach to brand-building. A discussion between these two people may strengthen the internal brand-building process.
2. To characterize your organizational culture, undertake an audit of the artefacts that surround you – for example:
    *   material objects
    *   architecture and office location
    *   language
    *   dress style
    *   stories
    *   ceremonies, rites and rituals
    *   styles of behaviour.
    Having undertaken this audit, work with a colleague to consider what these imply about the culture of your organization. Encourage colleagues in other departments to do a similar exercise. Convene a workshop with representatives from each department and explore the extent to which your

inferences concur. Where there are departments that have notably different perceptions about the organizational culture, focus on these domains and as a team explore whether these views represent (i) differences due to inferences or (ii) differences due to artefacts. Differences due to inferences are likely to reflect differences in thinking styles, and may not be as indicative of cultural diversity problems as would be the case given agreed differences in the artefacts.

3.   More insight on your organizational culture can be appreciated from auditing the core values of your staff. Involving each head of department, identify at least one person from each department who is thought to reflect the team working in that department. Gain the agreement of each of these individuals to participate in this exercise. Interviewing each person alone, ask them to consider what are the three most important activities their department undertakes. For the first of these activities, ask them why this is important. After recording this reason, probe again by asking why this is important. Continue with this procedure until you have elicited the first values. Repeating this process for the other two activities will enable you to elicit the three core values from the employee. By conducting similar interviews with the other members of staff you should be able to surface the values that characterize your organizational culture. Tabulating these values, in descending order of frequency of mentions, provides an appreciation of the more widely held organizational values.

4.   Another assessment of your organizational culture can be found from surfacing managers' assumptions. This can be completed using the card sort technique. Approach those individuals who participated in exercise (3) above to gain their agreement to take part in this exercise. Interview each person alone, with the respondent at a table, and ask that person to state who he or she sees see your organization competing against. As the person specifies competitors, write the names of these on separate cards. Write your organization's name on a card, shuffle all of the cards and give them to the respondent, asking that they arrange the cards on the table in such a way that those competitors who are competitively similar are placed close to each other. Record the map, either by taking a photograph or making a drawing. Ask your respondent to explain why the cards were arranged in this manner, and probe to surface the respondent's justifications. The replies will provide the assumptions held by that person. Repeat this procedure with the other members of staff, and summarize the findings by

showing the frequencies with which each type of comment was mentioned. This enables you to have an understanding of the dominant assumptions as well as an appreciation of how these assumptions vary by department.

5.   To assess how appropriate the organizational culture is for the brand's envisioned future, write the brand's envisioned future on the left-hand side of a page and, from activity (4) above, on the right-hand side of the page record the dominant assumptions. By comparing the right- and left-hand statements, spend time thinking about whether the assumptions are going to help or hinder achieving the envisioned future.

6.   To evaluate how appropriate the organizational culture might be for helping the brand to achieve its purpose, complete the three blocks in Figure 5.10.

     Check the impact from the assumptions by considering whether these work for or against the brand's purpose. Likewise, consider how suitable the artefacts are for helping to bring about the brand's purpose.

7.   An appreciation of the alignment of the values of your organizational culture with the values of your brand can be found by recording on the left-hand side of a page the espoused values of your brand. On the right-hand side of the page, record the values that were surfaced in exercise (3) in this section. To understand how well matched these are, try to rearrange the values on the right-hand side of the page so that those surfaced values which directly match the brand values are on the same lines. By inspecting this tabulation you can see whether there is a good fit, and it will also show where there are gaps that need further work amongst employees.

8.   In some successful organizations, the founder, as an active executive, can be regarded as being so influential that he or she is perceived as being the brand – for example, Sir Richard Branson and Virgin. The problem is that, without planning, when they retire the brand is perceived to have

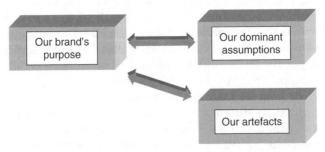

Figure 5.10   *Does the culture help achieve the brand purpose?*

lost something. This can be overcome by the founder strengthening the organizational culture so the culture lives on after his or her retirement. Questions to help integrate the founder into the organizational culture include:

- Do the artefacts include a wall on which there is a record of the staff heroes who have provided, and continue to provide, strong leadership?
- Are there values workshops, where everyone exchanges views about the organization's values?
- Are there six-/twelve-monthly reports that review how managers' assumptions about their market have changed?

9. From activity (3) in this section, it is possible to identify whether there is a counter-culture in the organization. For each department where activity (3) was undertaken, compare the elicited values against the espoused values of the organizational culture. Where there are instances of conflicting values, this may be indicative of a counter-culture and warrant further investigation.

10. If your organization is considering a merger with another organization, use activities (2), (3) and (4) in this section to audit both of the organizational cultures and check the extent to which they are aligned. This can help the debate about the suitability of the merger, and can provide information regarding which aspects of the separate cultures will need most attention to produce a more unified culture.

11. To enhance the performance of your corporate brand, evaluate:

- whether your current organizational culture is suited to the current and future external environment
- how adaptable your organizational culture has been and, if it has remained firmly entrenched, consider why it should not be fine-tuned to fit the environment better
- whether, from a staff audit, there is respect for the senior leaders and, if not, what actions could be taken
- whether meeting the needs of staff, customers and shareholders is recognized by each individual.

References and further reading

Assael, H. (1998). *Consumer Behavior and Marketing Action*. Cincinnati OH: South-Western College Publishing.

Bettis, R. and Prahalad, C. K. (1995). The dominant logic: retrospective and extension. *Strategic Management Journal*, **16** (1), 5–14.

Brown, A. (1995). *Organizational Culture*. London: Pitman Publishing.

Buchanan, D. and Huczynski, A. (2004). *Organizational Behaviour*. Harlow: Pearson Education.

Collins, J. and Porras, J. (1996). *Built to Last*. London: Century.

Deal, T. and Kennedy. A. (1982). *Corporate Cultures: The Rights and Rituals of Corporate Life*. Reading MA: Addison-Wesley.

de Chernatony, L., Daniels, K. and Johnson, G. (1994). Competitive positioning strategies mirroring sellers' and buyers' perceptions? *Journal of Strategic Marketing*, **2** (3), 229–48.

Denison, D. (1990). *Corporate Culture and Organizational Effectiveness*. New York: John Wiley.

Deshpande, R. and Webster. F. (1989). Organizational culture and marketing: defining the research agenda. *Journal of Marketing*, **53**, 3–15.

Doyle, P. (1992). What are excellent companies? *Journal of Marketing Management*, **8** (2), 101–16.

Gordon, G. and DiTomaso, N. (1992). Predicting corporate performance from organizational culture. *Journal of Management Studies*, **26** (6), 783–98.

Hofstede, G. (1980). *Cultures Consequences*. Beverley Hills CA: Sage.

Hofstede, G. (1998). Identifying organizational subcultures: an empirical approach. *Journal of Management Studies*, **35** (1), 1–12.

Huff, A. (1997). A current and future agenda for cognitive research in organizations. *Journal of Management Studies*, **34** (6), 947–52.

Jackson, D. (1997). *Dynamic Organizations: The Challenge of Change*. Basingstoke: Macmillan.

Kanter, R. (1989). *When Giants Learn to Dance*. New York: Simon and Schuster.

Kotter, J. and Heskett, J. (1992). *Corporate Culture and Performance*. New York: The Free Press.

Kroeber, A. and Kluckhohn, C. (1952). *Culture: A Critical Review of Concepts and Definitions*. New York: Vintage Books.

Legge, K. (1995). *Human Resource Management*. Basingstoke: Macmillan.

Martin, J. (1992). *Cultures in Organizations: Three Perspectives*. Oxford: Oxford University Press.

Mazur, L. (2000). When brands and cultures clash. *Marketing*, **16 March**, 22–3.

Meyerson, D. and Martin, J. (1987). Culture change: an integration of three different views. *Journal of Management Studies*, **24** (6), 623–47.

Mistry, B. (1998). Life and soul of the brand. *Marketing*, **26**, 47–9.

Morgan, G. (1986). *Images of Organization*. Thousand Oakes CA: Sage.

Nicholson, J. (1997). Sashaying on the ice floe. In *Advantivity: Building Competitive Advantage through Creative Cultures*. Leeds: Elmwood Design.

Peters, T. and Waterman, R. H. (1982). *In Search of Excellence*. New York: Harper & Row.

Rijkens, R. (1992). *European Advertising Strategies*. London: Cassell.

Schein, E. (1984). Coming to a new awareness of organizational culture. *Sloan Management Review*, **Winter**, 3–16.

Schwenk, C. (1988). *The Essence of Strategic Decision Making*. Lexington NJ: Lexington Books.

Smirchich, L. (1983). Concepts of culture and organizational analysis. *Administrative Science Quarterly*, **28** (3), 339–58.

Thornbury, J. (1999). KPMG: Revitalising culture through values. *Business Strategy Review*, **10** (4), 1–15.

Wilkins, A. and Ouchi, W. (1983). Efficient cultures: exploring the relationship between culture and organizational performance. *Administrative Science Quarterly*, **28**, 468–81.

Chapter 6

Setting brand objectives

Summary

This chapter focuses on the brand objectives block of the process for building and sustaining brands (see Figure 6.1). The purpose of this chapter is to consider brand objectives and devise catalytic mechanisms to ensure that staff focus on striving to achieve these objectives. The chapter opens by focusing on long-term objectives, which need to be easily understood, gain interest and motivate everyone. Breaking down long-term objectives into shorter-term goals helps managers to fold back the future, and to facilitate this process the use of the market cube is described. To help focus people's attention on those strategies best suited to meet the stretching objectives, the concept of catalytic mechanisms is reviewed.

Long- and short-term brand objectives

From the brand vision there should emerge a sense of direction for the brand. For example, Kingfisher, the group of retail businesses in DIY, electrical and general merchandise, has an encompassing objective of enabling people to enjoy their homes and lifestyles better than through any other retailer in the world. This provides a stretching objective and suggests implications for brand strategy. The next stage in the process of building and sustaining brands, as shown in Figure 6.1, is to take the ideas encapsulated in the brand vision and transform these into concrete objectives. The model developed in this book adheres to the views of Hamel and Prahalad (1994) that managers should roll the future back to the present, rather than incrementally project the present forward. As

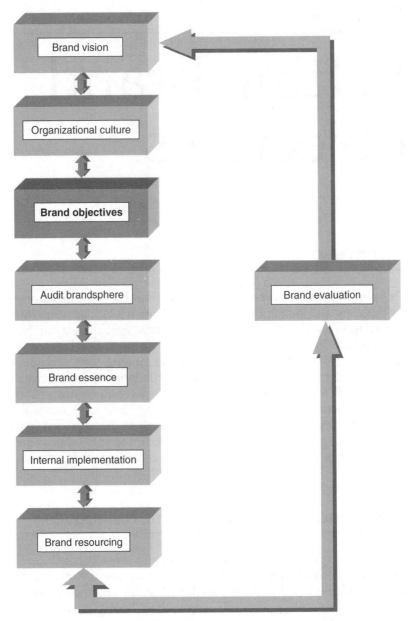

Figure 6.1   *Brand objectives in the process of building and sustaining brands*

such, the challenge managers face is putting down clear markers about what the brand must achieve at specified times.

To help managers transform the brand vision into some quantified objectives, it may help to consider the two-stage process shown in Figure 6.2.

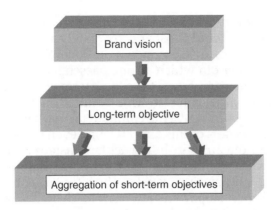

Figure 6.2   *Transforming the brand vision into brand objectives*

For example, Starbucks, on its 2005 website (www.
starbucks.com), set itself the objective of establishing Starbucks
as the most recognized and respected brand in the world.

Activity 6.1

Given the long-term brand objective of establishing Starbucks as the most recognized and respected brand in the world, how would you envisage this being broken
down into smaller objectives?

Discussion

The constituent objectives that could help to achieve this long-term goal include:

- rapidly expanding its retail operations
- growing its speciality sales and other operations
- selectively pursuing opportunities to leverage the Starbucks brand through
  introducing new products and developing new distribution channels.

This chapter will first concentrate on long-term brand objectives,
then address shorter-term objectives.

Long-term brand objectives

Boeing's brand purpose is always to be at the leading edge of
aeronautics. Collins and Porras (1996) present an interesting
insight as to how this part of the brand vision led to a series of
long-term brand objectives. In 1952 there was a growing view
within Boeing that aircraft in the future would have jet engines.
At the time, Boeing had a significant presence in the military
market and its image amongst airlines was firmly one of building

bombers. Furthermore, it was estimated that to develop a proto-type jet aeroplane would cost approximately a quarter of the cor-poration's net worth. Convinced of Boeing's views about a future environment in which airline passengers would be flying in jet aircraft, the company set the long-term objective of launch-ing a commercial jet aircraft. This resulted in the Boeing 707, which brought jet travel to the commercial market.

With the success of this aircraft came even more challenging requests from the airlines. In particular, Eastern Airlines voiced a desire for what was then seen as an extremely daunting option: a jet that could land on a runway too short for any conventional jet aeroplane, fly non-stop from New York to Miami, be wide enough for six-abreast seating, and carry 131 passengers. Having met its first long-term objective in the commercial jet market, true to its values, purpose and the same envisioned future, Boeing took this incredible challenge as its next long-term objective. Eventually this resulted in the Boeing 727.

From these examples, and others, several points can be made about powerful long-term objectives. The first observation is that long-term objectives should be easy to understand, everyone should feel compelled to act, they should be able to appreciate where their individual efforts need to be focused, and the object-ives should act as an internal catalyst. The intent is to move from merely having a goal to having a long-term daunting challenge. In the early 1960s, President Kennedy was faced by many who doubted the scientific viability of a moon mission. He did not issue an objective of beefing up America's space programme; rather, in 1961 he proclaimed the daunting challenge of landing a man on the moon and returning him safely to earth before the end of the decade. This long-term objective rapidly engaged NASA's employ-ees, who were excited by the challenge and felt strongly motivated to satisfy this. Furthermore, its clarity was instantly appreciated.

Activity 6.2

What other characteristics would you associate with a powerful long-term objective?

Discussion

When thinking of the Boeing and NASA long-term objectives, both of these would have raised questions about whether they were unreasonable. In effect, what is hap-pening with a powerful long-term objective is that each person is being forced to put aside his or her existing mental model of how things work and to develop a new model. This is an unpleasant situation to face (hence the cries of unreasonable), but if a brand is to thrive it needs to bring about change. You may have come up with other ideas, and we will explore some other points.

A powerful long-term objective is one that is constantly revisited as brand development progresses, and thus should lead to other exhilarating long-term objectives.

Activity 6.3

Think either about a successful brand in your organization, or of another organization. Can you identify a *series* of long-term objectives for that brand?

Discussion

The Boeing case is a classic example of managers setting even more stretching long-term objectives for higher-specification jets. These resulted in the 737 and then the 747 jumbo jet, which nearly bankrupted Boeing. In Sony's case, one of its long-term objectives was to become *the* company best known for changing the image of Japanese consumer products from poor to high quality. Its next long-term objective was to miniaturize bulky electrical products, and resulted in innovations such as the transistor radio and the Sony Walkman.

A long-term brand objective is powerful when there is commitment at all levels inside the organization, even though the firm is facing high levels of risk. Two particularly powerful examples of this are IBM and Zantac.

IBM set itself the long-term objective of reshaping the computer industry in the early 1960s and developed the IBM 360, which was a multibillion dollar project. IBM embarked on satisfying this objective, knowing that the new brand would make many of their existing brands obsolete. Everyone was committed to this long-term objective, whose announcement resulted in a drastic drop in sales of other IBM lines, providing a further stimulus for staff to beat the sceptics, with an 'all or nothing' attitude prevailing throughout the organization.

When Glaxo had developed Zantac to compete against SmithKline Beecham's Tagamet, they anticipated a challenging battle, particularly because of Tagamet's dominant position in the anti-ulcer drug market. At the time of Zantac's launch, Tagamet commanded a 90 per cent market share in the UK. Yet Glaxo's senior management had memories of not exploiting Ventolin when it was launched. A market research study recommended that Zantac should be launched at a price 10 per cent below that of Tagamet. Recalling the higher price that Ventolin could have obtained, and forcing the organization to recognize the superiority of its brand, Sir Paul Girolami, Glaxo's CEO, ordered that Zantac be launched at a price premium over Tagamet. If the brand were to achieve its objective of being a brand leader, staff needed to be committed to delivering a quality offering at a quality price.

Through a series of well-conceived strategies supported by a committed team, Zantac overtook Tagamet.

While both these examples illustrate success stories, it should be realized that to thrive a brand needs to have a series of stretching objectives. Both IBM and Zantac subsequently faced competitive challenges, which may not have had such impact if a rolling series of stretching objectives had been set.

From the growing number of cases of successful brands, inside the organization there needs to be considerable confidence in being able to reach the stretching objectives. When an objective catches everyone's imagination, it makes people become more focused and their confidence grows. These long-term objectives force everyone to think beyond their current capabilities and environments, and creatively to explore new ideas. The result is that powerful long-term objectives are not risk-free, yet everyone is aware of the risks they are facing and are spurred on, through a collective spirit, to overcome the odds and reach the goal.

When the innocent drinks company (www.innocendrinks. co.uk) set itself the objective of being a major player in the pure fruit smoothie market, it had to think far more creatively. The concept was tested by the three founders buying £500 of fruit, crushing it into smoothies and then selling them from a stall at a music festival. Above their stall was a sign, 'Do you think we should give up our day job?' People were asked to reply by throwing their used container into either a 'Yes' or a 'No' bin. Enthused by the response, they resigned from their previous jobs and formed the company. They decided to make one of their points of differentiation humour on their labels, which are frequently changed. For example, one packs says:

> Gently pasteurized, like milk.
> Separation sometimes occurs*
>
> *but mummy still loves daddy.

Powerful long-term objectives act as a motivating force, stronger than that of a charismatic leader and capable of outliving the tenure of that leader. However, the objective must always be true to the three elements of the brand vision. One has only to think about the purpose of Disney, 'bringing happiness to millions', to appreciate the logic of long-term objectives – which took Disney from its origins to films and then theme parks.

It is possible to assess whether a powerful long-term objective has emerged by asking:

- Does it stimulate progress?
- Is it exciting and adventurous?
- Is it clear to understand?

- Does it force staff to think differently?
- Does it provide a clear sense of direction for individuals who appreciate how their role needs to change?
- Is it consistent with the brand vision?
- Does it have a risk, but at the same time the scope for gaining full commitment and unifying staff to work outside their comfort zone?
- Does it suggest other long-term objectives to sustain momentum?

Short-term brand objectives

In the previous section, examples were given of brands with stretching long-term objectives stimulating managers and their staff to embark on a challenging but focused route forward. It is not always clear from the long-term objective how this can be rolled back to the present day to enable managers to appreciate how to move forward. Just as a problem is no longer a problem when it's broken down into its different constituents, so a long-term objective may become easier to grasp when broken down into shorter-term objectives.

A helpful starting point is to think of the typical marketing objective. This specifies the expected level of sales of a brand to a particular customer group by a specific time. If we draw on this, we are saying that to achieve a long-term brand objective we have to be clear about which group of *customers* are going to benefit from this brand. The nature of the potential benefit from the brand needs to be reflected in the underlying customer *motivations* for buying the brand. However, the brand's consumers' purchase varies according to the *context* they are in. For example, the motivation for wearing shoes may be primarily because of the desire to protect one's feet and to feel comfortable. Yet when people choose a pair of shoes to go to work, these may reflect a need to conform to the conservative office style of clothing. After work the same person might be going out to a dinner party and a different pair of shoes may be selected, reflecting the need to dress fashionably.

By thinking about the potential market for a brand in terms of the three dimensions of customer group, motivation and context, as shown in Figure 6.3, managers have a tool for taking a long-term brand objective and breaking it down into shorter-term objectives.

The way to identify short-term objectives using the market cube in Figure 6.3 is to start with the long-term brand objective, which might, for example, be a sales intention ten years ahead.

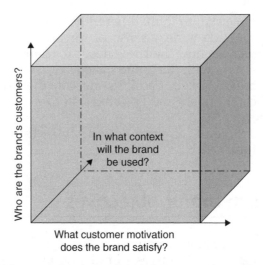

Figure 6.3   *The market cube to define the potential brand market*

The first task is to consider what categories, in the tenth year, will constitute each of the three dimensions of the market cube. For argument's sake, assume the brand's team of a car manufacturer has as its long-term objective to bring pollution-free freedom to travel on roads to everyone over the age of seventeen.

A helpful way to approach the market cube is for the brand's team to work together at a workshop. Taking the first dimension of customer motivation, from the long-term objective the team needs to identify the primary reasons why customers might want this new range of cars. This could be for environmental reasons – for example, because the car does not degrade the quality of air and does not create noise pollution. A second motivation might result from the term 'freedom to travel', and here the motivation may be a desire for stress-free driving without the worry of getting lost when travelling. By translating the long-term objectives into possible consumer motivations, ideas should start to emerge in terms of shorter-term brand objectives.

Activity 6.4

From these potential customer motivations described in the case of the car manufacturer, what functional attributes might the brand have?

Discussion

A revolutionary engine will be needed that does not emit any pollutants. The whole concept of the physical form of the car will need to be reconsidered to ensure that every part of the car is produced in a pollution-free manner, and that at the end of the car's useful lifetime every part can be recycled or is rapidly biodegradable. The design of the car needs to ensure that it is relatively quiet when driven. Each car needs to have an onboard navigation system that guides the driver throughout the journey and also 'senses' traffic delays, revising the recommended route to ensure minimal traffic jams.

Next, the team will need to identify contexts within which their futuristic range of cars might be used. Some of the contexts could be to learn to drive, to go to work, to go shopping, to go on holiday/away for weekend, to visit friends/relatives or to take children to school. Finally, the team needs to clarify who their customers might be ten years ahead. They might feel that the most appropriate way of categorizing potential customers is by age, specifically in four age groups – i.e. those aged 17–25, 26–40, 41–59, and over 60.

The market cube in this example is characterized by two categories on the motivation dimension, six categories on the context dimension and four categories on the customer dimension. In other words, by taking each element of this cube, the team has $2 \times 6 \times 4$ variants for the brand as it strives to deliver the desired level of sales.

Arriving at the possible categories constituting the three dimensions takes time, and all members of the brand's team need to be given a document summarizing the categories. At the next workshop, the team will need to explore each of the 48 cells of the market cube, since these constitute the range of options for the brand. Some of the cells may be deleted as being inappropriate – for example, there may be too small a market potential for those aged over 60 who want the car to learn to drive. By taking the remaining cells and considering how each one might help to achieve the long-term objective, the team has a tool to stimulate ideas about shorter-term objectives. As ideas start to become more concrete when working through these cells, the team should always consider whether an attractive 'cell' will be a natural consequence of each of the three components of the brand vision.

Activity 6.5

What criteria could be used to assess the attractiveness of each cell in the market cube?

Discussion

Criteria to assess the attractiveness of each cell include:

- To what extent does this idea help the organization to achieve its long-term objective?

- How will the values from the vision shape the form of the brand?
- How will this idea help to bring about the envisioned future?
- To what extent will this idea support the stated purpose of the brand?

Depending on the scoring criteria the team chooses, so the opportunities from each cell can be prioritized.

Out of these workshops should emerge short-term objectives that enable the long-term objective to be rolled back to the present. In addition, this tool helps the brand team to put forward a stretching sales forecast. In the example, when the new range of this car brand is launched, each of the sales forecasts for every one of the cells will need to be aggregated to identify the total forecast sales for the end of the first year. Market cubes for each of the subsequent years need to be completed and again, by summing the cells for a particular year's market cube, each year's sales can be identified.

From the series of workshops focusing on the market cube, shorter-term objectives can be surfaced. However, once these have been agreed, systems need devising to ensure that appropriate strategies are enacted.

Catalytic mechanisms

Even though stretching objectives have been set, it is not unusual to see bureaucratic actions emerge which slow down progress in trying to achieve the desired objective. Much of the effort that has gone into defining objectives can become dissipated by actions that create a lot of work but make few strides towards the goal. One way to focus attention on strategies that achieve the objective is to devise catalytic mechanisms. This concept was introduced by Collins (1999), and an example helps with appreciating it.

Granite Rock is an established firm that sells crushed gravel, sand and asphalt. A stretching objective was set of providing total customer satisfaction and achieving a reputation for service that would meet or exceed that of Nordstrom (an upmarket American department store renowned for its customer service). The catalytic mechanism introduced to focus attention on achieving this objective was that of short pay. At the bottom of all invoices was a section, 'If you are not satisfied for any reason, don't pay us for it. Simply scratch out the line item, write a brief note about the problem, and return a copy of this invoice along with your cheque for the balance.'

Activity 6.6

What impact would you anticipate Granite Rock's catalytic mechanism having?

Discussion

This particular catalytic mechanism:

- provided impactful information
- acted as a powerful stimulus for managers to resolve customer problems
- signalled to stakeholders that the firm was serious about service
- kept everyone alert.

The result of this attentiveness to customer service was continual gains in market share, while charging a 6 per cent price premium.

The story is told of a business development manager going to the owner of a Formula 1 racing car team with a presentation to pitch for becoming the supplier of all their promotional clothing. The owner listened to the presentation, then asked the question, 'And how will this help my racing cars go faster?' Unprepared for such an unexpected question, a weak reply was given and the owner concluded the meeting. A few weeks later the persistent business development manager was able to meet with the owner again, but this time started the presentation along the lines 'With the money you'll make from the idea I'm going to present, you can invest in engine and body refinements which will make your racing cars faster.' With such a focused owner, any action not meeting the objective of greater speed would be ignored.

The challenge for the brand's team is to invent catalytic mechanisms that help to realize the objectives. To devise an appropriate catalytic mechanism, the nature of the objective first needs to be understood by all concerned, then creative ideas are needed to instigate actions which are concentrated in the desired direction. Several examples may help.

1. A student wanted to be an entrepreneur, building his own business. However, he realized that he would need a job to build sufficient capital. He recognized that he might become too comfortable with his job. As such he wrote a letter of resignation, dated five years ahead, and gave it to his friend with instructions to post this at the future date.
2. 3M has a stretching objective of continually introducing new products. The danger is that overt control may stifle this objective. As such, it introduced the catalytic mechanism of enabling scientists to spend up to 15 per cent of their time on research that particularly interests them.

3.   Nucor Corporation, a successful American steel company, has the objective of workers and managers sharing the common goal of being the most efficient, high-quality steel operation in the world. Its factory employees work in teams, and team productivity rankings are posted daily. Significant bonuses, based on team productivity, are paid weekly to the teams that achieve results. The return of poor-quality products directly reduces the teams' bonuses. When sales decline, workers' pay drops by 25 per cent, plant managers' by 40 per cent and more senior managers' by 60 per cent.

Each of these catalytic mechanisms was devised to focus everyone's attention on those activities critical to achieving the brand's objective. By identifying catalytic mechanisms that have teeth, any transgression will soon feel the impact. The more impactful the catalytic mechanism, the more the organization signals to its brand's team that it is serious about having a focused brand.

Conclusions

Guided by the brand vision, stretching brand objectives need to be identified in order that the brand's team can consider how they can roll the desired future back to the current time with innovatively appropriate brand strategies. Having stretching brand objectives provides guidance about future direction; however, this can be daunting. It is suggested that this task can become less challenging by spending time identifying long-term objectives, then breaking these down into shorter-term ones. If a long-term objective is to be powerful, it should be easily understood, act as a catalyst, lead to other objectives and gain the commitment of everyone.

To achieve the long-term objective, the three dimensions of the market cube need considering – i.e. types of customers, motivations, and consumption contexts. Each element in the cube can provide ideas about new variants of the brand and, for those that are particularly attractive, annual forecasts can be made, which when aggregated help the brand team to realize how the stretching goal might be achieved.

Once an objective has been defined, suitable catalytic mechanisms need to be identified to ensure that everyone focuses on critical activities to bring about the desired future. It is not difficult for people to be deflected from the original goals in their daily tasks, and the purpose of the catalytic mechanism is to keep everyone concentrating on the central objective.

Brand marketing action checklist

This chapter has presented ideas to help organizations focus on brand objectives. Undertaking some of the following exercises could be beneficial.

1. In your brand planning document, focus on the section relating to your brand's objective. Critically consider the extent to which this is a more concrete manifestation of your brand vision. If there is insufficient linkage between the brand vision and the brand objective, take time with other colleagues to focus on developing a more challenging objective which better links with the vision.

2. If you are developing a new brand, take the brand vision statement and, as a brand's team, identify what stretching objective reflects this vision. As a consequence of this long-term objective, what are the implications for the shorter-term objectives?

3. To strengthen your brand objective assess it against the criteria:
    - easily understood
    - motivating
    - everyone can appreciate implications for their roles
    - likelihood of leading to other objectives
    - forces staff to think differently
    - consistent with the vision.

    In those criteria where the brand objective looks weak, consider how it could be improved.

4. To capitalize on the stretching long-term objective, as a stimulus for shorter-term objectives, apply the market cube technique to your brand objective. First identify how the long-term objective will come about through:
    - specified customer groups
    - different motivations
    - varied consumption contexts.

    Once you have considered the categories that could constitute each of these dimensions, summarize them along the three axes of the market cube and circulate this to members of the brand's team, inviting individuals to add and delete any of the categories.

    Summarize the team's overall replies on another market cube, and make this the subject of a workshop. Convening all members of the brand's team, surface views about the criteria that should be used to evaluate the attractiveness of each element of the cube. Having reached some consensus, divide the cube into smaller cubes for small groups to focus on. Specifically, each group is required to evaluate the attractiveness of each element of their cube. Running a plenary session should not only help with understanding the attractiveness of alternatives, but also with forecasting the likely performance of the brand variant over time. As a result of narrowing down the alternatives, produce a summary of the short-term objectives.

5. Ask colleagues to let you know how they spend their time in their jobs, itemized per activity, and for each of those activities ask them to consider the extent to which these contribute to achieving the brand objective. This exercise will give you an assessment of the extent to which non-value adding activity is being undertaken.

6. If activity (5) shows a group of busy people, but who are making little headway specifically on the road towards the long-term objective, it will be helpful to identify a suitable catalytic mechanism. Identify:
    –   the nature of the objective
    –   the deflecting activities and the claimed rationale for their existence.

    From this analysis, consider what catalytic mechanism could be introduced which makes people more focused on actions to achieve the long-term objective. Do not try to identify this by yourself – involve those who work on the brand.

References and further reading

Collins, J. (1999). Turning goals into results: the power of catalytic mechanisms. *Harvard Business Review*, **July/August**, 70–82.

Collins, J. and Porras, J. (1996). *Built to Last*. London: Century.

Doyle, P. (1998). *Marketing Management and Strategy*. London: Prentice Hall.

Hamel, G. and Prahalad, C. K. (1994). *Competing for the Future*. Boston MA: Harvard Business School Press.

McDonald, M. (2002). *Marketing Plans*. Oxford: Butterworth-Heinemann.

Chapter 7

Auditing the brandsphere

Summary

This chapter focuses on the audit brandsphere block of the process for building and sustaining brands (see Figure 7.1). The chapter presents the five forces of the brandsphere as a basis for systematically analysing the factors that could enhance or impede brand success. The chapter goes through each of the brandsphere forces individually – i.e. the corporation, distributors, customers, competitors and the macro-environment. It encourages managers to score 1 where the overall evaluation of the force is favourable for the brand and 0 when the force impedes brand progress. The procedure should enable the brand's team to consider how it could capitalize on opportunities, or protect the brand for the future.

The five forces

As Chapter 6 indicated, breaking down the long-term objective into several shorter-term objectives will suggest ideas to the brand's team about potential brand strategies. However, in order then to consider how the brand might be developed to capitalize on such objectives, an audit is required of the forces that might enhance or impede the brand.

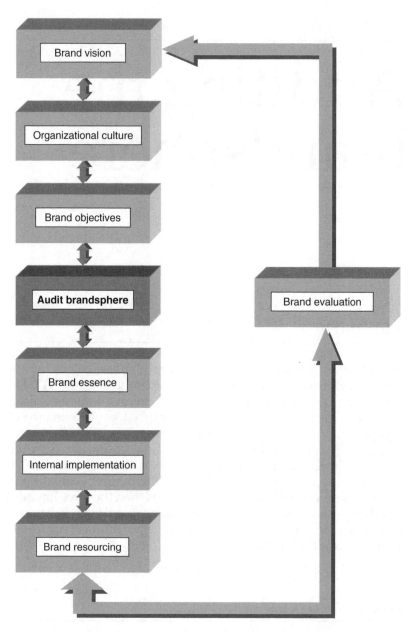

Figure 7.1   *Auditing the brandsphere in the process of building and*
sustaining brands

Activity 7.1

If you were asked to audit the key forces that enhance or impede brand performance, what factors would you focus on?

Discussion

No doubt you have identified many forces – for example, changes in the economic environment, new technology on the horizon, and the likely introduction of new legislation. When first faced with this challenge on a brand strategy project, many issues were considered; the problem was that with so many factors it proved challenging to summarize the impact of different forces. To make the audit feasible, and thus to enable the results to be analysed, the brandsphere, shown in Figure 7.2, was devised. This summarizes the five enhancing or impeding forces, and is the subject of this chapter. Without knowledge of these factors it is difficult to appreciate what promise the brand should aim to deliver.

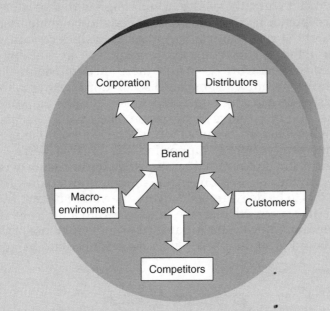

Figure 7.2 *The five forces of the brandsphere*

The corporation

The first force that has a considerable influence over the brand's future is the corporation. It is here that paradoxes may become evident. For example, some corporations talk about staff being their most important asset, yet they issue short-term contracts. Another paradox that might be surfaced is organizations espousing the virtues of long-term brand visions, yet they focus on short-term measures. When auditing the impact of the corporation on the current or potential brand, the following points need addressing:

1. *Co-ordination.* Due to the size and diversity of some organizations, where numerous pan-company activities take place, it is not uncommon for the firm to be under-utilizing its brand resources and processes as a result of an inability to co-ordinate activities effectively. This lack of co-ordination may also adversely affect the brand when staff in different departments do not communicate frequently with each other. All of the value-adding processes behind the brand should be identified and then, by walking through these processes, the strength of linkage between activities can be assessed.

2. *Values.* As Chapters 4 and 5 explored, brands are more likely to succeed when the values of staff align with the values of the corporation. There therefore needs to be some assessment of the extent to which employees' values concur with those of the organization and the brand they are working on, as depicted in Figure 7.3. Where there is a dominant reliance on the corporation's name, as discussed in Chapter 2, there needs to be a strong concurrence between the employees' values and those of the organization. There will be instances, though, where the organization will have a portfolio of line brands which, while supporting the organization's core values, will also have unique values, and thus will not overtly draw on the corporation's name in their brand name. If the brand is to be delivered effectively, the values of employees working on a particular line brand need to align both with the unique values of the organization and with those of their line brand. Auditing these values, as described in Chapters 4

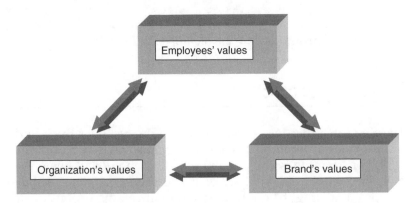

Figure 7.3   *The need for internal alignment*

and 5, enables insights to be obtained about where more attention is needed to gain alignment.

3. *Employees' understanding and commitment.* As was reviewed in Chapter 4, some employees may not fully understand the brand's promise and therefore are unsure about the strategy that they should be contributing towards. There may also be employees who are not particularly committed to achieving the brand's vision. The intellectual and emotional buy-in matrix, reviewed in Chapter 4 (see Figure 4.6), enables an assessment of the extent to which employees understand the brand strategy and are committed to enacting it.

4. *Departments' cultures.* Chapter 5 highlighted the fact that different departments, or different operating companies belonging to the corporation, or even different country operations, may exhibit some unique cultural characteristics. As such, variations in organizational cultures can be anticipated, but where counter-cultures emerge these can, in effect, pull the brand apart. A regular audit of the subcultures in the organization can surface insights about where there is conflict, and strategies can then be introduced to minimize this.

5. *Heritage.* In a world of change, people appreciate stability. Organizations that have stood the test of time not only give customers confidence about their greater likelihood of surviving but also have some values relating to tradition, which can act as a welcome haven of tranquillity in a world of strife and upheaval. When it becomes difficult to sustain a point of difference, being able to draw on a heritage can help create a competitive advantage. During the corporation audit, questions need to be raised about the extent to which the brand draws on its heritage, particularly since there may be instances when it is inappropriate to do so (e.g. for a hi-tech brand).

6. *Communications.* An organization communicates its brand's benefits in a variety of ways, other than just through the classical promotions mix of advertising, exhibitions, sales presentations, etc. As Chapter 3 explored, these could be through the attitude of customer-facing staff, the concern taken over customer service, the distributors being used, etc. The audit can help to appreciate whether any conflicting messages are being transmitted by assessing all the cues that different stakeholders use to appreciate the brand. For existing brands, an audit of the visual manifestations of the organization's communication symbols can show whether they are still appropriate. It is not uncommon for firms to form alliances, for example in the airlines market. As time progresses, consumers learn to appreciate the benefits from

such alliances. To communicate the benefits of individual firms forming an alliance, for example Thai Airlines and SAS being part of the Star Alliance, new visuals are needed for the brand identification.

7. *Distinctive capabilities and core competencies.* If an organization has succeeded with one or several of its brands, it becomes strongly associated either with the category or with the competence that underpins the brand. For example, people talk about the 'Starbucks effect' (Vishwanath and Harding 2000) due to the significant impact that Starbucks has had on the whole of the coffee sector. Likewise, because of the innovations brought about by Danon in yoghurts, it is strongly associated with the yoghurt market. Another example is Amazon.com, which has built a set of competencies that allows it to be the place where customers can find and discover anything they want on-line. Thus, part of the corporation audit needs to investigate the historical competitive advantages or the core competencies that have led to the brand having dominant market associations. Consideration then needs to be given to whether these associations limit the scope for brand development in new markets – in which case there may be a need for a new brand identity, with a naming strategy that does not rely on the corporation.

    Competitive advantage relates to the way the brand delivers outstanding added values or offers a cost advantage over competitors. When seeking to understand the source of the current or potential brand's competitive advantage, the brand's team needs to be attentive to the difference between operational effectiveness and strategic positioning.

    As Porter (1996) clarifies, operational effectiveness means performing similar activities better than rivals, while strategic positioning means performing different activities from rivals – or performing similar activities in different ways. If managers focus too much on operational effectiveness, they are in danger of their brand becoming similar to others through concentrating on benchmarking and outsourcing. By contrast, being more oriented towards strategic positioning encourages the brand's team to consider how the brand could become different. Examples of brands that have focused on strategic positioning rather than operational excellence are easyJet, Amazon.com and eBay.

8. *Employees' identification with the organization and its brands.* A problem that brands might face is employees being half-hearted about their work and having undesirable attitudes. This is more of an issue when these employees have regular contact with customers, since their behaviour and attitude

may be at variance with that desired for the brand. If employees relate well to an organization and its brands, they are likely to want to make the brand a success. By assessing their identification with the organization, it is possible to evaluate where there are internal problems.

Mael and Ashforth (1992) define organizational identification as 'the perceived oneness with the organization and the experience of the organization's successes and failures as one's own'. They measure this concept using six statements:

(i) When someone criticizes [our organization/brand], it feels like a personal insult

(ii) I am very interested in what others think about [our organization/brand]

(iii) When I talk about [our organization/brand], I usually say 'we' rather than 'they'

(iv) [Our organization's/brand's] successes are my successes

(v) When someone praises [our organization/brand], it feels like a personal compliment

(vi) If a story in the media criticized [our organization/brand], I would feel embarrassed.

9. *Brand citizenship behaviour*. Organizations such as Starbucks realize the criticality of staff acting in a manner that supports the desired brand. A continual concern for management is ensuring that their staff 'live the brand' through their daily actions which support the desired brand. Burmann and Zeplin (2005) developed the construct 'brand citizenship behaviour', which can be used to gauge the extent to which employee behaviour is 'on brand'. Brand citizenship behaviour describes employee behaviours that enhance the brand identity. Specifically, Burmann and Zeplin identified seven dimensions characterizing this construct:

(i) Helping behaviour – positive attitude, friendliness, helpfulness and empathy towards staff and consumers

(ii) Brand compliance – adherence to brand-related behaviour guidelines

(iii) Brand initiative – showing initiative in brand-related behaviour

(iv) Sportsmanship – lack of complaining, even if actions supporting the brand cause inconvenience

(v) Brand endorsement – recommending the brand in both work and social situations

(vi) Self-development – willingness continuously to enhance brand-related skills

(vii) Brand advancement – contribution to the adaptation of brand identity due to changing market needs or new organizational competencies.

10. *Relationships with stakeholders.* An organization and its brands
     thrive because relationships with other participants in the
     value chain result in a supportive environment. Unfortunately
     there are some economic players who wish to own a dispro-
     portionately larger share of the overall gains, leading to
     rivalry rather than harmony. It is therefore wise to audit
     how supportive the relationships with each of the key stake-
     holder groups are, and to surface an understanding of any
     tension between the organization and stakeholders. This
     issue will be addressed in more detail shortly, when audit-
     ing the impact distributors can have on the current or poten-
     tial brands.

Having completed this detailed evaluation of the impact that different corporation issues can have on the brand, the brand's
team needs to arrive at an overall assessment. After reviewing
each of these ten issues, the team needs to decide whether *overall*
these issues result in the corporation force enhancing or impeding the likelihood of brand success. If it is felt that overall the corporation force enhances the likelihood of brand success, a score
of 1 should be given. However, if this force is thought to impede
brand success, it gets a score of 0. By forcing this 1/0 decision it
necessitates the team evaluating whether the *critical* issues overall work for or against the brand.

Distributors

If an organization distributes its brands directly to its users, as is
the case with numerous financial services brands, this is unlikely to
be a dominant force. However, where the organization uses third
parties to distribute its brands, the impact from the distributors
should be considered. Some of the factors to be considered include:

1. *Alignment of goals.* Just as the brand producer has a clear
    understanding about the vision and objectives it has for
    its brand, so each distributor has its long- and short-term
    objectives. To enable both parties to thrive, there needs to be
    a shared understanding about how both supplier and dis-
    tributor can use the brand to their mutual benefit. There
    therefore needs to be an understanding of exactly what the
    visions and objectives are for each distributor, and how the
    brand will help each distributor to achieve these. The analysis
    may reveal little overlap between the goals of some distribu-
    tors and the brand owner, apart from short-term sales/profit
    goals. Where there is little congruence between the goals of

the brand owner and specific distributors, there needs to be consideration about whether this could damage the brand, and therefore what actions should be taken to protect the brand.

It is worth undertaking, on a regular basis, a key account audit, drawing on the knowledge from the sales team. For each of the major accounts it is worth considering:

- what their objectives are for the next five years
- how they are going to achieve these
- what role is expected of the supplier's brand to help that account to achieve its goals
- what role is expected of competitors' brands to help that account to achieve its goals.

2. *Power.* Even though it is widely accepted that we are in a relationship era, it is not unusual for distributors or brand owners to use their relative strength as a basis for negotiating better terms. Some brand owners seek to assess whether they or their distributors are more powerful. While this knowledge can help to formulate a negotiating strategy, this is tactically focused. Rather than thinking just of brand strength, some consideration of the attractiveness of each retailer could provide more strategic insight. By combining these two sets of information, the brand owner is better equipped to consider the appropriateness of each distributor. This not only helps to formulate a short-term negotiating strategy, but also provides a strategic review. The strategic review helps to prioritize the allocation of resources to different distributors. Using the brand strength–distributor attractiveness matrix in Figure 7.4 facilitates this exercise.

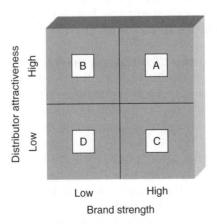

Figure 7.4   *The brand strength–distributor attractiveness matrix*

The first requirement is to evaluate the *brand strength* through each current and potential distributor. A brand is strong if it scores well on the factors critical for brand success. This information could be obtained by talking directly with each distributor, or by talking with the sales team members who are in contact with distributors. The organization therefore needs to identify distributors' views about the factors they consider when listing a brand. Their criteria could include issues such as profit, likely sales level, extent to which the brand's image matches that desired by the retailer, extent to which the brand has a sustainable functional advantage, etc. With knowledge of the critical success factors each distributor uses, the brand can then be evaluated against these and scores assigned, showing how the strength of the brand varies by individual distributor.

The next action is to evaluate the *attractiveness of each distributor*. In a workshop, the brand's team needs to discuss and agree the attributes that make a distributor attractive. These might include such issues as likely sales level, extent to which it attracts customers who fit the brand profile, geographical coverage, etc. Using these attributes, a score for the attractiveness of each distributor can be calculated.

For each distributor, its location on the matrix can be identified by plotting its position relative to the brand strength and the distributor attractiveness dimensions. By then examining the quadrants in which each distributor is located, this part of the audit enables managers to prioritize their distributor investment strategy.

Those distributors who are in quadrant A of the matrix in Figure 7.4 should be considered primary distributors for the brand. In this quadrant the brand and distributors are ideally matched and, in the (probably unlikely) event of these distributors demanding better terms the brand owner is in a strong position to counter such demands by clarifying the value of the brand. These distributors are ideal partners for joint marketing campaigns to reap the benefits of the brand.

The next priority distributors are those in quadrant B, where the brand is not particularly strong but the distributor is attractive. This represents an opportunity for the brand, since the changes to make the brand strong are under the control of the brand owner and the attributes needing attention will be known from the scoring procedure. Once these changes have been addressed, the strengthened brand can capitalize on the synergistic effects from trading with highly attractive distributors. The danger in this quadrant is that the distributor also regularly reviews its brand mix portfolio, and this brand would be regarded as underperforming.

The third priority distributors are those in quadrant C, where the brand is strong but the distributors are not particularly

Table 7.1 *Power analysis*

Deskpros sales through:	%	Share of office equipment brands through Brightspace	%
Officerite	27	Alpha brand	36
Brightspace	25	Companion brand	33
Ranger	17	Deskpro brand	16
Workspace	16	Other brands	15
Designer	15		
Total	100	Total	100

attractive. The audit needs to identify whether there are any joint initiatives that could make these distributors become attractive (e.g. joint advertising, better training for the distributors' merchandisers, etc.). If it is felt that investment in this type of distributor is unlikely to improve its attractiveness, questions need to be asked as to why the distributor is being employed.

Finally, distributors in quadrant D need considering. Where the brand is weak and the distributors are not attractive, serious consideration needs to be given to cutting any ties (if they exist). Where the brand is of mediocre strength and the distributors are of mediocre attractiveness, thought needs to be given to whether any investment might transform the situation over the longer term.

By undertaking a brand strength–distributor attractiveness audit on a regular basis, an organization is able to prioritize its investment and working relationship with individual distributors. This can also stop the 'knee-jerk' response of many brand owners when faced with a demand from a distributor for a larger discount. By identifying in which quadrant the distributor lies, an appropriate response can be formulated.

It is not uncommon to hear about managers feeling forced into a particular position because the distributor has the 'upper hand'. Another way to appreciate the balance of power between a brand owner and distributor is to analyse the proportion of a brand's sales through each distributor, and then for each individual distributor to make an assessment of how important the brand is for that distributor. For example, Table 7.1 shows a hypothetical analysis for an office equipment manufacturer, Deskpro.

In this particular example, Deskpro is more reliant on Brightspace than Brightspace is on Deskpro. A quarter of Deskpro's sales depend on maintaining distribution through Brightspace, yet Brightspace only achieves 16 per cent of its office equipment sales through Deskpro. This type of analysis enables brand owners better to appreciate which distributors might exert pressure on their brand.

Activity 7.2

What actions can Deskpro take in this hypothetical example if it wants to counter the threat from Brightspace flexing its muscle?

Discussion

To stop selling its brand through Brightspace would hurt Deskpro more than Brightspace. It therefore needs to find ways of growing business for its brand through those distributors other than Brightspace, at a *faster rate* than is envisaged through Brightspace.

The factors highlighted in this section provide a good basis for understanding the way distributors can influence brand success. Readers wishing to have a broader appreciation of the impact of distributors on brands should consult de Chernatony and McDonald (2003).

After completing the review of the impact that distributors can have on the brand, the brand's team needs to arrive at an overall assessment about this force. Again, just as was the case at the end of the analysis of corporation issues, so a decision is needed about whether distributors enhance (a score of 1) or impede (a score of 0) brand success.

Customers

The term 'customer' is used, yet there is a distinction between end-users in classical consumer markets and customers in business-to-business markets. Each of these two segments will be addressed.

End consumers

Time rich or money rich

The organization needs to appreciate how consumers buy their brand, and what role the brand will play in enhancing their lifestyle. Consumer research can be particularly helpful, but may again surface several paradoxes. For example:

- consumers are being presented with more brand choice, yet have less time to choose
- consumer wealth is notable, yet value is a key influencer
- consumers welcome brands that are tailored to their needs, yet they do not like the perceived intrusion from direct mail and Internet activity.

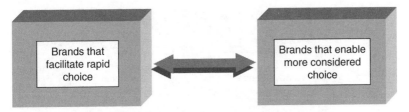

Figure 7.5   *Branding opportunities in a time-pressured society*

Such paradoxes create brand opportunities. For example, in the bookstore market, Waterstone's appeals to readers who wish to take advantage of the variety of choice and enjoy browsing through books. Juice bars are part of their retailing format where, over a light refreshment, consumers can skim through texts. By contrast, Amazon.com appeals to readers who wish to be efficient with their time. Not only is their website easy and rapid to negotiate, but recommendations are suggested about other books, based on the consumer's previous selections, in addition to the availability of critiques by other readers. Figure 7.5 summarizes the brand typology opportunity – i.e. designing brands that act as rapid decision devices and those that are 'pamper me' brands, providing more information for the person who wants to make a considered choice.

In many societies there is an increasing number of consumers who have exceptionally full lifestyles, leaving little time for brand decisions. There are also those who do not have such pressured timetables. Brand marketers are developing brands that match the time consumers have. However, by also interlinking this time availability issue with an assessment of consumers' personal disposable incomes, a more insightful appreciation of brand opportunities results, as shown in Figure 7.6.

By auditing where the core target market resides on the matrix in Figure 7.6, the brand's team can check the appropriateness of its brand strategy and, by undertaking this audit over time, can consider how the brand needs fine-tuning to reflect the movement of consumers around this matrix.

Tight or loose control

For those brands that are marketed predominantly over the Internet, the brand's team needs to consider the extent to which the organization is exerting a tight or loose control over the brand. In an Internet environment, rather than having consumers an organization has a community, all of whom share an interest in the brand. Brands are welcomed in an Internet environment not just

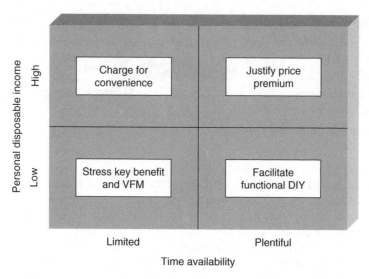

Figure 7.6   *Branding opportunities in a money- and time-constrained society*

because of their functional and emotional values, but also because of their experiential values. The experiential values arise because of what an organization *does* to its community and because of the way the community *co-creates* value with the brand. Recognizing this, the brand's team should have a chat room on their website that encourages discussion about the brand, and through listening in the brand's team should consider how the brand could be fine-tuned to meet the evolving needs of the community.

The ultimate for a loose-control brand on the Internet is for the organization to post the brand's values, educate its community about how the brand's values provide guidance about what the brand can and cannot do, and then leave the community to provide ideas about the future development of the brand. In effect, the brand's team is acting as the conductor, providing leadership guidance for the brand. Its community is the orchestra, interpreting the leadership in terms of the type of music the musicians want to produce.

As consumers become more experienced with a brand, they expect more. Thus there is a need continually to audit the extent to which the organization is exerting a tight or loose degree of control over the brand and whether there is a need for change.

How well does the brand fit the consumer's buying process?

When consumers buy brands, the stages they go through, and therefore their expectations of brands, vary according to the

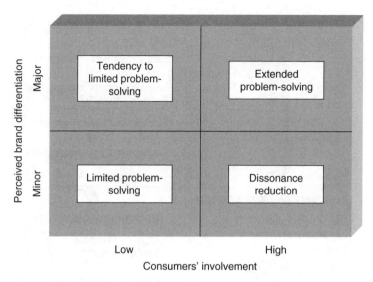

Figure 7.7   *A typology of consumers' buying processes (adapted from Assael 1987)*

degree to which they are involved in the brand-buying process and the extent to which they perceive competing brands to differ. Consumers' brand-buying typologies can be characterized by the matrix in Figure 7.7.

By auditing which brand-buying process the consumers are following, the brand's team can consider how effective its strategy is in supporting its brand, as is next considered.

- *Extended problem-solving*. This buying process characterizes highly involved consumers who perceive significant differences between competing brands in the same product field. It occurs for high-priced brands which are generally perceived to be a risky purchase due to their complexity (e.g. washing machines, cars, PCs) or brands that reflect the buyer's self-image (e.g. clothing, cosmetics, jewellery). It is characterized by consumers *actively* searching for information to evaluate alternative brands. When making a complex purchase decision, consumers pass through the five stages shown in Figure 7.8.

The decision process starts when the consumer becomes aware of a problem – for example, a young man may have heard his friend's new audio system and become aware of how inferior his sounds. This recognition might trigger a need to replace his system, and he is likely to become more attentive to information about audio brands.

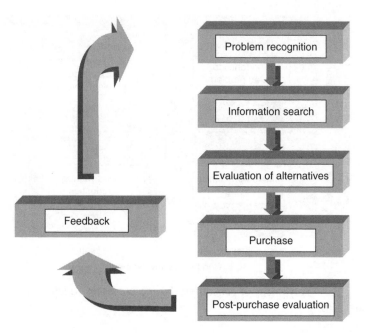

Figure 7.8   *Stages in extended problem-solving*

The search for information will start first in his own memory and, if he feels confident that he has sufficient information, he will be able to evaluate the available brands. Often, though, consumers do not feel sufficiently confident to rely on memory alone (particularly for infrequently bought brands), so they will scan the external environment (e.g. visit shops, become attentive to certain advertisements, talk to friends). As they get more information, highly involved consumers will start to learn how to interpret the information in their brand evaluation.

Even so, consumers do not single-mindedly search out brand information. It has been estimated that in any one day people are bombarded by around 1500 different marketing messages, of which they are attentive to less than 2 per cent. Consumers' perceptual processes protect them from information overload. Should something interest them, their attention will be directed to this new source. However, of the few advertisements they take notice of, they are likely to ignore the points that do not conform to their prior expectations and interpret some of the other points within their own frame of reference.

As consumers mentally process messages about competing brands, they evaluate them against criteria important to them. Brand beliefs are then formed (e.g. 'the Sony system has a wide range of features, it's well priced', etc.). In turn, these beliefs

Activity 7.3

What are the communication challenges a brand has to overcome when consumers are following an extended problem-solving buying process?

Discussion

There are at least three main problems when communicating a brand proposition. First, the brand has to fight through the considerable 'noise' in the market to be noticed. The next challenge is to develop the content of the message in such a way that there is harmony between what the marketer puts into the message and what the consumer takes out of the message. Having overcome these two hurdles, the next challenge is to make the message powerful enough to reinforce the other brand-marketing activities.

begin to mould an attitude and, if sufficiently positive, there is a greater likelihood of a positive intention.

Having decided which audio brand to buy, the consumer then makes the purchase. Once the audio is installed, he will assess how well his expectations were met. Satisfaction with different aspects of the brand will strengthen positive beliefs and attitudes towards the brand. If this is the case, the consumer will be proud of his purchase and praise its attributes to his peer group. With a high level of satisfaction, the consumer will look favourably at this company's brands in future purchases.

Should the consumer be dissatisfied, though, he will seek further information after the purchase in the hope of having reassurance that the correct choice has been made. Without such positive support, he will become disenchanted. The danger is that this consumer not only vows never to buy that brand again, but also talks to others, leaving little doubt in their mind that they should not buy that brand.

- *Dissonance reduction.* This type of brand-buying behaviour is seen when there is a high level of consumer involvement with the purchase, but consumers perceive only *minor differences* between competing brands. Without any firm beliefs about the advantages of any particular brand, a choice will most probably be made based on other reasons – such as, for example, a friend's opinion, or advice given by a shop assistant.

Following the purchase, consumers may feel unsure, particularly if they receive information that seems to conflict with their reasons for buying. The consumer experiences mental discomfort, 'post-purchase dissonance', and attempts to reduce this state of mental uncertainty. This is done either by ignoring the dissonant information, for example by refusing to discuss it with the

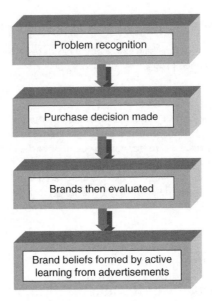

Figure 7.9   *Brand purchasing under dissonance reduction*

person giving conflicting views, or by selectively seeking those messages that confirm prior beliefs.

In this type of brand purchase decision, consumers make a choice without firm brand beliefs, then change their attitude *after* the purchase – often on the basis of experience. Finally, learning occurs on a selective basis to support the original brand choice by the consumer being attentive to positive information and ignoring negative information. This brand-buying process is shown in Figure 7.9.

Activity 7.4

How can brand marketing be used to ensure the consumer buys a brand with confidence when following this buying process?

Discussion

Any form of advertising should predominantly be used to reduce post-purchase dissonance by providing reassurance *after* the purchase. Advertising's role is not to stimulate the purchase, but rather is to reassure once a purchase has been made. Wallpaper paste is relatively inexpensive, yet wallpaper is expensive and the resulting decoration is very visible to the homeowner and visitors. Consumers do not have the ability to evaluate the technical differences between brands of wallpaper paste, which is seen as a risky decision. Polycell once ran a series of advertisements using the strap line 'You've chosen well' deliberately to reassure consumers after the purchase.

Also, close to the point of purchase, as consumers are unsure about which brand to select, promotional material is important in increasing the likelihood of a particular brand being selected. Likewise, any packaging should try to stress a point of difference from competitors, and sales staff should be trained to be 'brand reassurers' rather than 'brand pushers'.

- *Limited problem-solving*. When consumers do not regard the buying of certain categories as important, and when they perceive only minor differences between competing brands (e.g. packaged groceries, household cleaning materials), their buying behaviour can be described by the 'limited problem-solving process'. The stages that the consumer passes through are shown in Figure 7.10.

Problem recognition is likely to be straightforward. As consumers are not particularly interested in the purchase, they are not motivated actively to seek information from different sources. Whatever information they have will probably have been passively received, for example via a television commercial that they were not paying particular attention to.

Alternative evaluation, if any, takes place *after* the purchase. In effect, fully formed beliefs, attitudes and intentions are the

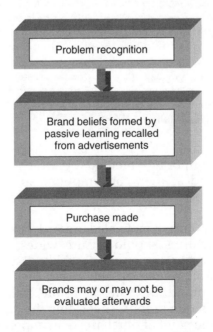

Figure 7.10   *Limited problem-solving brand purchase*

outcomes of purchase and not the causes. The consumer is likely to regard the cost of information search and evaluation as outweighing the benefits.

Promotions providing information, however, still do have a role to play in low-involvement brand purchasing, but whilst they have a positive role, it is different from that in high-involvement buying. Consumers passively receive information and process it in such a way that it is stored in their memories without making much of an impact on their existing mental structures. Having stored the message, no behavioural change occurs until the consumer encounters a purchase trigger (e.g. an in-store display of the brand) at the point at which they need to purchase the brand. After trying the brand, the consumer can then decide how satisfactory it is. If the brand is satisfactory, there will be a belief in the brand, albeit a fairly 'weak' one, which will lead to the likelihood of repeat brand buying.

Activity 7.5

How can marketers overcome the challenges brands face when consumers are following a limited problem-solving buying process?

Discussion

Consumers pay minimal attention to advertisements for these kinds of brands. Consequently, the message content should be kept simple and the advertisements should be shown frequently. A single (or low number) of benefits should be presented in a creative manner which associates a few features with the brand. In low-involvement brand buying, consumers are seeking acceptable rather than optimal purchases – i.e. they are seeking to minimize problems rather than maximize benefits. Consequently, it may be more appropriate to position low-involvement brands as functional problem-solvers (e.g. a brand of washing-up liquid positioned as an effective cleaner of greasy dishes).

Trial is an important method by which consumers form favourable attitudes after consumption, so devices such as money-off coupons, in-store trials and free sachets are particularly effective.

As consumers are not motivated to search out low-involvement brands, manufacturers should ensure widespread availability. Any out-of-stock situations will probably result in consumers switching to an alternative brand, rather than visiting another store to find the brand. Once inside a store, little evaluation will be made of competing brands, so locating the brand at eye level, or very close to the point of purchase, is an important facilitator of brand selection. Packaging should be eye-catching and simple.

- *Tendency to limited problem-solving.* While the 'limited problem-solving' aspect of the matrix describes low-involvement
purchasing with *minimal* differences between competing
brands, this can also be used to describe low-involvement
brand purchasing when the consumer perceives *significant*
brand differences. When consumers feel minimal involvement, they are unlikely to be sufficiently motivated to undertake an extensive search for information – so even though
there may be notable differences between brands (e.g.
a pleasing dispensing nozzle on Heinz's tomato ketchup),
because of the consumers' low involvement they are less
likely to be concerned about any such differences. Brand
trial will take place and, in an almost passive manner, the
consumer will develop brand loyalty.

How does the brand fit the consumer's needs?

Consumers buy brands that match their needs most closely.
Maslow's hierarchy of needs (Assael 1987) argues that consumers'
needs can be arranged in a hierarchy, as shown in Figure 7.11.
Before any of the higher-order needs can act as strong motivators, the lower needs must first have been satisfied.

This concept has been used by others, for example Swiss Re
(1999), which have considered how this can be translated into a

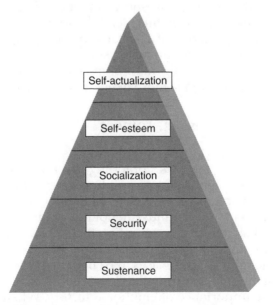

Figure 7.11   *Maslow's hierarchy of needs*

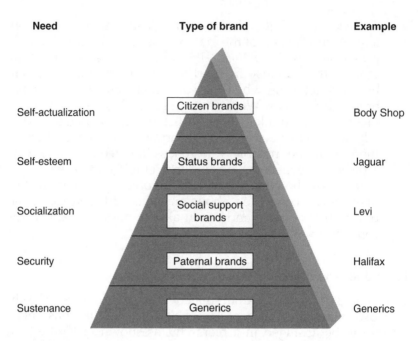

Need	Type of brand	Example
Self-actualization	Citizen brands	Body Shop
Self-esteem	Status brands	Jaguar
Socialization	Social support brands	Levi
Security	Paternal brands	Halifax
Sustenance	Generics	Generics

Figure 7.12   *Matching brands with consumers' needs (adapted from Swiss Re 1999)*

brand environment. By adapting their model, it is possible to conceive brands thriving by meeting consumers' needs at different levels of the hierarchy, as shown in Figure 7.12.

The implications from this hierarchy for brand management relate to the importance of regularly tracking changes in consumers' needs. By fine-tuning existing brands to better meet these needs, or launching new brands that major on specific needs, the organization is more likely to thrive with its brands.

Business-to-business customers

Brands are as important in business-to-business markets as they are in consumer markets. Branding in business-to-business (BTB) markets is about people building long-term relationships with people who are very time constrained. One of the reasons for many thinking that brands are not important in BTB markets is because of an incorrect assumption that choice is solely rationally based, without any emotional influences. As a result of the much greater costs of purchases in BTB markets there is a greater reliance on rational considerations, but there are numerous cases showing the importance of emotional factors. When two organizations have virtually similar offerings, it is not unusual to hear buyers saying they can 'get on with people better' in one of the firms and choosing to do business with that firm. Emotional considerations occur in the evaluation of BTB brands from numerous directions. For example, these may arise due to evaluations about prestige, friendship, self-interest, trust, status and security.

One way of appreciating why emotions play a role in brand selection in BTB markets is through an understanding of the concept of perceived risk. From Chapter 2, recall discussing the brand as a risk reducer; people do not make brand choices to maximize their utility, but rather to reduce their perceived risk (Bauer 1960: 389–98). In other words, some buyers seek to minimize their perception of uncertainty as to whether there will be an unfavourable outcome from their purchase decision. Perceived risk is an aggregate of components (Derbaix 1983) such as:

- performance risk – will the brand meet the functional specifications?
- financial risk – will the firm get good value for money from the brand?
- time risk – will the firm have to spend more time evaluating unknown brands and if the brand proves inappropriate how much time will have been wasted?
- social risk – what associations will colleagues link with the purchaser as a result of the brand choice, and will the decision enhance promotion prospects?
- psychological risk – does the purchaser 'feel' right with the decision?

It is important not to overlook the risk dimension in career advancement. Some managers are particularly ambitious to gain rapid promotion, and are keen to show what improvements they can make for their firm. If approached by a new supplier with a particularly attractive brand proposition, they are likely to be receptive. By contrast, the manager who has gradually achieved promotion may be more cautious and thus less receptive.

In conclusion, there is a significant opportunity for branding in BTB markets through understanding buyers' perceptions of the different components of risk. By then designing a strategy promoting the brand as a promise to reduce those components of risk important to the buyers, the firm should have an advantage over competitors. This challenge is, however, greater, since there are often several people, the Decision-Making Unit (DMU), involved in the brand selection decision. Their roles typically encompass:

- users
- influencers
- deciders

- buyers (those administering the purchase)
- gatekeepers (those controlling the flow of information within the purchasing organization).

The sales force needs to identify who is playing which role and what their risk concerns are. With this knowledge, and knowledge of the way that evaluation occurs at different stages of the decision-making process, they can then address differing concerns, striving to promote an overall position for their brand as a company-wide risk reducer.

Having audited the impact of customers on the current or potential brand, the brand's team needs to make a judgement as to whether overall this force is helping (scores 1) or impeding (scores 0) brand success.

Competitors

The fourth force that impacts on the well-being of brands is that of competitors. Several issues need considering under this heading.

Defining the competitive set

People rarely buy a brand without comparing it against others, and thus managers need to evaluate their brand against key competitors. However, a frequent assumption is that all members of the brand's team share the same views about which competing brands constitute the collection of competitors. This is an erroneous assumption, as is now clarified.

The personal backgrounds of managers, and their jobs, bias the way they seek and process information (Glaister and Thwaites, 1993). For example, the technical director who is part of the brand's team may focus more on brands in the market that are technology leaders, overlooking some of the followers, while the marketing director may be more concerned with price-leading brands, paying little attention to pricing laggards. All members of the brand's team are unlikely to receive the same information about the market, as they read different trade journals, go to different trade shows and interact with different groups of stakeholders. Even if they all read the same journals, perceptual selectivity leads them to focus on different news items, selective comprehension may result in the same message being interpreted differently, and selective retention results in different recall rates (Solomon *et al.* 1999).

Managers, like everyone, have limited cognitive capabilities (Larson and Christensen 1993). A far greater emphasis is placed on searching memory rather than external search. Even then, managers employ simplification processes to make sense of their external search (Schwenk 1984), one of the popular procedures being simplification by categorization (Bogner and Thomas 1993). Over time, managers develop knowledge structures, known as schemas, or cognitive models that enable them rapidly to appreciate different competitors on the basis of beliefs about them having similar characteristics to other members of their mental categorizations. Grouping competitors mentally, on the basis of the extent to which they match certain characteristics, is an effective simplification process for drawing inferences about the nature of competing brands. Again, because of perceptual processes, managers in the same brand team will exhibit differences in their categorizations.

Thus it is unlikely that all members of the brand's team will have the same perceptions as to which brands constitute the competitive environment and, of these brands, which ones are similar. Evidence supporting this has been published by de Chernatony *et al.* (1993). To help managers appreciate any diversity of perceptions about competition, the card sort technique can be employed. Managers in the brand's team are interviewed individually by someone external to the organization and are asked to name the brands they consider to be competing against their brand. These brands are written on separate cards, along with the team's brand name. The cards are shuffled and given to the managers, asking them to place the cards on their desk in such a way that those brands perceived as being similar to each other are placed close together. A photograph is taken to record this. Managers are then asked to explain their cognitive maps, and this elicits the dimensions they use to evaluate competitive similarity.

A further reason for having regular independent assessments of competitions is that manager perceptions of the composition of competitors may not be the same as those of consumers. Figure 7.13 helps with appreciating why managers' and consumers' views about competitors may differ.

While a manager may have full knowledge of all brands, because consumers are less knowledgeable the number of brands they are aware of may be smaller. Of these, only a small number are acceptable (evoked set), some are unacceptable and others are overlooked. Even then, of the acceptable brands some are rejected (inert set) as they are not perceived as having any unique advantages.

Through undertaking in-depth interviews, followed by accompanied shopping trips with consumers, market researchers can provide considerable insight into consumers' perceptions of the competitive structure of markets. By then presenting this to

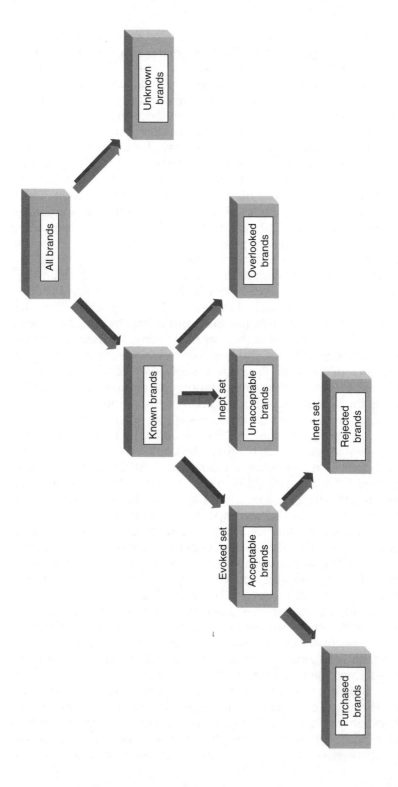

Figure 7.13 *Consumers' views about brands (Schiffman and Kanuk 1987)*

the brand's team, with photographs of their mental maps, managers can appreciate how better to focus their competitive brand strategy.

Thus one part of the competition audit is first to ensure that the key competitors are focused upon.

How are competitors differentiated?

With the plethora of competitors entering markets it is becoming more difficult to sustain a valued functional advantage, and after a quick glance at competing brands one is struck more by their similarity than their dissimilarity. For example, within their particular segment of the market, competing brands of cars, laptop PCs and televisions appear, on quick perusal, to exhibit more similarity than dissimilarity.

The use of eye-catching designs, novel logos and innovative blending of colours gives a brand an attractive outward appearance. The innovative style the brand proclaims may be welcomed by customers, and soon other brands walk with the trendsetter, clad in a similar fashion to ensure they belong to the welcomed group. Continuing with the personification analogy, it is when you speak with a smartly dressed person that you start to appreciate the difference arises more from the person's sense of direction, beliefs and the whole cluster of emotional issues that constitutes his or her personality. Likewise, when considering the brand, its point of difference is not just in its features, but rather the ethos, the values and the direction that give rise to a unique identity. Just as the artefacts are the veneer of a culture, so the design, logo and name are physical manifestations of the soul of a brand. Of more value when seeking to understand the real points of difference of a brand is its identity.

The concept of identity is one that has attracted a lot of interest and has been interpreted in many ways (Whetten and Godfrey 1998). Recall, from Chapter 2, that a particularly helpful interpretation of identity is that of Hatch and Schultz (2000), who regard it as the distinctive or central idea of a brand and how it communicates this idea to its stakeholders. A useful conceptualization of brand identity is provided by Kapferer (2004). His hexagonal identity prism helps to explain the essential differences between competing brands, and is shown in Figure 7.14.

The six dimensions of this prism enable managers to assess the differentiating features of a brand. Adapting Kapferer's model slightly,

- *Physique* relates to the tactile features of the brand that are recognized by our senses. The FT majors upon its pink

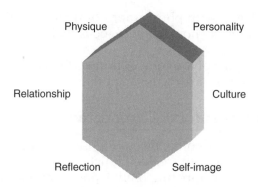

Figure 7.14   *Kapferer's (1997) brand identity prism*

pages, Toblerone on its pyramid shape, Chanel No. 5 on its sophisticated fragrance, Fairy Liquid on its gentleness, Guinness on its creamy taste and Rolls Royce on its silent yet powerful engine. For services brands, the physical cues associated with the brand provide a basis for distinction – for example, the uniform staff wear, the tone of voice over the telephone, the logo employed and the behaviour of staff.

- The *personality* of the brand reflects the set of human characteristics associated with a brand (see Activity 7.6).
- Each brand comes from a unique *culture*. While the culture of the Co-operative Bank could be described as ethically-oriented, Virgin is about being a challenger.
- Brands thrive through the *relationships* they form with customers. For example, because of the way breakfast cereal eaters like to have some variety in their limited repertoire of preferred brands, this is akin to a casual friendship. By contrast, the relationship someone might have with a private health insurer, e.g. BUPA, is that of trust.
- A brand provides a basis for the customer *reflecting* externally something about themselves to their peers through owning the brand. For example, Jaguar car owners are making a statement about their success.
- Self-image, or internal reflection, relates to the way a brand enables users to make a private statement back to themselves. A secretary who has had a difficult and argumentative day at work may have a favourite brand of tea that he or she drinks when back home alone. Part of the pleasure of the brand of tea relates to the way the secretary can silently think about the day and, while sipping the tea, say 'I know I was right – and what's more, I got through the day.'

Activity 7.6

Choose a market and assess how competing brands differentiate themselves by their personalities.

Discussion

Joie de Vivre Hospitality has developed a string of hotels in the USA that are inspired by magazine titles and differentiated through their personalities. For example, Phoenix is based on *Rolling Stone* and its personality is characterized as being young, adventurous, irreverent and fun. By contrast, Nob Hill Lambourne is inspired by *Men's Health* and its personality is male and health conscious. Interestingly, the personalities of these brands have led to different brand strategies. The Phoenix has music-minded staff and caters for late-night parties, while Nob Hill Lambourne provides free vitamins, yoga videos, and algae shakes for breakfast.

Not only does this tool help managers to assess the competitive differentiation of brands, but it also provides an evaluation of the coherence of the brand. For an integrated brand, each of the six identity components should reinforce each other.

Activity 7.7

Use Kapferer's brand identity prism to consider the uniqueness of the Volvo car brand and to assess whether this is a coherent brand.

Discussion

From the perspective of having seen and been driven in Volvos, their brand identity would appear to be:

Physique	Square, rugged
Personality	Solid, safe, family-centred
Relationship	One of the family, loyalty
Culture	Caring, Swedish social benefits
Reflection	I'm responsible and want to ensure my family is safe
Self-image	I've overcome the fear of not surviving an accident

Each of these dimensions supports the others, and this therefore suggests that Volvo is a coherent brand.

Strategic strength of competing brands

To appreciate fully the strategic strength of the firm's brand and competitors' brands, it is necessary to consider the following issues:

1. What are the objectives of competing brands, and how could these impact upon the firm's brand?

Some indicators of competitors' objectives can be gleaned from:

- their attitude – for example, organizations such as Mars, Procter & Gamble and General Electric have always aimed to have leading brand shares, thus their signalling of moves into a new market would suggest that any existing brands should raise their protective shields
- their historical development – for example, if a firm has failed in a market it has gained knowledge, and if it again enters the market there is a greater likelihood that it will be using a revised strategy
- their investment in competencies and assets, such as training, production facilities, advertising, distribution, etc.
- satisfaction levels amongst customers, with a likelihood that areas of dissatisfaction will be the focus for new entrants.

2. How important is your market to each competitor and what is their commitment? This gives some indication of the ferocity with which key competitors are likely to respond to any of your brand initiatives. Markets where competitors are likely to show a high degree of commitment to supporting their brands are characterized by:
    - high growth
    - high profitability
    - a high proportion of company's sales coming from a low number of their brands
    - the firm's heritage.

3. What is your brand's strategic direction and, by understanding the strategic direction of your competitors, who is posing the greatest challenge? The strategic directions of brands could be categorized as being to:
    - enter new market with new allocation of resources
    - improve competitive position
    - maintain current position
    - harvest current position, intentionally emphasizing short-term profits and cash flow, but not at the risk of losing business in the short term
    - exit promptly from a market.

4. What are your and your competitors' strengths and, judged against the critical success factors, where does the real brand strength reside?

5. What are your and your competitors' weaknesses, and where is each brand notably vulnerable?

6. What are your brand's and other brands' competitive positions? These can be categorized as:
    - leadership, having the greatest impact on market dynamics

- strong, enabling the brand to capitalize on a variety of strategies and not be vulnerable to competitors' actions
- favourable, having the capability to exploit specific brand strengths often in niche sectors
- tenable, whereby performance still justifies continuation, albeit without a startling recent track record
- weak, with an unsatisfactory performance record.

7. Are there any indications that competitors are likely to change their brand strategies, and how could this affect your brand?

By addressing these issues, managers should be in a better position to appreciate the strategic strength of competing brands. One of the challenges in doing this exercise is to summarize succinctly the findings in order to consider the overall question of what the strategic effect of competitors' activities will be on the firm's brand. To help complete this task, the template in Figure 7.15 provides a means for managers summarizing this strategic brand audit.

By considering the issues relating to the competitive force, the organization should be better able to understand the impact that this force has on their brand. Again, as was done with the previous three forces, the brand's team needs to make a judgement as to whether overall this force is helping (score 1) or impeding (score 0) brand success.

The macro-environment

Finally, the brand's team can benefit from regularly scanning its marketing environment to identify the much wider opportunities and threats, by considering the following factors:

- political
- economic
- social
- technological
- environmental.

By anticipating change, plans can be prepared to enable the brand to capitalize on any relevant opportunities, or to be protected against likely threats. Drawing the analogy with military thinking, good surveillance enhances the likelihood of success.

Again, after considering the impact of the different factors in this last force, a judgement needs to be made as to whether overall this force is helping (score 1) or impeding (score 0) brand success.

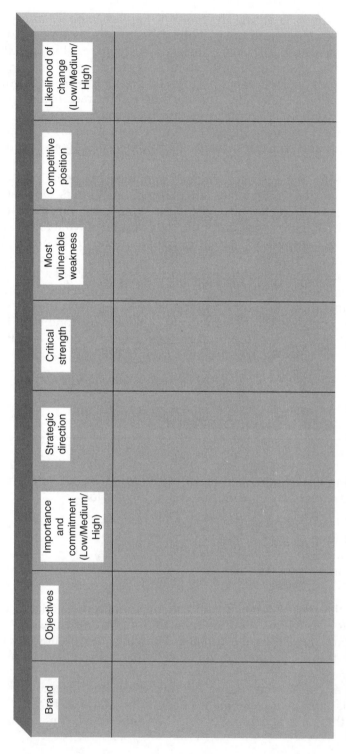

Figure 7.15   *Template to summarize strategic strengths of competing brands*

Corporation	Distributors	Forces impacting on the brand			
		Customers	Competitors	Macro-environment	
Co-ordination	Goals aligned	**End consumers**	Competitive set	Political	
		Time/money rich			
Values	Power	Tight/loose control	Differentiation	Economic	
Understanding & commitment		Buying process		Social	
		Match needs	Strategic strength	Technological	
Diverse cultures		**BtB customers**		Environmental	
Heritage		Perceived risk			
Communications		DMU			
Capabilities & competencies					
Identify with brand					
Brand citizenship behaviour					
Stakeholder relationships					
OVERALL SCORE	0/1	0/1	0/1	0/1	TOTAL

Figure 7.16 Template to summarize the impact of the brandsphere

Summarizing the impact of the five forces

At the end of each of the five forces' analyses, the brand's team should have made a decision as to whether overall each force is likely to enhance or restrict the likelihood of the brand succeeding. By scoring 1 for an enhancing and 0 for an impeding force, the team can aggregate these scores and arrive at an overall view about the impact from the five forces of the brandsphere on its brand. The ideal scenario is that of a brand scoring 5, and the most daunting scenario is a score of 0.

By deliberately forcing the brand's team to use this 0/1 scoring system, it encourages the team, within each of the forces, to adopt a holistic perspective and consider how each of the issues interacts to arrive at an overall view about whether these will or will not favourably affect the brand. Figure 7.16 presents a template that summarizes the components constituting the five forces in the brandsphere and enables the brand's team to record its 0/1 scores.

This audit has concentrated the brand team's attention on considering whether the environment is going to help or hinder the brand's progress towards achieving its goal. By breaking the forces into their individual components, it enables the brand's team members to appreciate those issues they need to capitalize upon and those that they need to brace themselves against. It forces team members to consider what strategies they needs to put in place to achieve the stretching objective. However, it may unearth issues that had not earlier been envisaged, and thus result in the brand's team having to return to the brand vision and brand objective, since these could have been far too optimistic. If this is the case, further internal workshops are needed to reconsider how the brand vision and brand objectives may need revising.

Conclusions

Through addressing the five forces of the brandsphere, the brand's team should be better equipped to understand the forces that will either work for or against the brand. By using the 0/1 scoring procedure it pushes the brand's team to consider, for each individual force, how the different issues interact, and thus from an overall perspective whether the force is or is not likely to be favourable. The value of this process is that it enables the brand's team members to consider how they could capitalize on each issue and how they should protect the brand against potentially damaging factors. Ultimately, it encourages them to reconsider the original brand vision and objective, in case they should have been excessively optimistic.

Brand marketing action checklist

Undertaking some of the following exercises may help you to develop your brand further, using some of the concepts in this chapter.

1. By taking the first column of the template shown in Figure 7.16, undertake an audit of the factors constituting the corporation force. Convene a workshop with members of the brand's team and, after explaining the summary of your audit, encourage colleagues to assess whether overall these factors are likely to help or hinder your brand (finally scoring 1 or 0). For those factors that are unfavourably affecting the brand, consider what actions could be taken to minimize these, or what else could be done to transform the problems into strengths. Ideally, this exercise should be repeated for each of the five forces in Figure 7.16.

2. One of the factors within the corporation force that influences the well-being of a brand is the extent to which staff identify with it. Mael and Ashforth's (1992) six statements have been shown, in 'The corporation' section above, as a way of assessing this. Circulate these six statements amongst those employees who work on your brand and, using a postal questionnaire, ask respondents to assess the extent to which they strongly agree (5), agree (4), neither agree nor disagree (3), disagree (2) or strongly disagree (1) with each statement. By taking the average across the six statements for each employee, you can evaluate the extent to which the employees identify with your brand. This exercise should enable you to evaluate whether there are any problems amongst staff that warrant further attention.

3. Draw on Burmann and Zeplin's (2005) construct, brand citizenship behaviour, to gauge the extent to which staff are living the brand through behaviour that supports it. The seven dimensions described in 'The corporation' section earlier in the chapter enable you to profile the extent to which key employees are 'on brand'. For each of the seven dimensions use a five-point scale, where 1 = not adhering to this characteristic and 5 = strongly adhering to this characteristic. As a result of the profiles, you can consider the actions that might enhance employees' brand-supporting behaviour.

4. When undertaking the annual distributor review, use the brand strength–distributor attractiveness matrix (Figure 7.4) to evaluate how to prioritize activities with different distributors.

5. If your brand is targeted at a consumer, rather than business-to-business market, the following exercise may be helpful. Do you know which of the four buying processes in Figure 7.7 your consumers follow? If this has not been made explicit, it would be wise to consider using a qualitative market researcher to undertake some accompanied shopping visits with consumers. In essence, the market researcher gains the confidence of the consumer and observes how the consumer goes about making decisions, encouraging the consumer to talk about his or her reasoning/feelings as purchases are made. As a consequence of knowing the buying process, consider how you are marketing your brand and, from the recommendations made following Figure 7.7, evaluate the changes that may be needed.

6. In the section 'How are competitors differentiated?', Kapferer's brand identity prism was presented as a tool to evaluate differentiation of competing brands. Furthermore, by considering the interrelationship between the six elements of the brand identity prism, it also provides insight about the extent to which they support each other, and therefore whether the brand is coherent. Apply this tool to your brand, and to its closest competitor, to consider:
    *   is there a critical point of differentiation?
    *   to what extent is each brand coherent?
    This exercise should help you to consider how you could strengthen your brand's point of differentiation and undertake changes to ensure that each identity component supports the others better.

7. Figure 7.15 provides a template that can help you to assess the strategic strength of your brand and those of your closest competitors. Use this to evaluate your brand and the few critical competitive brands presenting the greatest challenges. As a result of this analysis, consider what changes may prove beneficial in protecting your brand.

8. As a result of completing a thorough analysis of the brand-sphere, use the template in Figure 7.16 to evaluate the extent to which the five forces are conducive to the brand thriving (i.e. the maximum score of 5) or are serious impediments to progress (i.e. the minimum score of 0). If scores of 2, 1 or 0 result from this analysis, consider whether the brand vision or brand objective are too stretching.

References and further reading

Assael, H. (1987). *Consumer Behavior and Marketing*. Boston MA: Kent Publishing.

Bauer, R. (1960). Consumer behaviour as risk taking. In *Dynamic Marketing for a Changing World* (Hancock, R. S., ed.), 43rd Conference of the American Marketing Association. Chicago IL: American Marketing Association.

Bogner, W. and Thomas, H. (1993). The role of competitive groups in strategy formulation. *Journal of Management Studies*, **30**, 51–69.

Burmann, C. and Zeplin, S. (2005). Building brand commitment: a behavioural approach to internal brand management. *Journal of Brand Management*, **12** (4), 279–300.

Davidson, H. (1987). *Offensive Marketing*. Harmondsworth: Penguin.

Davidson, H. (1997). *Even More Offensive Marketing*. London: Penguin.

Davies, G. (1993). *Trade Marketing Strategies*. London: Paul Chapman Publishing.

de Chernatony, L. and Macdonald, M. (2003). *Creating Powerful Brands in Consumer, Service and Industrial Markets*, 3rd edn. Oxford: Butterworth-Heinemann.

de Chernatony, L., Daniels, K. and Johnson, G. (1993). A cognitive perspective on managers' perceptions of competition. *Journal of Marketing Management*, **9**, 373–81.

de Chernatony, L., Daniels, K. and Johnson, G. (1994). Competitive positioning strategies mirroring sellers' and buyers' perceptions. *Journal of Strategic Marketing*, **2** (3), 229–48.

Derbaix, C. (1983). Perceived risk and risk relievers: an empirical investigation. *Journal of Economic Psychology*, **3**, 19–38.

Glaister, K. and Thwaites, D. (1993). Managerial perception and organizational strategy. *Journal of General Management*, **18**, 15–33.

Hatch, M. J. and Schultz, M. (2000). Scaling the tower of Babel. In *The Expressive Organization* (Schultz, M., Hatch, M. J. and Larsen, M. H., eds). Oxford: Oxford University Press.

Kapferer, J.-N. (1997). *Strategic Brand Management*. London: Kogan Page.

Kapferer, J.-N. (2004). *The New Strategic Brand Management*. London: Kogan Page.

Larson, J. and Christensen, C. (1993). Groups as problem solving units: towards a new meaning of social cognition. *British Journal of Psychology*, **32**, 5–30.

Mael, F. and Ashforth, B. (1992). Alumni and their alma mater: a partial test of the reformulated model of organizational identification. *Journal of Organizational Behaviour*, **13**, 103–23.

Porter, M. (1996). What is strategy? *Harvard Business Review*, **November/December**, 61–78.

Quinn, J. (1999). Strategic outsourcing: leveraging knowledge capabilities. *Sloan Management Review*, **40** (4), 9–21.

Schiffman, L. and Kanuk, L. (1987). *Consumer Behavior*. Englewood Cliffs NJ: Prentice Hall.

Schmidt, B. and Simonson, A. (1997). *Marketing Aesthetics*. New York: The Free Press.

Schwenk, C. (1984). Cognitive simplification processes in strategic decision making. *Strategic Management Journal*, **5**, 111–28.

Solomon, M., Bamossy, G. and Askegaard, S. (1999). *Consumer Behaviour: A European Perspective*. New York: Prentice Hall.

Swiss Re (1999). *The Insurance Report 1999 Life Results*. London: Swiss Re.

van Riel, C. and Balmer, J. (1997). Corporate identity: the concept, its measure and management. *European Journal of Marketing*, **31** (5/6), 340–55.

Vishwanath, V. and Harding, D. (2000). The Starbucks effect. *Harvard Business Review*, **March/April**, 17–18.

Ward, S., Light, L. and Goldstine, J. (1999). What high-tech managers need to know about brands. *Harvard Business Review*, **July/August**, 85–95.

Whetten, D. and Godfrey, P. (1998). *Identity in Organizations*. London: Sage Publications.

Wolff Olins (1995). *The New Guide to Identity*. Aldershot: Gower.

Chapter 8

Synthesizing the nature of a brand

Summary

This chapter focuses on the brand essence block of the process for building and sustaining brands (see Figure 8.1). The purpose of this chapter is to help the reader to appreciate how the central core nature of the brand can be summarized. Brand essence is put forward as a way of visually summarizing the brand using a brand pyramid with a crisp brand promise. Recognizing that different people have different styles of thinking, some alternative perspectives on brand essence and brand models are reviewed to enable the brand's team to employ a process it feels most comfortable with. Striving to ensure an integrated brand, the linkage between the brand pyramid and the two constructs of brand positioning and brand personality is clarified. The chapter concludes by characterizing brand positioning and brand personality.

The shape of the promise

As the flow process involved in building or strengthening the brand is followed, by this stage (see Figure 8.1) the brand's team will have considerable insight, from the brandsphere analysis covered in Chapter 7, into the forces affecting the brand. This analysis can then be used to consider what the core nature of the brand should be.

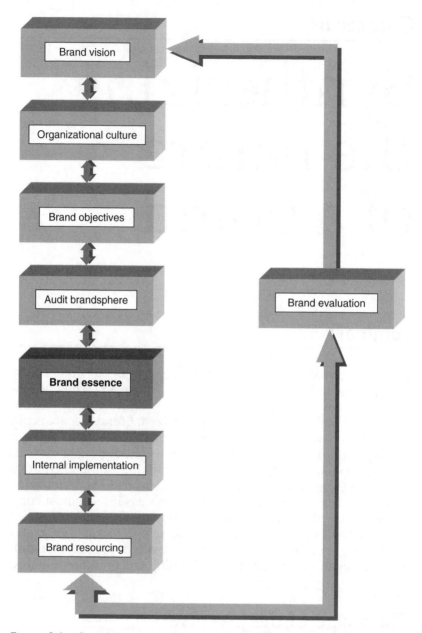

Figure 8.1   *Brand essence in the process of building and sustaining brands*

Rational analysis now becomes combined with creative insights to conceive the core of the brand. However, as you are no doubt aware, particularly after reading Chapter 2, brands are complex entities. Different members of the brand's team may have different mental models about the way they conceive their brand. The problem becomes even more pressing when recognizing that the core nature of the brand needs to be communicated to everyone inside the organization to ensure that they all appreciate how they can contribute to building the brand.

The brand essence is a useful means of conceptualizing the core of the brand, then communicating this to everyone. As will be shown in this chapter, there are different interpretations of the brand essence concept. Within the context of brand planning, brand essence is the centre of the brand and defines its central nature, enabling staff to have a clear representation of its uniqueness and to appreciate how they can then contribute to delivering the brand promise.

Visually, the brand essence can be appreciated as a pyramid summarizing the key functional benefits that allow the brand to make a rational claim which has been superbly linked with emotional rewards through welcomed values, all of which are understood through personality traits. Verbally, the brand essence can be understood from a short statement that summarizes the distinctive and welcomed promise of the brand which has been portrayed in the brand pyramid. This will be addressed in more detail.

Understanding the brand essence through the brand pyramid

To enable effective internal communication and encourage all staff inside the organization to pull in the same direction, the brand pyramid enables the core promise of the brand to be characterized. Figure 8.2 shows how the brand pyramid describes the core of a brand.

The logic behind the brand pyramid is as follows. When managers devise a new brand, they are initially concerned with finding unexploited gaps in markets, then majoring on their core competencies to devise a brand supported by a novel technology (or process) that delivers unique attributes. However, consumers are less concerned with attributes (e.g. a multifunction remote controller for a videocassette recorder) and more attentive to the benefits gained from these attributes (e.g. ease of recording a TV programme). With experience, consumers begin to understand the brand better and the benefits lead to emotional rewards. For example, one of the benefits of Emirates Airline, as an early innovator which installed individual TV screens in front of each economy class seat in all their aircraft, is in-flight entertainment, leading to the emotional reward of fun during the flight. If the

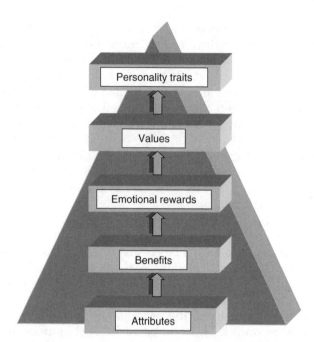

Figure 8.2   *Summarizing the brand essence using the brand pyramid*

emotional reward is to be appreciated, it must lead to a value that is welcomed by consumers. Thus the emotional reward of fun could lead to the value 'relaxation'. For some passengers, this value could be the key reason for them travelling with one airline rather than another. As was explored in Chapter 7, consumers rarely spend long seeking and interpreting information about brands. Therefore, at the top of the pyramid is a personality representing the personality traits associated with the values of the brand. By using a personality who exhibits the traits of the brand (e.g. a film star, pop star, athlete, etc.) to promote the brand, consumers draw inferences that the brand has some of the values of the promoting personality. Ultimately, the laddering in the pyramid is used to enable the brand to make a unique and welcomed promise. For example, following the airline case, it could relate to the brand promising to ensure travellers feel rested on arrival.

The use of a brand pyramid can also be justified from means–end theory (Gutman 1982), which was addressed in Chapters 2 and 4 (see Figures 2.8 and 4.5). The theory states that the attributes defining a brand (the 'means') have consequences for the person, and these reinforce that individual's values (the 'ends'). This is portrayed in Figure 8.3.

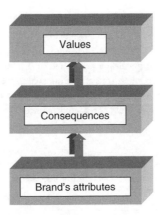

Figure 8.3   *Means–end laddering: how a brand's attributes are linked to values*

Recall that the aims of the brand pyramid are to communicate internally the core characteristics of the brand and to reflect the critical components of the brand that are important to consumers. Since choice decisions are based on a low number of attributes (Miller 1956), only the three most important attributes are to be included at the base of the pyramid. This necessitates the brand's team discussing and agreeing what the critically unique brand attributes are that are welcomed (or likely to be welcomed) by consumers. Once these have been identified, the brand's team members then need to work together in a workshop to develop the three 'ladders'. Focusing on the first attribute, they need to consider what rational benefit this leads to, then what emotional reward arises from this, followed by a debate about which values result and finally what personality traits arise from this value. This laddering is repeated for the other two attributes, resulting in three unique chains. By examining the personality traits, the brand's team needs to consider which well-known person might represent the elicited personality traits. Given these core facets, the team then needs to build on these to define the brand's promise.

There is an advantage in undertaking this work with the brand's team together, rather than as a series of individual exercises. It requires people to 'spark off' each other, and a more creative environment results from the team being together, drawing on their diverse backgrounds. The time needed to devise a brand pyramid will vary depending on the group, but it should be considered in terms of a low number of hours. Once the five levels have been completed, it is advisable to take a break and then, when refreshed, to return to identify the brand's promise.

Activity 8.1

To gain confidence in using the brand pyramid, try the following exercise. A car manufacturer is planning to develop a new car brand. The three key attributes that will differentiate it from its competitors are its unusual shape/looks, the fact that it sits close to the road, and that it has a lot of air bags inside the passenger compartment. By undertaking a laddering process for each attribute, devise a brand pyramid.

Discussion

The brand pyramid might look like that shown in Figure 8.4. The brand promise could be 'This brand promises to confidently liberate you from the tedium of life, getting heads turning.'

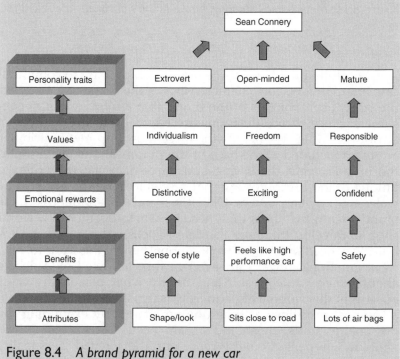

Figure 8.4   *A brand pyramid for a new car*

The fact that you might have different elements from Figure 8.4 shows why it is good to do this with the brand's team together. As different elements are put forward by different members, so these evoke debate and eventually consensus should be reached, resulting in a rich brand essence.

In Activity 8.1, the personality traits of the brand were pushed to form a view as to whether there is a personality to reflect the brand. This may make it easier for staff to understand the brand,

and may be a useful recognition device for customers. However, it may be felt by the brand's team that with only three personality traits, it is not particularly appropriate to specify a particular person who is the representational embodiment of the brand. When therefore thinking about the top sections of the brand pyramid, the brand's team needs to be flexible as to whether members wish to stop at the personality traits level, or push the pyramid and specify a specific person who summarizes the brand.

By completing the brand pyramid, a visual reflection of the brand is available for everyone in the organization. However, to ensure that everyone really appreciates what the brand stands for, the components of the brand pyramid need synthesizing into a short statement – the brand promise – that hopefully will motivate staff. A powerful brand promise has the characteristics of being:

- simple
- concise
- enduring
- capable of providing a sense of direction.

An examples of a brand promise is:

> VSO: promises to tackle disadvantage by realizing people's potential.

A particularly insightful example of arriving at a brand promise was provided in a presentation given by Bates Dorland. During the latter half of the 1990s, they developed a new advertising campaign for Heinz. Their analysis resulted in the summary brand pyramid shown in Figure 8.5 – note that their interpretation omitted the emotional rewards level.

Activity 8.2

Given the brand essence of Figure 8.5, what brand promise might summarize this?

Discussion

The Bates Dorland work led to the promise 'Heinz promise you' reassuring simplicity. In a world of rapid social change which makes family relationships even more complicated – for example, single-parent families, fathers working long, unsociable hours making it difficult to be with their young families – it was decided that the Heinz brand is about providing comfort through reassuringly simple food. A series of campaigns was developed making the point that, regardless of the complexity of the family relationship (for example, when mothers cannot be home to greet their children at the end of each school day), Heinz can provide warmth and comfort. The campaigns used life scenes to portray complex family relationships, with South African music in the background, showing different varieties of Heinz brands as having a reassuring simplicity.

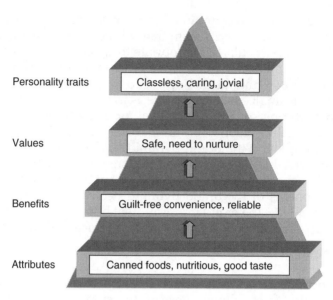

Figure 8.5   *Summarized brand pyramid for Heinz*

Arriving at the brand essence through this process provides rich inspiration for creative leaps of faith, which for the more rationalistic, left-brain biased manager can be justified through a logical system. However, the process should be seen as a series of stepping stones that help the team to arrive at the essence, and not as a straitjacket which imposes a particular style of thinking. The creative members of the team are no doubt right-brain biased, and they seek inspiration from material presented as stimulants, rather than wishing to have long, detailed presentations about the brand. Workshops that recognize that managers feel more comfortable with different styles of thinking, and are therefore flexible and tolerant of different forms of behaviour, are more likely to result in powerful brand essences.

Alternative perspectives on brand essence

There are different views about the meaning of the brand essence concept, and therefore alternative approaches. Such variety is not problematic, since it offers the opportunity of choosing an interpretation and a process that better meet the thinking style of the team. However, if the conceptualization is grounded in a model of the brand, this can provide logical justification for the process and helps the workshop convenor to recognize when to introduce different information stimulants to spark creativity amongst the brand's team members. Different terminology is also used by different writers when talking about brand essence.

Interbrand has a comprehensive model, 'Interbrand's brand blueprint', shown in Figure 8.6 (Blackett and Boad 1999). This particularly thorough model enables the brand's team to appreciate how the brand essence relates to different facets of the brand. The Interbrand brand blueprint results from customer research and internal workshops. It regards brand essence as being 'the distillation of the brand proposition and values – the ultimate promise to the customer'.

VanAuken (2000) defines brand essence as a two- or three-word phrase that captures the heart and soul of the brand. He gives the example that the brand essence of The Nature Conservancy is 'sharing great places'. The brand essence is the first thing an employee might say to describe the brand quickly to another employee. In contrast with the brand pyramid approach and Interbrand's brand blueprint, this is more of a *gestalt* approach to summarizing the core nature of a brand. Rather than having a detailed building-block perspective which is then summarized, it takes a holistic stance.

For Upshaw (1995), the essence of a brand is the core of its identity. This is justified by Upshaw's model of brand identity, shown in Figure 8.7, which locates brand essence at the heart of brand identity.

Upshaw explains that the essence of a brand includes everything that the brand hopes to register with prospects and customers about why it is the preferred choice. While this could encompass much (e.g. the brand's vision, its performance, its community relations policy, etc.), Upshaw points out that the essence of a brand can sometimes be represented by a single-word association.

Activity 8.3

What would be the single-word brand essence of Marlboro, of Visa and of Disney?

Discussion

Upshaw (1995) specifies these as:

- Marlboro: independence
- Visa: ubiquitous
- Disney: magic.

You may have arrived at other terms. For example, Visa may have provoked more than one word, since just one word could be too constraining and force generalities. Universally recognized payment may more fully describe Visa's brand essence, but then it generates more words.

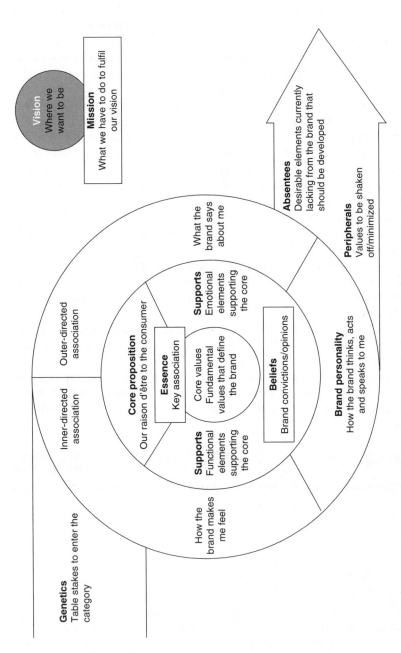

Figure 8.6 *Interbrand's brand blueprint (Source: Interbrand Newell and Sorrell)*

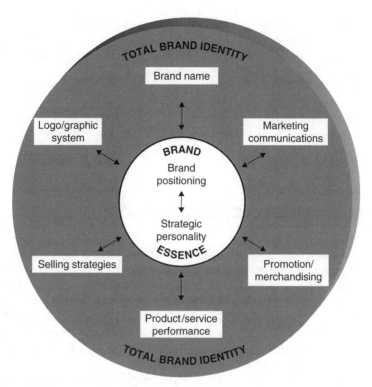

Figure 8.7   *How Upshaw relates brand essence to brand identity (Source: Upshaw 1995)*

Michel and Ambler (1999) conceived a brand as a social representation structured as a central nucleus and a peripheral system. The peripheral system relates to the interface between the central nucleus and the brand's situation, while the central nucleus is the group of associations that are seen as being inseparable from the brand by the majority of people. Brand essence is similar to the central nucleus, albeit a difference results from the methodology to identify it. Qualitative research helps to generate brand associations. Each association is then tested according to whether it is a central or peripheral association; this is done using a seven-point scale from certainly not (1) to certainly is (7), with the question 'If the product is not ... (association), to what extent would it be a result of ... (brand)?' As Michel and Ambler explain, if the majority of respondents answer 1 or 2, that association is a central association. If the majority do not answer 1 or 2, the association is a peripheral association of the brand. Using this approach, they investigated how a brand's essence varied across three countries. This approach has the advantage of being grounded in psychology, and encourages a standardized process. However, it can generate a notable list of terms that constitute the brand's essence, and may lead to the challenges of internal communication and memory retention.

Macrae (1996) regards brand essence as the communications connections that give a brand a historical basis to strive for a leadership position. Macrae argues that brand essence work-shops can be a helpful navigational tool for aligning brand's teams.

Models characterizing brands

The previous section reviewed different conceptualizations of brand essence. Some of these made brand essence the focus of their attention (for example, the brand pyramid), others related brand essence to diverse components of the brand. All these approaches enable the characteristics of a brand to be crisply summarized so that all personnel working on the brand can rap-idly appreciate the core nature of their brand and thus recognize their roles in the brand-building process.

There are, however, other ways of describing the character-istics of a brand, albeit possibly not as concerned with brevity. The richness of these alternative ways of characterizing brands comes from their detail and their logical structure, as for example is the case with Kapferer's (2004) brand identity prism, reviewed in Chapter 7. It is thus appropriate to overview some alternative ways of characterizing brands.

Vyse (1999) proposes that a brand can be characterized by its 'brand fingerprint'. Through investigating nine attributes, he argues that managers should be better able to track their brand's development. Enshrining this information into a brand docu-ment, everyone should be clear about the nature of their brand and, even though the composition of the team may change over time, the brand document helps to ensure brand continuity. To arrive at a brand's fingerprint, the following need to be audited:

- Target – a description of the target market
- Insight – a statement summarizing consumers' needs when buying the brand
- Competition – from the consumer's perspective, the com-petitors they consider and the relative values of these com-petitors
- Benefits – a statement of the functional and emotional bene-fits motivating purchase of the brand

- Proposition – the compelling reason why consumers would buy the brand
- Values – what the brand stands for and believes
- Reason to believe – the proof the organization has to substantiate the positioning
- Essence – the distillation of the brand's genetic code into a clear thought
- Properties – the tangible things that, with any tactile sensation, would evoke recall of the brand.

Vyse notes that there are organizations that strive to compress the brand fingerprint into a single statement, akin to a brand essence.

Activity 8.4

While recognizing that it would involve a considerable amount of work to produce a brand fingerprint, by taking a more holistic perspective from seeing (and maybe driving) a Mazda MX5, what brand essence would summarize this brand?

Discussion

Vyse reports that Mazda devised the statement, 'It is a rugby player in a dinner jacket.'

Research Business International has developed a proprietary model, BrandWorks™, which enables a brand to be characterized. The analogy, so insightfully drawn by Gordon (1999), is that of a diamond. When a stone is being assessed, it is only by looking through different facets that its value can be appreciated. Likewise, by considering six dimensions of a brand, a better understanding of its nature is provided. The Research Business International model is shown in Figure 8.8.

The first facet, user image, relates to customers' perceptions of the likely user of the brand. It can be most revealing when contrasting the brand team's intentions against customers' perceptions. A strong brand is likely to be one where customers equate with the user image and talk in terms of 'people like me'. It is worth spending time to differentiate between whether customers *feel* part of the user group, or have an *aspiration* to be part of the user group. Thus, if respondents describe their perception of the typical user as being above them, probing should then consider whether or not this is a motivator.

The product image facet throws light upon customers' perceptions of the functional attributes of the brand. Issues that

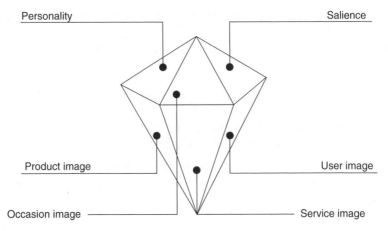

Figure 8.8   *Research Business International's BrandWorks™*

would be surfaced here relate to look, feel, taste, smell, sound, size, performance, etc.

All brands have a product and service component; it's just the importance of these that varies according to the category. As such, the service image facet enables perceptions to be explored about how the brand is delivered and how it performs, bearing in mind the way interactions between customers and staff affect perceptions.

The context within which brands are consumed influences perceptions.

Activity 8.5

Select a brand and consider how context can favourably or unfavourably affect perceptions.

Discussion

Places are brands. Someone going to Florida for a late winter break may do so because he or she perceives it to be a sunny and warm location. Yet, if during the five-day break it rains every day, that person's perceptions of Florida are likely to be less favourable.

The BrandWorks™ model seeks to understand when the brand would be most likely to be used, and why customers hold these views.

The personality facet throws light on the emotional and rational values of the brand and helps to gauge the relationship that the customer has with the brand. In other words, it is rather superficial just to elicit personality traits, but more useful also to surface

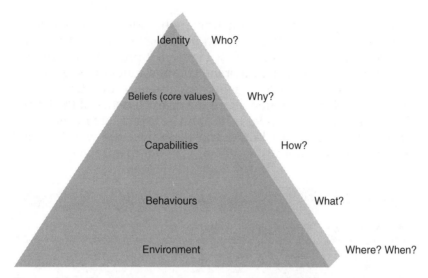

Figure 8.9   *Brand identity triangle (Source: Jones 2000)*

from the customer how these traits form a particular relationship. Thus an airline may be perceived as being 'young, professional and adventurous', but by then knowing that 'this helps take the planning concerns out of my diary' provides a clue about how the brand has been integrated into the customer's life.

Salience binds together the other five facets through the concept of emotional closeness or distance. People's feelings about a brand result from previous, current and anticipated experiences. Brand salience is the emotional distance between a customer and a brand over a time continuum (Gordon 1991). By explaining to customers a timeline diagram, they are able to locate a brand in terms of their emotional closeness to it.

Not only does this model help to characterize a brand, but it also enables an assessment to be made of the extent to which the different facets interact.

When dealing with brands that are predominantly services based, Jones (2000) argues that BrandWorks™ is still appropriate, with the addition of the following facets:

- Corporate values – addressing customers' perceptions of the organization's values, whether these are admirable and whether they encourage the customer to want to do business
- Personnel imagery – seeking customers' views about perceptions of staff, and thus inferences about the brand
- Capabilities imagery – what customers perceive the brand is capable of achieving for them
- Tone of voice – how the brand speaks to its customers.

Another helpful way of characterizing brands is the brand identity triangle (Jones 2000), adapted from the hierarchy of communication model (Gordon 1999). Figure 8.9 presents this model. The model reflects the way a brand communicates messages about itself at different levels. Against each level a question can be asked to elicit information about the characteristics of the brand. The strength of this model is its ability to stimulate ideas for the future direction of the brand and to analyse the way different brands are communicating messages about themselves.

Activity 8.6

A stockbroking company is thinking of developing a brand to reflect its new business of telephone stockbroking. By using the questions against each of the levels of the brand identity triangle, what might be the characteristics of the brand?

Discussion

Building on Jones's (2000) presentation, the stockbroker might devise a brand whose characteristics are those shown in Figure 8.10.

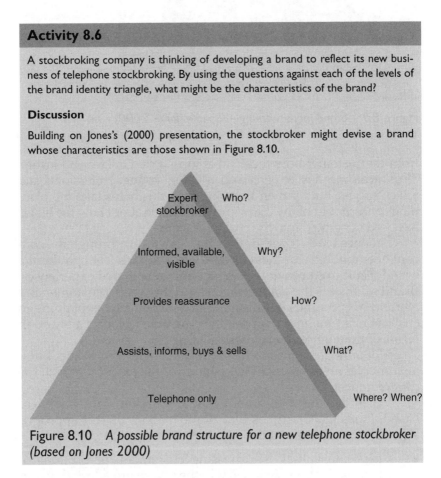

Figure 8.10   *A possible brand structure for a new telephone stockbroker (based on Jones 2000)*

From brand essence to brand positioning

Through succinctly summarizing the brand using the concept of the brand essence, or another of the models reviewed in this chapter, everyone inside the organization will become more aware of the core nature of their brand. This needs translating into two further brand characteristics that help the brand to thrive externally: the brand positioning and brand personality. The process of devising the brand pyramid will have given insights to potential positioning and personality options, which can be further refined.

One of the challenges brands face is numerous brands jostling to catch customers' attention. Positioning is a process for ensuring that a brand can fight through the 'noise' in a market, and enables the brand to occupy a distinct, meaningful and valued place in target customers' minds. For example, Harley-Davidson has succeeded in positioning itself as the authentic motorcycle experience. Positioning is concerned with registering the brand's functional capabilities on a low number of attributes. Following the theme of brevity in the brand's essence, positioning is about customers holding in their memories the one or two functional attributes that differentiate the brand. Brevity has a notable value in society – for example, the Declaration of Independence which differentiates America is based on around 300 words. To thus focus the brand team's attention on crisply associating their brand with a unique functional attribute is pointing them down a road of likely success.

Finding a crisp and focused statement that summarizes the outstanding functional dimensions of a brand should help both internal and external cohesion, through everyone understanding and pulling in the same direction. Sir Richard Branson's positioning of his portfolio of business from the perspective of standing for certain principles, the consumer champion, instantly signals to staff something about the activities desired of them, and promptly enables consumers to appreciate the functional benefits they can anticipate.

Thompson (2003) provides an interesting case study as to how an integrated brand positioning can emerge from the strategic insight that starts with a brand vision. The new CEO of Symantec, a network and security systems company with the brand Norton AntiVirus, instigated a programme to help the company become the leader in Internet and security solutions in consumer and corporate sectors. Market studies showed that competitors all positioned themselves as detectives hunting viruses and hackers. People were becoming concerned at the proliferation of viruses and the growth of hackers gaining unlawful access to databases. In this context, a brand vision was devised that sought to bring about a future in which people should be free to work and play in a connected world without interruptions. From this a brand positioning was devised, summarized as 'pure confidence', underpinned by the values such as customer-driven, trust and innovation.

While the brand's team strives to evoke a unique functional association with a brand, customers' mental simplification processes can affect the intended positioning. Thus while Van den Bergh successfully positioned 'I Can't Believe It's Not Butter' away from margarines, it was more fortunate than many banking brands, many of whom tried to major on subtle points of difference yet were perceived as similar to each other. Markets are becoming more diffuse, as new entrants see market opportunities from originally unrelated markets. Several grocery retailers have worked hard to build consumer confidence in their corporate brands, enabling them to enter financial services markets and to be perceived as differentiated through the level of trust and consumer confidence they offer.

Creativity enables the brand's team to devise novel perspectives on the brand's core functional advantage. For example, Procter & Gamble uses the happy baby positioning for its Pampers brand, allowing it to extend into any related area which engenders happy babies, looking continually through a baby's eyes.

Defining a positioning statement for a brand is best considered as an iterative process, whereby the brand's team proposes the positioning, gauges consumers' responses, then builds on feedback to refine the team's thinking. In other words, the brand positioning is managed. An alternative perspective, of predominantly relying on customer research, can miss opportunities. For example, Lefkoff-Hagius and Mason (1993) reported that what is important when customers judge the similarity of brands does not match what is important when they evaluate which brand to purchase.

The bottom levels of the brand pyramid provide suggestions, rather than precise statements, about the brand positioning. The communications' agencies, design agencies, technical team and the brand's team need to know precisely how the brand is to be positioned. The three attributes and the three benefits of the brand pyramid define boundaries regarding the brand's positioning. The challenge then becomes that of deriving a crisp statement which rapidly communicates the brand's functional advantage, but does not lose any meaning through being so brief. For example, Rijkens (1992: 7) states that the positioning of After Eight mints was:

> Consumers should perceive After Eight as a uniquely presented, wafer-thin, high quality mint chocolate, which is enjoyed after a relaxed dinner or on comparable occasions. It should be associated with the elegance, sophistication and social status of the good hostess and of her guests. As an affordable token of friendship or appreciation, it reflects the good taste of the giver and will flatter the receiver.

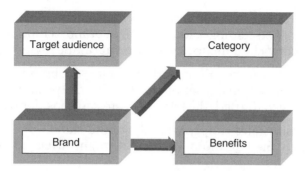

Figure 8.11   *Ensuring structured links for a brand's positioning*

While this is a thorough statement, its length may result in readers forgetting some of the detail. The variety of functional advantages in this statement may dissipate appreciation of the brand's central functional advantage.

Rossiter and Percy (1997) proposed a helpful structure which balances brevity against depth. They argue that a good positioning statement should have the structure:

> *To .... (target audience)*
> *............... (brand name) is the brand of .... (category)*
> *that offers .... (benefit)*

This positioning structure is concerned with linking the brand to three dimensions, as Figure 8.11 shows.

Activity 8.7

Use Rossiter and Percy's brand positioning structure to identify what might be Diet Coke's positioning.

Discussion

Your brand positioning statement could have been of the form:

> *To weight-conscious adults, Diet Coke is the brand of diet cola that offers the best taste.*

Taking the bottom part of the brand pyramid, combining it with Rossiter and Percy's brand-positioning structure and adding creative flair to give the brand some magic can help to derive the brand positioning statement. However, this may result in a statement that:

- does not lead the buyer to perceive anything special
- could lead to too narrow a perception of the brand (for example, Club 18–30 has people outside this age band)

- may cause confusion due to several claims being made
- may not be credible – for example, a branded film-processing company claiming top quality prints at the lowest prices.

This problem can be minimized by testing the brand's positioning statement against a set of criteria. Once a positioning statement has been drafted, the brand's team can consider whether it:

- communicates simply what the brand stands for
- reflects the key motivations that might drive customers to buy it
- clearly differentiates the brand from competitors
- captures the imagination and understanding of staff
- provides a direction for all staff to follow
- does not restrict the brand's scope for future extensions.

Sometimes, the brandsphere audit combined with the brand pyramid analysis may result in the finding that, due to the plethora of competing brands, all the functional motivators and discriminators have been employed by the competing brands. In this situation, it is worth looking inside, rather than outside, the organization. The intent of this analysis is to identify whether there is something valuably unique amongst the organization's resources and competencies, or whether its heritage might be a source for positioning.

An example of looking inside the organization and drawing on any heritage is the Rabo Bank in Holland. This organization has been in existence for many years, and competes in a market where functional advantages can be rapidly emulated. Internal analysis showed that the organization started as a co-operative bank for farmers. It had taken the time to get to know its customers and, through a relationship of respect, was a trusted financial advisor. This type of relationship came about through a unique culture, which it was difficult for a competitor to copy, and therefore became a basis for positioning.

Enabling staff to appreciate the brand positioning

Having completed the journey of translating the brand essence into a crisp brand positioning, the brand's team should be better informed about the functional strength of the brand. However, while it may be felt that the brand positioning enables the team and its external agencies to develop strategies to communicate this to customers, shorter statements might help staff to appreciate their role in reinforcing these functional capabilities. Keller (1999) put forward the idea of brand mantras, short three- to five-word phrases that capture the spirit of the brand positioning. The aim of devising brand mantras is not only to guide staff's behaviour but also to help them to screen out those actions that might lead to inappropriate customer perceptions.

Keller argues that a brand mantra is composed of three terms:

1. Brand functions – this describes the nature of the product or service, and/or the type of experiences or benefits provided by the brand
2. Descriptive modifier – this further clarifies the brand functions
3. Emotional modifier – this is another qualifier about how the brand delivers its benefits.

Thus Nike's brand mantra is:

Emotional modifier	Descriptive modifier	Brand function
Authentic	Athletic	Performance

Activity 8.8

What would you anticipate to be Disney's brand mantra?

Discussion

Disney's brand mantra is:

Emotional modifier	Descriptive modifier	Brand function
Fun	Family	Entertainment

The power of a mantra derives from the combination of the three terms, its simplicity and its ability to guide employees.

Working with managers in brand strategy workshops has shown that this concept is rapidly understood. However, as was earlier mentioned, people think in different ways, and an adaptation of this approach helped a team to arrive at a brand mantra. The adaptation was of the form:

• Emotional modifier becomes the primary emotional value
• Descriptive modifier becomes the target market
• Brand function remains constant as the critical functional strength.

Thus, having summarized the nature of the brand through its brand essence, this enables a logical process to be followed which links the brand's positioning to the lower sections of the brand pyramid. Criteria have been reviewed to enable the brand's team to assess the brand positioning. In the search for an integrated brand, the final check should ensure that the brand positioning aligns with the brand vision.

From brand essence to brand personality

Recalling that a brand is a cluster of functional and emotional values, the previous section focused on functionalism. In view of this being less sustainable than the emotional content of a brand, attention will now focus on the upper part of the brand pyramid.

When following through the different stages in Figure 8.1 of building and strengthening brands, some time will have elapsed between the brand team's addressing the brand vision (one component of which is values) and finally devising the brand pyramid (one aspect of which includes values). This passage of time may result in the brand team's memory of the values in the vision becoming a little hazy. To help ensure that the brand is an integrated entity, it could therefore be helpful to check for internal consistency.

Two checks for internal consistency could be considered. The first check is one that assesses whether there is concurrence between the values elicited during the laddering exercise, when devising the brand pyramid, and the values specified in the brand vision. The second check can evaluate whether there is any conflict between the three values elicited in the laddering work for the brand pyramid. Should there be any inconsistencies from either of these checks, the brand's team would be advised to reconsider its assumptions for each of the earlier stages of the brand-building process.

While brand positioning focuses on what the brand can *do for* the consumer, brand personality concentrates on what the brand *says* about the consumer and how they feel being associated with it. Brand personality represents an efficient summary device for customers since, through seeing people associated with the brand, customers are rapidly able to recognize the values it stands for. It also acts as a purchasing motivator, since consumers prefer brands whose values reflect those they respect (Sheth *et al.* 1991). Particularly for conspicuously consumed brands, people choose brands on the basis of brand personalities, since by owning the brand they are non-verbally signalling to their peer group the values they wish to be associated with (Aaker 1997). For example, a consumer may choose a particular suit brand, not just because of the design (one of the core attributes at the bottom of the brand pyramid) but because the consumer values being a trend-setter. When therefore thinking about what personality could represent the three values of the brand, there is virtue in the brand's team reconsidering the brand audit stage earlier in the brand planning process and asking:

- How well will each possible personality fit the lifestyle of the target market?
- What aspect of the consumer will the brand express?
- Will consumers feel right using the brand in different usage situations?

Recall from Chapter 2, when the interpretation of a brand as personality was discussed, that consideration was given, using Figure 2.7, to the way that situation influences brand choice.

Associating a brand with a particular person saves consumers the effort (if they are prepared to make it) of quickly considering the values of the brand. The problem is that the person ages, or dies, or may suddenly act in a way that managers would not wish their brand to be associated with, and because the brand is so strongly linked with that personality this can adversely affect the brand. Over time, certain brands become strongly associated with particular groups from which consumers develop mental images of the personality of the brand and its users. For example, *The Guardian* newspaper reader has been stereotyped as a well-educated person, likely to be working in local government or education.

Brand personality also acts as a symbolic or self-expressive function. People don't buy a Mercedes just because of the brand's performance, but rather because of the meanings of status and lifestyle represented by the brand. Brands acquire symbolic meanings in society and, through people interacting with each other, the meanings represented by a brand become better understood by people (Holbrook 1995). The symbolic connotations of brands are reinforced through the way that consumers conceive brands as human personalities – for example, well-known historical figures, or celebrities (Rook 1985). In part this results from the interactions between different people; in part it is due to the way some advertisers deliberately associate their brand with a person.

Assessing a brand's personality

For existing brands, it is helpful to appreciate whether there is a chasm between the desired brand personality and that perceived by consumers. Unearthing consumers' perceptions of a brand's personality can be done through qualitative in-depth interviews.

Some of the prompts to surface consumers' views about the brand's personality include:

- 'If the brand were to come to life, what sort of person would it be?'
- Using analogies – for example, 'If the brand were a politician/sports person/film star, etc., who would it be?'
- Using drawings – for example, 'If AMEX were a person, draw the type of house they would live in. Now draw the type of car they would drive.'
- 'If BMW died, what would be said at the funeral?'
- Free association – for example, 'Tell me the first thing that comes to mind when I say … (brand)'
- Sentence completion – for example, 'People like McDonald's because …'

While these qualitative procedures provide an insight into a brand's personality, qualitative research programmes have to be undertaken each time a brand personality project is necessary, and are time-consuming. If a measurement scale is produced, it tends to be unique to that brand (or small cluster of brands) involved in the original project. Therefore, to measure changing perceptions over time amongst consumers about a varying number of brands is problematic, since a generalizable scale that is reliable and valid is required. This problem was addressed by Aaker (1997), who claimed to have developed a reliable, valid and generalizable brand personality measurement scale.

The first stage in devising the brand personality measurement scale was a literature review and qualitative research which identified 309 personality traits. To reduce this list to a more manageable number, 25 people were recruited and asked to rate how descriptive the 309 traits were of brands in general. This resulted in 114 traits being regarded as descriptive of brand personalities. The next stage in reducing the list of personality traits was a further series of consumer interviews across a broad category of brands.

The brands were selected on three criteria: they needed to

- be well known
- encompass a broad range of brand personality types
- cover both symbolic and utilitarian products.

A study amongst consumers involved 131 brands in 39 product and service categories being assessed on the above criteria. Cluster analysis revealed that these brands represented 9 different personality profiles. Four brands were randomly selected from each cluster, to ensure a good spread of symbolic and utilitarian categories. Eventually, 37 brands were selected.

Questionnaires were sent to 1200 people, representative of the American population, who were asked to rate the extent to which each of the 114 personality traits described a specific brand. To reduce the effect of respondent fatigue and boredom when undertaking this task, for each of the 37 brands a balanced design was used such that each group focused on a particular set of 9 brands, plus Levi jeans. Approximately 55 per cent returned the questionnaires (631 returns).

The resulting correlation matrix for the 114 personality traits was factor analysed, using principal component analysis and a varimax rotation. A five-factor solution resulted, explaining 92 per cent of the variance in brand personality. The generality of the five brand personality dimensions was checked, running separate principal component analysis on sub-samples, and good similarities resulted. To identify the traits that constitute each of the five personality dimensions, the sets of items in each factor were factor analysed individually. Test–retest reliability and Cronbach's alphas were addressed, showing the five brand personality dimensions giving consistent, reliable results.

To check that the five dimensions were not the result of a particular group of brands, or a particular sample, a further assessment was undertaken with a new sample (180 subjects) who used 42 of the personality traits to assess a different set of brands. A good fit was found for the five personality dimensions, further strengthening confidence in its generalizability. Readers wishing to become more familiar with the techniques employed should consult Nunnally (1978) and Hair *et al.* (1995).

Figure 8.12 shows the five dimensions of a brand's personality, as well as the two to four facets that describe each of these dimensions.

While the thoroughness of Aaker's (1997) work has given rise to greater confidence in the use of a personality measurement scale, researchers have raised cautions about its generalizability. Azoulay and Kapferer (2003) argue from the personality literature that Aaker's (1997) scales of brand personality merge a number of dimensions of brand identity. Austin *et al.* (2003) concluded after further fieldwork that the framework did not generalize to individual brands in the restaurants category, even though this was one of the categories in Aaker's research. They argued that the personality measurement framework does not generalize to situations in which personality is measured at the individual brand level. One reason for this is an interaction between brands and respondents' interpretations of the personality traits. For example 'cool' evoked thoughts about 'in' (e.g. TGI Friday), but for other brands (e.g. some quick service brands) this prompted impressions about being cold or unfriendly. They

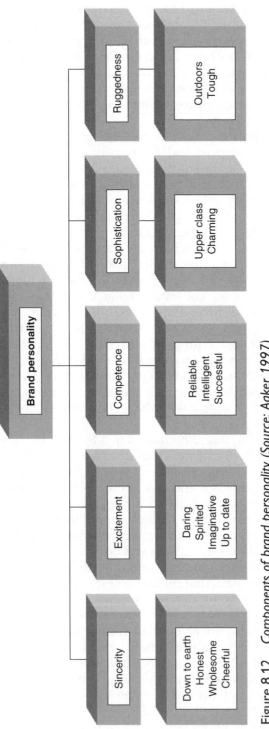

Figure 8.12   Components of brand personality (Source: Aaker 1997)

recommended that additional research is needed to produce multiple-brand personality frameworks. Furthermore, they recommended that descriptive phrases be used in Likert-type scales, rather than using one- or two-word descriptive phrases for the personality traits.

Smith (2003) sought to use Aaker's (1997) personality scale to assess the brand personality of UK political parties. When undertaking the initial stage of fieldwork, it became apparent that two of the traits (Western and small town) had to be omitted as respondents were unsure what these meant. When then undertaking a factor analysis using the reduced number of traits, he did not find the five personality dimensions of Aaker, but rather six personality dimensions which he labelled honesty, spirited, image, leadership, toughness and uniqueness.

In view of these findings, Aaker's (1997) work has notably advanced our abilities to assess brand personalities, but before using this scale researchers should consider the suitability of the personality traits.

Conclusions

This chapter has focused on appreciating the core nature of a brand. It argues that the brand essence is a helpful way of summarizing the central nature of the brand. The core nature of a brand can be represented through the brand pyramid and a crisp brand promise.

The logic for the brand pyramid is grounded in means–end theory. Not only does the brand pyramid give rise to a process for synthesizing the core of the brand (i.e. through laddering), but it also results in a visual presentation of the brand's central characteristics. The brand pyramid enables rapid appreciation of a brand's core nature through its unique attributes, benefits, emotional rewards, values, personality traits and, if the brand's team feels sufficiently confident, a personality to summarize these. The visual elements of the brand pyramid are then summarized in the brand's promise.

When formulating ideas about the core nature of a brand, the brand pyramid and brand essence statement should not be regarded as rigid templates, but rather as a framework to enable people creatively to express ideas about the brand. Different people think in different ways, and therefore, by reviewing in this chapter alternative perspectives on brand essence as well as different models characterizing brands, people can choose the summary devices they feel more comfortable using.

A strength of the brand pyramid is the way that it links the logic of the brand planning process of Figure 8.1 to brand positioning and brand personality, striving to achieve an integrated brand. Both positioning and personality are again the subject of brevity, to ensure everyone concurs about the brand's functional and emotional values.

Brand marketing action checklist

This chapter contains ideas and frameworks that can help organizations to strengthen and build brands. To capitalize upon these ideas, undertaking some of the following exercises may prove beneficial.

1.   What is the brand pyramid for your brand? Even if you have a summary of the core of your brand, it is still worth undertaking this exercise to sharpen this essence. Convene the brand's team. If, from Figure 8.1, you have the results of analysing the brand vision, brand objective and audit of brandsphere, it would be helpful to circulate these to the team prior to the workshop. The exercise can still be undertaken without this analysis, albeit the team will have less background information.

Working in a room that has several flip charts and marker pens, start the session by getting the team to consider what are, in descending order of importance to customers, the three critically unique attributes of your brand. Market research reports may be helpful. Write one of these attributes at the bottom of a flip chart and pose the question, 'why is this important to our customers (or our potential customers for a new brand)?' Record, in a causative manner, comments made until there is consensus about the benefit from this specific attribute. On your summary flip chart you can record at the bottom the attribute, with an arrow leading to the benefit. Returning to a blank sheet, ask your colleagues what emotional reward customers feel they get from this attribute. Recording each of the replies, open the debate to arrive at a consensus about the resulting emotional reward, which should be written onto your summary pyramid.

Returning to another new blank sheet, get your colleagues to consider what value is implied by the agreed emotional reward. It may be useful at this stage to remind colleagues that the term 'value' relates to a particular form of behaviour, or end-state of existence, that the customer considers worthwhile – for example, courage and peace. All of the comments should be written on the flip chart to enable a consensus. The agreed value should be recorded on the summary pyramid.

Colleagues should then be encouraged to consider what personality trait is linked to the value and, once agreement is reached, this should be recorded on the summary pyramid.

This process should be repeated for the other two attributes, taking the second most important attribute next, then finally the third attribute.

Having completed a summary brand pyramid, consisting of three ladders, consider as a group whether it is possible to summarize the brand's personality traits through a particular personality.

After having produced this brand pyramid, work together and summarize this in terms of the brand's promise, which should be simple, enduring and capable of providing a sense of direction.

2. Having produced the brand pyramid and brand promise, consider the following:
   - Are there any conflicts between the elements of each of the three ladders?
   - Do all elements of the three ladders reinforce the brand vision and brand objectives?
   - Do the elements of the three ladders capitalize on any opportunities identified in the brandsphere audit?
   - How do any of the elements in the three ladders protect the brand against threats unearthed in the brandsphere audit?

3. If a brand is successful, the branding intent of the management team should be mirrored in stakeholders' perceptions. Select small numbers of people (between six and eight) who are representative of particular stakeholder groups. Using the process described in exercise (1), undertake similar workshops with them to identify their brand pyramids, and how they might be summarized in brand promises. Compare the brand team's findings with those of each of these stakeholder groups. Where there are disagreements between the brand's team and specific stakeholder groups' brand pyramids, these indicate areas where further work is needed to (i) understand the source of conflict and (ii) resolve this. Discrepancies should be addressed by undertaking further interviews to identify why conflicting views are held, and therefore how matters could be resolved.

4. Recognizing that different people think in different ways, run a brief seminar for your colleagues to explain the alternative perspectives on brand essence and the brand models. Having

clarified these, working as a team, take your brand and get the team to apply the alternatives to analyse your brand. An open discussion should then ensue, with the aim of agreeing upon whether there is an alternative process the team prefers to employ. Once the alternative has been identified, try using it in exercises (1), (2) and (3) above, to see how your brand could be strengthened.

5.   Take your current brand positioning statement and compare this with the elements of your brand pyramid. Is there any incongruity? What changes are needed to resolve any conflict?

6.   Do you have a brand positioning statement that is several sentences long, or takes up several lines? If so, consider using Rossiter and Percy's (1997) structure to summarize crisply the brand's positioning. In other words, consider how you would describe your brand using the structure:

> To .... *(target audience)*
>
> .... *(brand name) is the brand of* .... *(category)*
>
> *that offers* .... *(benefit)*

7.   Check your brand positioning statement to consider:
   * Do buyers perceive anything special?
   * Does this lead to too narrow a perception of the brand?
   * Are several claims being made?
   * Is the claim credible?

8.   If your analysis at exercise (7) indicated that your competitors are making similar claims, look inside your organization to consider whether an internal source of difference can be identified. Search out your company's old brochures and annual reports and see whether there was something about your organization that was once unique. Augment this exercise by undertaking interviews with your longest-serving members of staff.

9.   Working together as a brand's team, identify your brand mantra, based on the three word scheme:

> *(emotional modifier) (descriptive modifier) (brand functions)*

or

> *(primary emotional value) (target market) (brand functions)*

As a brand's team, reach an agreed view about whether you feel it best to circulate the brand pyramid, the brand promise, or the brand mantra (or any combination of these) to everyone working on your brand. According to the final decision, ensure that everyone receives a copy. In particular, liaise with the human resources director to ensure that this is part of the induction pack for new employees.

References and further reading

Aaker, J. (1997). Dimensions of brand personality. *Journal of Marketing Research*, **34**, 347–56.

Austin, J., Siguaw, J. and Mattila, A. (2003). A re-examination of the generalizability of the Aaker brand personality measurement framework. *Journal of Strategic Marketing*, **11** (2), 77–92.

Azoulay, A. and Kapferer, J.-N. (2003). Do brand personality scales really measure brand personality? *Journal of Brand Management*, **11** (2), 143–55.

Blackett, T. and Boad, B. (1999). *Co-Branding. The Science of Alliance*. Basingstoke: Macmillan.

Cowley, D. (1991). *Understanding Brands By 10 People Who Do*. London: Kogan Page.

Gordon, W. (1991). Accessing the brand through research. In *Understanding Brands* (D. Cowley, ed.). London: Kogan Page.

Gordon, W. (1999). *Goodthinking*. Henley-on-Thames: Admap Publications.

Gutman, J. (1982). A means–end chain model based on consumer categorization processes. *Journal of Marketing*, **46**, 60–72.

Hair, J., Anderson, R., Tatham, R. and Black, W. (1995). *Multivariate Data Analysis with Readings*. Englewood Cliffs NJ: Prentice Hall.

Holbrook, M. (1995). *Consumer Research*. London: Sage Publications.

Jones, J. (2000). How do you understand a financial services brand? Paper presented at Branding in the Financial Services Industry 2000. London: Centaur Conferences.

Kapferer, J.-N. (2004). *The New Strategic Brand Management*. London: Kogan Page.

Keller, K. L. (1999). Brand mantras: rationale, criteria and examples. *Journal of Marketing Management*, **15** (1–3), 43–52.

Lefkoff-Hagius, R. and Mason, C. (1993). Characteristic, beneficial and image attributes in consumer judgements of similarity and preference. *Journal of Consumer Research*, **20**, 100–110.

Macrae, C. (1996). *The Brand Chartering Handbook*. Harlow: Addison-Wesley Longman.

Michel, G. and Ambler, T. (1999). Establishing brand essence across borders. *Journal of Brand Management*, **6** (5), 333–45.

Miller, G. (1956). The magic number seven, plus or minus two: some limits on our capacity for processing information. *The Psychological Review*, **63** (2), 81–97.

Nunnally, J. (1978). *Psychometric Theory*. New York: McGraw Hill.

Pinker, S. (1998). *How the Mind Works*. Harmondsworth: Penguin.

Rijkens, R. (1992). *European Advertising Strategies*. London: Cassell.

Rook, D. (1985). The ritual dimensions of consumer behaviour. *Journal of Consumer Research*, **9**, 287–300.

Rossiter, J. and Percy, L. (1997). *Advertising Communications & Promotion Management*. New York: McGraw Hill.

Sheth, J., Newman, B. and Gross, B. (1991). Why we buy what we buy: a theory of consumption values. *Journal of Business Research*, **22** (2), 159–70.

Smith, G. (2003). Assessing the brand personality of UK political parties: an empirical approach. Paper presented at Political Marketing Conference. London: Middlesex University Business School.

Sternberg, R. (1997). *Thinking Styles*. Cambridge: Cambridge University Press.

Thompson, A. B. (2003). Brand positioning and brand creation. In *Brands and Branding* (Clifton, R. and Simmons, J., eds). London: Profile Books.

Trout, J. and Rivkin, S. (1995). *The New Positioning*. New York: McGraw Hill.

Upshaw, L. (1995). *Building Brand Identity*. New York: John Wiley.

VanAuken, B. (2000). Developing the brand-building organization. *Journal of Brand Management*, **7** (4), 281–90.

Vyse, K. (1999). Fingerprint clues identify the brand. *Marketing*, **30 September**, 30.

Chapter 9

Implementing and resourcing brands

Summary

This chapter focuses on the internal implementation and brand resourcing blocks of the process for building and sustaining brands (see Figure 9.1). The chapter opens by considering internal brand delivery systems, recognizing that any change to an internal delivery system for a brand does not affect just the functional or just the emotional values of a brand, but both these values. Within this context, the chapter focuses initially on mechanistic implementation considerations, because these predominantly influence functional values, then staff implementation considerations are addressed since these mainly influence emotional values. The mechanistic implementation considerations cover value chain analysis, strategic outsourcing, core competencies and, specifically for services brands, critical incident technique and service blueprints. The staff implementation issues reviewed include the impact on brands from employees' values, empowerment and relationships. Finally, each of the eight components of the atomic model of the brand is explored, since these provide the detail about the final form of the brand.

Structuring to deliver the brand with its unique mix of resources

Returning to the route plan of Figure 9.1, the process for building or strengthening a brand should have led the brand's team to be

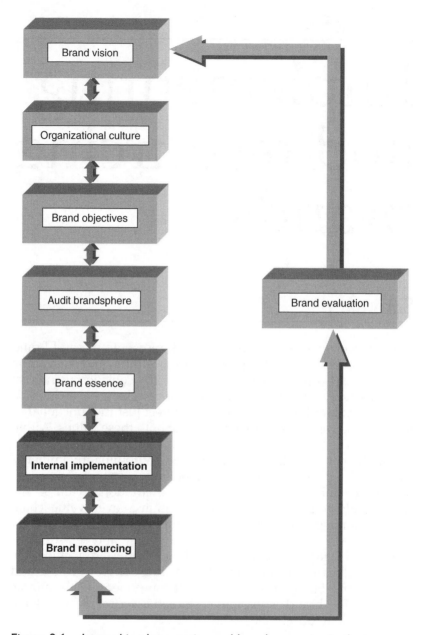

Figure 9.1   *Internal implementation and brand resourcing in the process*
of building and sustaining brands

more specific about the core nature of the brand through models
such as the brand pyramid, the brand promise and the development of more integrated brand positionings and brand personalities. A challenge faced at the next stage of the route plan in

Figure 9.1 is the internal consideration that needs addressing to implement the desired form of the brand. For example, an airline may have defined one of its values as being caring yet, through management not being attentive to the problems of promptly serving drinks and collecting used glasses on short flights, the stern replies from the cabin crew to passengers requesting extra glasses of water run counter to the behaviour implied by this value. Through management and staff thoroughly understanding their brand, they should be better able to devise appropriate processes and types of behaviour to enact the desired format of the brand.

As the brand's team sets about designing suitable internal processes, members will evaluate the suitability of these against the detailed form that the brand will take. In other words, in Figure 9.1 they will iterate between considering the internal implementation stage and the brand resourcing stage. To help managers appreciate the detail about their brand, the atomic model is presented. This model translates the brand essence into eight resourcing components – for example, the brand's name, its functional capability and the level of after-sales service. Just as a marketing strategy is characterised by a particular marketing mix, so a brand essence is enacted through a particular combination of the eight resourcing elements of the atomic model of the brand. This chapter addresses the internal issues involved in designing processes to deliver the brand essence and the detail regarding the mix of resources defining the brand.

Internal considerations about the value chain

It is difficult to take the brand pyramid and focus upon the delivery system necessary *solely* to ensure the brand's functional values, then the delivery system that can *solely* bring about the brand's emotional values. Each part of the delivery system has an impact on *both* the brand's functional and emotional values. For example, consider a firm of solicitors where all the staff adhere to the principle of returning telephone calls to clients as soon as possible. The secretaries have been told to take notes about the clients' calls, then give these to the solicitors as soon as they are available. A promptly returned telephone call gives rise not only to the emotional value of caring, but also the functional value of professionalism. When developing a delivery system, thought needs to be given to the way that its implementation influences both functional and emotional values.

One way of considering the internal delivery system is from the perspectives of the mechanistic and the staff components. The mechanistic component encapsulates issues that could be considered more overtly to influence the functional values. Specifically, these are the value chain, core competencies, outsourcing of activities and, for services brands, service blueprints and critical incident technique. The staff component relates to the values, empowerment and relationship-building capabilities of the people working inside the organization who have a notable impact on the emotional values. This input perspective on delivering a brand concurs with the logic of Grönroos (2000), who argues that the quality of a service consists of a technical dimension and a process-related dimension. The technical dimension focuses on *what* the customer receives and, because of its strong functional orientation, can often be measured objectively in terms of the technical solution to a problem. The process-related dimension refers to *how* the customer receives the service, and has stronger emotional connotations.

However, even with this mechanistic and staff-based analysis of internal processes, while two factors will relate predominantly to functional values and predominantly to emotional values, there is an interaction effect. Recognizing this caveat, we will consider the internal implementation processes using these two categories.

Mechanistic internal implementation considerations

One way of considering how the firm should structure its value delivery system for a new brand, or evaluate its current system for an existing brand, is Porter's (1985) value chain. The array of activities involved in designing, producing, marketing, delivering and supporting a brand can be captured in the generic value chain shown in Figure 9.2. These value activities can be divided into:

- primary activities
- support activities.

The way that each activity is performed determines whether the resulting brand will be more or less expensive than competing brands, and also how effectively it contributes to the buyer's needs. Understanding the functional values of the brand should guide the structures of activities in the value chain.

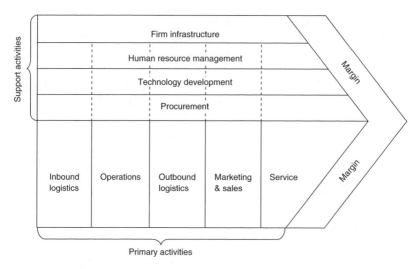

Figure 9.2   *The value chain (Source: Porter 1985)*

To evaluate the appropriateness of an internal delivery system, a flow chart of the value-creating processes that transform raw material into brands is needed. The activities should be plotted onto the template in Figure 9.2, first for the primary activities using the stages:

- inbound logistics – for example, materials handling, stock control, receiving goods
- operations – for example, production, quality control, packing
- outbound logistics – for example, storing finished goods, order processing, delivery
- marketing and sales, e.g. promotions planning, pricing
- service, e.g. installing, training, repairing.

The support activities then need plotting. They are categorized into purchasing (procurement), technical development, human resource management and infrastructure (e.g. legal and financial affairs). These are presented in the format shown in Figure 9.2, since each of these services can support many of the value-creating processes. For example, different departments within the firm may be raw material purchase, well-qualified staff, delivery lorries, creative advertisements, and after-sales support unit.

By breaking down all the primary and secondary activities, this template enables the brand's team to have an overview of all the activities involved in delivering the brand. An advantage of the generic value chain is the way it captures all the activities on a sheet of paper. By having such a succinct overview of the value delivery process, it makes it easier to assess its appropriateness.

The first issue is to consider linkages between activities. For example, buying higher-quality raw material at the inbound logistics stage links into the lower costs of quality control at the operations stage, as well as the lower costs of after-sales service at the service stage. The brand's team could benefit from taking each of the activities, evaluating where in the value chain these have notable impacts, and considering whether different resources or new styles of working could be advantageous at different stages in the value chain.

At a more macro level, the organization is part of a bigger chain, as shown in Figure 9.3. There is scope for the brand gaining a cost advantage, and/or being perceived as having more added value (e.g. speed of response), through more efficient linkages between the supplier's, brand owner's, distributor's and buyer's value chains – for example, the way grocery retailers link their IT systems with brand producers to ensure more efficient stock levels and goods dispatching/receiving.

The second issue to consider is how well the value chain supports the brand's position regarding relative price and/or offering the buyer added value. If the brand is positioned as being good value for money, this is best achieved when each of the activities is reviewed to consider how costs can be curtailed – for example, identifying those activities that produce features which are not particularly welcomed by the target market and eliminating these. Consider the way that hand-held controllers for TVs/video players/DVD players can sometimes come with a plethora of buttons giving options that are rarely used. Also, note how low-cost airlines such as Ryanair regularly consider each aspect of their value chain to continually drive down costs. Prior to landing, the cabin crew collects rubbish into sacks, saving costs on cleaning and ensuring that the aircraft's time on the ground is kept to a minimum. Some have questioned, though, whether Ryanair is becoming too obsessed with curtailing costs, particularly when in 2005 they issued a note to staff forbidding them to use company facilities to recharge their mobile phones.

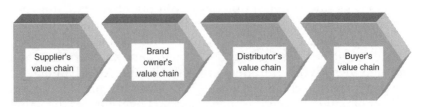

Figure 9.3   *A macro value system*

Porter (1985) identified several ways that brands can drive down their costs, resulting in better value for money. One of the key ways of achieving this is through striving for economies of scale and performing activities differently from key competitors. eBay is a classic example of driving down costs through highly effective use of the Internet and challenging the conventional way of individuals selling products and services. Some of the other ways include experience and learning effects, working towards continual capacity utilization and efficient linkages between all parties in the value-adding process. On a regular basis, management need to consider how well their value chain is structured to drive down costs.

By contrast, the brand could be positioned as offering the buyer more added value than competitors, then through, for example, continually scouring the world for new ideas and new technologies, each of the activities would be subject to continual review with the intention of regularly 'refreshing' the activities in the chain. There is a variety of ways to achieve added value. For example, in the legal services market, where the branding of legal practices is a relatively new concept, there are some legal professionals who add value by personally relating to their clients and offering qualities of friendliness and accessibility. By contrast, others regard adding value as being akin to acting as a rottweiler, and are as tough as possible when dealing with their opponents. In the business-to-business sector, Portakabin, which offers temporary mobile offices, adds value by offering a more comprehensive service through hiring out essential accessories such as alarm and fire systems, climate control and furniture, along with helping to gain planning permission for the temporary offices.

The challenge when positioning the brand as having more added value than competitors is the dynamic nature of markets and the need always to be thinking about the next series of enhancements. Furthermore, as buyers gain more experience of the brand they tend to take the view that what was regarded as added value yesterday is a taken-for-granted feature today.

A third issue to consider is how the brand can be more effectively delivered by:

- focusing more attention on the core competencies that underpin the brand, thereby providing an even better brand
- strategically outsourcing other activities, since other organizations can more effectively provide these.

For example, one of Nike's values is inspiration through its passion for sport. This is powerfully portrayed through high-profile marketing campaigns. Another of Nike's values is performance, which is backed by notable research and development activities. Nike concentrates on its core competencies of marketing and R&D, outsourcing its production using a carefully considered process to select production partners. The task facing the brand's team is to identify and appreciate their organization's core competencies underpinning their brand and to decide how to capitalize on these competencies in the value chain.

Core competencies can be recognized as:

1. The low number of skills, knowledge sets or activities that the organization has or performs better than its competitors
2. Providing scope for dominating a market
3. Enabling a brand to be stretched.

Activity 9.1

For each of the three points above, choose brands that bring these points to life.

Discussion

Swatch is able to innovate in its design competence.

Walt Disney's competence of customer service enables it to be a dominant player in the theme park market.

Toyota's process engineering enables it to stretch its brand into numerous different segments.

A core competence should produce a differentiating capability. Honda's core competence of small-engine manufacture has enabled it to extend its small-engine expertise into areas such as small cars, pumps and lawnmowers, because customers respect the added value that has elevated Honda above competitors through leveraging its core competence.

Quinn and Hilmer (1994) argue that an activity should not be outsourced until there is a clear appreciation of:

- the potential for gaining a competitive advantage from this activity, after allowing for transaction costs
- the vulnerability the organization exposes itself to by outsourcing an activity.

By incorporating these two factors in the matrix shown in Figure 9.4, a more balanced perspective can be taken. Where the potential for gaining a competitive edge is high and there is a high degree of vulnerability, there is a need for a high degree of control – suggesting not outsourcing, or a joint ownership or tight long-term contracts. At the other extreme, where there is

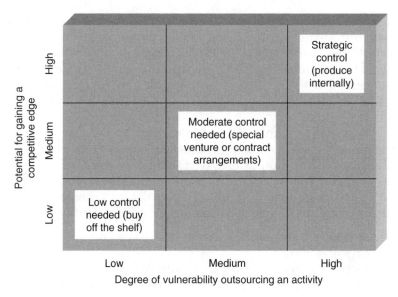

Figure 9.4   *A strategic approach to outsourcing (Source: Quinn and Hilmer 1994)*

little scope for gaining a competitive edge and there is minimal vulnerability, this is an automatic case for outsourcing.

In a knowledge-based economy, the issue of strategic outsourcing is still critical. As Piercy (1999) has shown, Dell has redefined its business model to be that of direct business, partnering with suppliers and customers, linked by processes of virtual integration and heavily supported by excellent electronic communications.

Activity 9.2

What do you perceive to be Dell's core competencies?

Discussion

Dell's core competencies include:

- excellent knowledge of its customers
- customer support systems
- shared information system to strengthen its relationships with suppliers.

Dell is a classic example of strategic outsourcing, with suppliers producing software and components for its computers. As Quinn (1999) has observed, by using IT to ensure that suppliers are aware of its production needs, it not only lowers suppliers' costs but also ensures greater customer responsiveness. It has devised its direct business model through good understanding of its customers, not only to capitalize on its core competencies but also to use these competencies to support its brand values of providing excellent customer support and flexible customization.

Where an organization's brands are knowledge intensive, e.g. brands of software and pharmaceuticals, success is enhanced when the organization focuses on a small number of intellectually-based knowledge activities and outsources other activities, using the matrix in Figure 9.4. The full potential for knowledge-based outsourcing can be achieved, argues Quinn (1999) by:

- ensuring congruence between the goals and values of both organizations
- recruiting and training managers with the long-term relationship management skills needed for outsourcing
- monitoring suppliers' movements to ensure they do not embark on directions potentially damaging to the relationship
- developing communication systems to ensure the widest sharing of knowledge between partners with the aim of encouraging more innovation.

Mechanistic implementation for services brand

The previous section has predominantly focused on product brands with some consideration of knowledge-intensive brands. The techniques previously discussed remain applicable; however, new techniques specifically for services have been devised, and these will be considered within the remit of mechanistic implementation. At the most basic level, all staff need to understand their brand's promise so that, regardless of points of contact, all stakeholders should get the same brand experience.

There is a caveat throughout this section brought about due to services brands being based on people interacting with other people. Regardless of the care taken over training staff to ensure that they have good technical skills, there is an impact from their personality which will result in variability of the service brand's functional value.

As a services brand is more about a promise, the performance of a deed or an experience, it is more challenging to describe the service delivery process. Service blueprints were devised to map the service systems, which involve all the people who are adding value to the customer's experience of the brand. A service blueprint breaks the service down into the steps or tasks in the service process at four levels:

1. Customer actions, which include the stages customers pass through as they interact with the service brand provider in buying, consuming and evaluating the brand
2. On-stage contact employees' actions, encompassing the visible actions of staff interacting with the customer
3. Back-stage contact employees' actions, which relate to the activities undertaken by supporting staff, unseen by the customer
4. Support processes, which include all the unseen internal supporting services.

A timeline is drawn across the page, and onto this are traced the activities taking place at each of the four levels. Where an interaction occurs between any of the four constituents, a vertical line is drawn. The example in Figure 9.5, showing the service received when staying overnight in a hotel, helps to clarify this technique. Note the way that the processes have been simplified. By keeping the blueprint relatively simple, it is easier to appreciate the important activities involved in the service delivery process.

There are several advantages to employing the service blueprint. It provides a much clearer understanding of:

• customers' roles in the service delivery process
• the way staff and supporting systems (e.g. IT) support the brand.

As a result of a clearer insight into the current process by which the service brand is delivered, just as with the value chain, activities can be evaluated in terms of:

• the extent to which they drive costs down
• the extent to which they produce further enhanced service experiences.

Within this context, staff need to be encouraged to consider how their service delivering behaviours reflect the brand. For example, if one of the brand's core values is being bold, reception staff should continually seek to take the initiative, instantly greeting visitors and making them feel welcomed. At all stages in the value-delivering process, staff need to be attentive to ensure that all their actions align with the brand's values.

According to the extent to which the brand is positioned to stress an inexpensive experience or a value-added experience, so the activities can be amended better to fit the brand. Likewise,

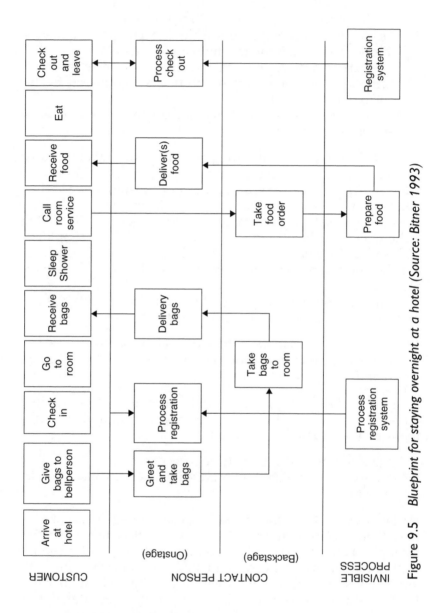

Figure 9.5 Blueprint for staying overnight at a hotel (Source: Bitner 1993)

the linkages between the four levels and between the different activities can be addressed in terms of ways that they can be changed to deliver the service brand promise better.

Activity 9.3

As a result of a small change in his circumstances, a man wishes to make a minor amendment to his will. What would the service blueprint look like for the service this man is likely to receive from his lawyer?

Discussion

Figure 9.6 presents a possible service blueprint for this small change to the will.

In the case of services-based brands, customers generally have more points of contact with the provider than they do with product-based brands, and these points of contact tend to be more built on people interactions, rather than technology interactions. With each service encounter, customers become aware of the service brand delivery and they start to form judgements. Thus, by using the service blueprint a tool is available to managers to enable them to work with customer-facing staff so each encounter provides the right impressions about the brand, reinforcing the espoused brand values.

The service blueprint also draws to managers' attention the full variety of encounters that take place, and thus encourages them to think about ensuring consistency of encounters by looking at each activity and assessing how well these align with the brand's values. A holistic approach to managing encounters is more likely to result in a coherent services brand offering. It is not advocated that only particular encounters be singled out for monitoring, however; as Zeithaml and Bitner (1996) reported, the importance of encounters in influencing perceptions varies. For example, Marriott Hotels found that four of the five most important encounters affecting customers' loyalty were experienced within ten minutes of a guest visiting a hotel.

A service blueprint provides an input approach to managing service brand delivery through focusing on consistency of encounters across the delivery process. A valuable output approach is provided by the critical incident technique, since this considers customers' views about their encounters with the organization's brand. Drawing on the methodology reported by Bitner *et al.* (1990), customers who have experience of the

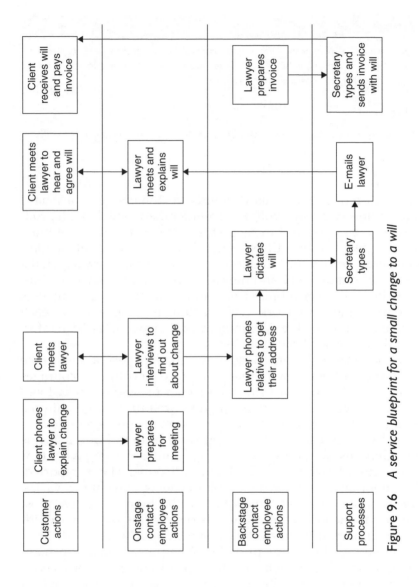

Figure 9.6 *A service blueprint for a small change to a will*

services brand are individually asked to think of a time when, as a customer, they had a particularly satisfying or dissatisfying interaction with … (brand). They are then asked:

- When did the incident happen?
- What specific circumstances led up to this situation?
- Exactly what did the employee involved say or do?
- What resulted that made you feel the interaction was satisfying or dissatisfying?
- What should or could have been done differently?

The information provided from these interviews can be plotted onto specific parts of the service blueprint. By then reflecting on those encounters that were either favourably or unfavourably assessed, the brand's team can consider where changes are needed in the services brand delivery system.

Further insights into the need to reconfigure the delivery system can be provided by undertaking the critical incident technique amongst customer-facing staff. By comparing customers' views of separate encounters with those of employees, the different perceptions can help staff to recognize that what constitutes satisfaction for them is not necessarily the same for their customers. Bitner *et al.* (1990) undertook critical incident technique research amongst customers and staff in three separate sectors – hotels, restaurants and airlines. Their findings showed notable similarities between the way staff and customers identified sources of satisfaction and dissatisfaction in service encounters. However, staff are less likely to attribute customer dissatisfaction to staff's attitudes or behaviour, and customers are likely to blame staff rather than themselves for problems.

Staff implementation considerations

Chapter 4 clarified that values are important because they provide guidelines about acceptable forms of staff behaviour. Therefore, when thinking about implementing the brand pyramid internally through staff, ensuring that they understand and are committed to the brand's values helps them to act in a manner that supports the brand. In the case of services brands, because of the greater interactions that take place between staff and customers, the importance of staff understanding and commitment to the brand's values is even more vital.

Through adopting a values-driven role to staff management there is less need for supervision, since committed staff know how they should act to support the brand. A logical progression is to provide employees with more information about their brand and its market, entrust them with resources and have confidence in their ability to make brand decisions – i.e. to empower staff. There are advantages and disadvantages to empowering staff, and its suitability varies between organizations.

By understanding the values of their brand and being entrusted by their managers to act within guidelines suggested by these values, employees will form particular types of relationships with their stakeholders. In the case of a coherent brand, the type of relationship between employees and their diverse stakeholders will be similar across stakeholders.

Thus, when considering the internal implementation of the brand pyramid relating to staff, the issues of values, empowerment and relationships are but some of the factors that need addressing. In view of their importance in implementing the brand pyramid, these three issues will be discussed.

Importance of values in internal implementation considerations

As Pine and Gilmore (1998) have argued, we have moved from an industrial economy to a services economy, and now to an experience economy. Restaurants originally reflected a services economy, but the evolution of themed restaurants (for example, the Rainforest Café) represents the move to the experience economy, where customers desire experiences. In a services economy, companies augment their brands to maintain sales while experience brands major on the provision of the experience. For example, traditional retailers of sports equipment and clothing provide a service, yet Niketown provides an experience.

Customers are more involved with an experience brand and, through their greater immersion, are more aware of the values of the brand. This point was also noted by Goyder (1999). The greater cognizance people have of organizations' actions, and therefore the realization of the way their actions conflict with their espoused values, makes organizations' brands more vulnerable to boycotts. It is therefore important that staff be involved in internal debates about what values underpin their brand, and be respected for pointing out situations where brand decisions go against brand values.

Ciulla (1999: 166) builds on this idea and writes that:

> We usually assume that values motivate us to act, but this isn't always the case. Some are satisfied to have a value and not act on it.

Successful brands are those that have well-founded values, with staff who take a stance as a result of these values. In other words, there are genuine value brands, with staff passionate about their values, and superficial value brands, where staff are less committed to the values and feign behaviour, almost as actors. When these superficial brands waver, confronted with challenges, customers see through them and leave.

A good example of a genuine value corporate brand is Merck Sharp and Dohme, which values health over wealth. Mectizan is the company's drug that counters the parasite causing river blindness, a disease threatening the eyesight of people in developing countries. Yet the countries that need Mectizan cannot afford it. Going back to its values, Merck Sharp and Dohme gave it away free. It was estimated that by the mid-1990s it had saved 6 million people from blindness in Nigeria, and this had cost the organization millions of euros.

After the Second World War, tuberculosis thrived in Japan, yet most Japanese people could not afford Merck Sharp and Dohme's drug Streptomycin. A large supply was given to the Japanese. They remembered this, and in 1983 they allowed Merck Sharp and Dohme to buy 50.02 per cent of Banyu Pharmaceutical.

In the case of a genuine value brand, staff who are recruited because of their beliefs and commitment to the values of the brand are a significant asset. Thus, staff recruitment campaigns that are based on the concurrence between potential employees' values and the brand's values in the brand pyramid should ensure a greater likelihood of brand success. Knowledge of a sector or of a technical skill is important, but these can be taught. By contrast, it is more difficult to teach someone commitment to a new set of values.

Two examples of recruiting on the basis of values are as follows. Kunde (2000) describes how staff in his agency worked together to make explicit their organization's values, attitudes and vision. A booklet called *Attitudes* was produced to summarize these. When screening potential employees, they are given this booklet to read and are then asked what they think about the ideas in this booklet. This helps to ensure that people with the desired values are recruited. Fairfield Inn, a division of Marriott Corporation, has as two of its values friendliness and cleanliness. When recruiting staff, regardless of their seniority or role, they are selected on the basis of having the appropriate attitudes and capabilities to deliver a friendly atmosphere.

While values alignment is critically important for brand success, many organizations face the challenge of recruiting good staff from a shrinking labour pool. As such, in addition to advertising its values to attract the right calibre of person, the organization also needs to make itself attractive to potential employees. Authors such as Ambler and Barrow (1996) and Ewing *et al.* (2002) argue that the 'employer brand' needs developing so the benefits package of working with an organization can be appreciated in terms of brand positioning and personality. By understanding their brand, managers can work together to create a galvanizing brand promise for staff that reflects the customer brand promise. Berthon *et al.* (2005) undertook a research project to identify the dimensions of an attractive employer brand, which is characterized by five dimensions. These are:

1. Interest value – providing an exciting work environment, novel work practices and making use of employees' creativity
2. Social value – creating an environment that is fun, provides good collegial relationships and a team atmosphere
3. Economic value – paying an above-average compensation package with job security and promotional opportunities
4. Development value – giving recognition, self-worth and confidence coupled with a career-enhancing experience and a springboard to future employment
5. Application value – opportunities for individuals to apply what they have learnt and to teach others in a customer-oriented and humanitarian environment.

By considering how these dimensions can be used, in conjunction with the brand's values, there should be a greater likelihood of attracting more suitable employees.

When involving staff regarding implications of the brand's values for their jobs, there may be confusion about terminology. Free (1999) argues that the language should be that of staff and customers, rather than managers. For example, quality could be regarded as being a 'fat' term, since it could be interpreted in different ways (for example, reliable or solid). By giving employees examples of how this value can result in particular outcomes, there is a greater appreciation of its meaning. For example, quality in a financial services perspective might mean that all consumers' transactions are error free, but for another customer it might mean knowledgeable staff who are always able to answer any questions.

By enabling employees in each department to appreciate how a brand's values are interpreted in other parts of the organization, promises that may not be delivered are less likely to be made to customers. Bringing together employees from different departments to discuss their departments' interpretations of the brand's values not only educates staff but also enables them to recognize conflicting tasks. Staying true to the brand's values, they can identify ways to resolve such conflict – which strengthens the coherence of the brand.

Rewards that reflect the brand's values are a further way of strengthening the brand through staff. Amazon.com has service to its customers as one of its values and, in a much publicized internal ceremony, awards the 'Just do it' prize to those employees who don't ask for approval and just take the initiative to provide better customer service. The challenge for the brand's team is to find ways of monitoring employees' behaviour relative to its brand's values, then finding suitable rewards.

Individuals' values give rise to their identity, which they manage in their groups, seeking confirmation from the group of their own identity. As Milton and Westphal (2005) have shown, people prefer to work and cooperate with others who positively confirm their identity as being that which the individual desires to project. This is important for brand management, since brand-building is a pan-company, team activity. At the recruitment stage, these authors therefore recommend that managers get their group to meet with the potential employee and not only think about the individuals' competencies and alignment of their and the brand's values, but also the applicants' potential fit with the group. As people often have erroneous assessments of other self-identities and assume these to be correct, another implication is that managers should help their teams to understand each other's identities. There are a variety of ways of achieving this – for example, personalizing attire, calling cards and their work spaces; getting people to communicate more about their selves; and through group-building exercises.

By adopting a values approach to management, an organization is investing in its culture – which it is more difficult for competitors to emulate. As a result of the pride employees have in working on a brand that resonates with their values, they are less likely to leave, further strengthening the sustainability of their unique culture.

The issue of empowerment as an internal implementation consideration

With increasing labour costs and the concerns managers have about ensuring consistent behaviours from every employee interacting with customers, many organizations have introduced more technology-based working practices. The danger is that they may be adopting a short-term orientation. An alternative strategy is to introduce technology for repetitive, non-value adding tasks by staff, then use this freed-up time to enable staff to add value through focusing on non-standard requests. In effect, this is transferring more resources (for example, information and finances) along with decision-making responsibility to staff.

Empowering employees, i.e. allowing staff more autonomy, discretion and unsupervised decision-making responsibility, is becoming more common (Buchanan and Huczynski 2004). The central assumption is that employees will feel more motivated through empowerment, particularly when the role of the line manager changes from supervising to coaching. However, because of personality differences between employees, whilst empowerment may motivate them, different approaches to empowerment are needed. Maccoby's (1988) research is helpful when considering ways of using empowerment to motivate employees. His research into social character types (i.e. the clusters of values that influence what different employees find motivating) unearthed five employee characteristics, as shown in Table 9.1.

Using this research, the way empowerment is approached needs to be tuned to an understanding of the type of employee. Experts will be enthused when they see empowerment giving them control and autonomy, while Innovators, if they see empowerment allowing them scope for creativity and trying out new ideas, will be more receptive. In a team there is likely to be a mix of employee types, and thought needs to be given to the way different individuals' motivations can be satisfied through empowerment.

Empowering employees runs counter to Levitt's (1972) argument for a production-line approach, which holds little confidence in employees' capabilities. This philosophy can be recognized when technology and systems take priority over staff. There is minimal scope for individual initiative, and tasks are simplified and codified, based on the assumption that this leaves little that can go wrong when staff are employed. For an organization whose brand values include innovation, responsiveness and being customer focused, this type of approach will not engender true delivery of the brand.

Table 9.1   *Social character types*

Category of employee	Dominant values
Expert	Mastery, control, autonomy
Helper	Caring for people, survival, sociable
Defender	Protection, dignity, power, self-esteem
Innovator	Creating, experimenting, glory, competition
Self-developer	Balancing mastery and play, knowledge and fun

Source: Maccoby 1988

One of the main influences on the appropriateness of empowerment relates to the brand's values. For example, Disney, with its focus on the importance of family values, in almost a parental manner, scripts precisely the roles staff must play. By contrast, Club Med values the magic of the holiday experience, and looks to its staff to find their own ways of evoking such sensations.

Another factor affecting the suitability of an empowerment approach is the organizational culture. If the culture is one that respects values such as openness, initiative, freedom, customer service and challenge, empowerment is suitable.

Activity 9.4

What other conditions do you consider encourage an empowerment approach?

Discussion

Several writers have provided guidelines about the suitability of an empowerment strategy. Bowen and Lawler (1992) identify five contingencies, as shown in Table 9.2.

Table 9.2   *The contingencies encouraging empowerment*

Contingency	Characteristics encouraging: Production-line approach	Empowerment
Business strategy	Low cost, high volume	Differentiation, customized
Tie to customer	Transaction, short time period	Relationship, long time period
Technology	Routine, simple	Non-routine, complex
Business environment	Predictable	Unpredictable
Type of staff	Low social and growth needs, weak interpersonal skills	High social and growth needs, strong interpersonal skills

Source: Bowen and Lawler 1992

Schlesinger and Heskett (1991) add that empowerment works best when:

- staff are selected who welcome empowerment, are trained to be competent in their empowered role and are rewarded on the outcomes of their empowered decisions and actions
- there is good internal communication
- non-performers are dismissed
- suitable resources are provided to help employees succeed.

From Packard (1993), it is also clear that managements' attitudes are important. Some managers regard empowerment as a challenge to their positions, and unless managers can change from being 'policemen' to being 'coaches' (Buchanan and Preston 1992), empowerment will not succeed.

An empowerment strategy has strengths and weaknesses. Some of its benefits include faster response, greater employee satisfaction, more genuine interactions between staff and stakeholders, and a source of greater efficiencies and new ideas. Some of the weaknesses are greater costs in selection, training and wages, and the risk of inappropriate decisions being made by employees and internal conflict as line managers feel threatened. However, if an organization is generally managing its brand through a value-driven philosophy, then allowing individuals and teams to work on brand development projects without excessive supervision should encourage more new ideas and greater commitment to new initiatives.

Running through any assessment of the costs versus benefits of empowering staff must be a consideration of consistency of brand values. Recall from the previous section the difference between genuine value brands and superficial value brands. In the case of genuine value brands, staff have been recruited who believe and are committed to the brand's values. Given regular training and good internal communication, these staff are ideally placed to thrive when empowered and, because they are in tune with their brand's values, they are capable of taking decisions that reinforce the brand's promise. The perceived values of the brand are likely to be constant across customer-facing staff and over time.

By contrast, staff working on superficial value brands are less committed to their brands. Training helps, but it takes a lot of effort to engender a strong commitment to the brand. As such, empowerment is likely to lead to greater variability of perceptions amongst customers about these brands' values.

Just as branding is not something marketers 'do to customers' but rather something 'customers do things with', the same point can be made about empowerment. This was powerfully summarized in Packard's (1993) research, reporting Ken Gulliver (Head of Management Development and Training at Ciba UK):

> *Empowerment is not a verb. 'You' cannot empower 'me'. It is more a state of mind and way of working.*

To talk about empowerment suggests there is only one generic approach; however, there are several different forms. Bowen and Lawler (1992) have developed a useful typology, portrayed in Figure 9.7.

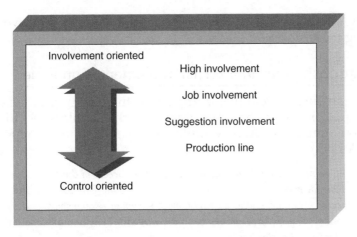

Figure 9.7   *Different levels of empowerment (Source: Bowen and Lawler 1992)*

In the case of high-involvement empowerment, staff are made fully aware of information about the organization and its markets. Skills in team-working, problem-solving and business operations are developed to enable staff to participate in decision-making. By involving staff in goal-setting and strategies to achieve goals, they become more committed members of a team (Schneider 2000). In the case of job involvement, jobs are redesigned, enabling staff greater freedom in deciding how to complete their work. Suggestion involvement represents a small move from the production-line approach by encouraging employees to make suggestions, but their daily activities do not change. In effect, they recommend but managers decide.

High-involvement empowerment is likely to engender genuine value brands. Job involvement empowerment is likely to be associated with transition brands. The owners of these brands have started to relax their rigid controls over the brand, typically as a response to market dynamics. For example, brands that took a 'brochureware' approach to the Internet (i.e. the Internet is a medium to tell customers about a brand), have shifted to an interactive approach. Suggestion involvement empowerment is likely to correlate with established brands that are slow to respond to opportunities and threats; whenever customer-facing staff have new ideas, these have to progress through a time-consuming administrative process.

Whatever the extent to which an organization empowers its staff, they will enact the values of their brand through particular relationships. In a production-control environment, stakeholders may sense that the relationship is rather forced, while in a high-involvement empowered environment it is perceived as being more sincere.

Relationships as an internal implementation issue

Relationships have a major impact on the health of brands, be they line brands or corporate brands. As the Royal Society for the Encouragement of Arts, Manufactures and Commerce reported (RSA 1995):

> The companies which will sustain competitive success in the future are those which focus less exclusively on shareholders and on financial measures of success – and instead include all their stakeholder relationships, and a broader range of measurements, in the way they think and talk about their purpose and performance.

It is widely documented that relationships are the foundations of successful business (e.g. Reichheld 1996; Gummesson 1999). As Goyder (1999) notes, values are critical for effective relationships, shaping the total business personality on which a firm's brands and its reputation depends. Numerous employees interacting with a plethora of stakeholders form different relationships, but when guided by the values of their brand are more likely to build similar types of relationships that engender greater trust in the brand. A powerful example of this is Unipart, which has skilfully developed shared destiny relationships with all parties in its supply chain. Each new supplier attends a course at the Unipart University, starting with a module on the firm's purpose and values. Partners are then introduced to a technique that enables them to evaluate their alignment with Unipart's and other partners' expectations. This 'open-book' approach enables all partners in the supply chain to benefit. Ultimately, therefore, building on Goyder's inclusive approach, the brand's team should ask against each relationship:

- Who is really behind the relationship?
- What is the end-user really looking for from this relationship? How far are the needs of the end-user and the capabilities and objectives of the supplying organization aligned?
- How can the brand team improve the alignment so they can genuinely create a relationship founded on a shared destiny?

With this information the team is better placed to work with staff to strengthen the relationship which reinforces expectations from the brand pyramid.

The challenge that the brand's team faces is translating the brand's values and personality into appropriate relationships. For example, Gordon (1999) gives an example of the personality of Famous Grouse whisky as being one of a Scottish laird striding through the heather with a dog bounding next to him. Consumers expect this to lead to a relationship that is reserved, polite and shows respect to all, regardless of their background. In this example, if the brand's team is satisfied with this relationship, the next stage is to work with customer-facing staff to get them to recognize the linkage shown in Figure 9.8.

Through this understanding, it becomes easier to work with staff to enable them to develop particular relationships with their stakeholders. This process was addressed in Chapter 2, looking at an interpretation of the brand as a relationship builder. Underpinning this is the idea that their brands act as relationship partners for consumers, and staff play an important role in ensuring this.

Building on Hinde (1995), a relationship is a connection or affinity between two parties characterized by:

- reciprocal exchange between active and interdependent partners
- purposive behaviour providing meaning to the participants taking a variety of forms which provide a range of benefits for participants
- evolution and change over interactions and also as a result of environmental changes.

Within this interpretation there are several implications for brand management. If a well-respected relationship is to occur between a stakeholder and the brand, the organization must be clear about what is being exchanged between the two parties. From the brand pyramid, there are clear points about the rational and emotional benefits that staff need to contribute.

Relations, from Hinde (1995), can take a variety of forms. From Gummesson (1999), some of the different types of relationships are characterized by:

- the extent to which parties collaborate
- the degree of commitment between parties
- the extent to which trust is engendered and risk reduced
- whether one party has greater power
- the longevity of the relationship;
- the degree to which there are frequent interactions

Figure 9.8 *Values drive relationships*

- whether the relationship is intensive or superficial
- the extent to which there is physical, mental or emotional closeness
- whether the relationship is formal or informal
- the degree of openness
- whether the relationship is routinized.

Other researchers have proposed different types of relationships. Wish *et al.* (1976) identified four dimensions of interpersonal relationships:

1. Power symmetry (e.g. equal versus unequal, dominant versus submissive)
2. Valence (e.g. co-operative and friendly versus competitive and hostile)
3. Intensity or extent of interdependence (e.g. deep versus shallow)
4. Social or work-related.

Iacobucci and Ostromn (1996) investigated these four groups of relationships in a business context, and found them to be applicable.

Fournier (1998) analysed consumers' relationships with their brands and identified fifteen emotional types of relationships, as shown in Table 9.3.

Not only does Fournier provide an insightful, emotionally-based relationship typology, but she also identified six facets that help to assess the strength of the consumer–brand relationship. This can be evaluated by considering:

- the extent to which there is a strong affection (i.e. love and passion)
- the degree to which there is a connection with the person's self-concept
- how much the brand has woven itself into the consumer's life (interdependence)
- whether consumers would remain committed to the brand
- the depth of familiarity with the brand's attributes (intimacy)
- the extent to which the brand has qualities expected from a friend (brand partner quality).

These different relationship typologies are presented as stimuli to be considered against the values and personality in the brand pyramid. The brand's team can consider which of these relationships might most usefully describe the affinity between employees and their stakeholders. Departmental managers can then explain the desired type of relationship to their team, and work with them to explore the implications in terms of their style of

Table 9.3 *Fournier's (1998) typology of brand–consumer relationships (adapted from Gifford 1997)*

Committed partner	Become advocate for brand
Marriage of convenience	Long-term bond from a chance encounter
Arranged marriage	Long-term bond imposed by someone, e.g. wax recommended by cabinet maker
Casual friendship	e.g. rotate between cereals
Close friendship	e.g. particular trainers just for jogging
Compartment friendship	Friendship depends on situation, e.g. choice of perfume according to activity
Kinship	Involuntary union, e.g. use same flour as mother
Rebound	Desire to replace a previous partner, e.g. divorcee switches brand of mayonnaise since it was ex-husband's brand
Childhood friendship	Buy brand to remember childhood
Courtship	Period of testing
Dependency	Obsessive attraction causing upset when brand is out of stock
Fling	Enjoy trying a new brand, followed by feeling of guilt
Adversarial	Intense dislike
Enslavement	Involuntary relation, e.g. use airline as there is no choice
Secret affair	Private, risky relationship, e.g. eating a cake while on a diet

actions. An example of this is the DIY retailer B&Q. Reflecting its values of having a down-to-earth approach, respecting people and being customer driven, it has been recruiting older staff who have considerable experience of DIY and have personalities that enable them to empathize with their customers. Regular staff meetings with their line managers help to reinforce the importance B&Q places on staff providing advice to customers.

Activity 9.5

Over time, relationships change – for example, through people taking more for granted. If an organization takes its brand relationship with customers for granted, this may weaken any bonds. How could you assess whether the affinity between an organization and its customers is weakening?

Discussion

By drawing on Fournier et al. (1998), some of the following questions could prove informative.

1. Is the dispatching of information about your brand co-ordinated or not? There is a danger that different parts of the organization send out different types of

information, leaving consumers baffled as to why they are receiving so much from different parts of the organization.

2. Which departments (and how often) are asking the customer to provide information? For example, a customer who stays on four occasions a year at a hotel has to provide the same information at each registration.

3. How does the company define a 'loyal' customer? Discussions with less frequent users can reveal antagonism when these infrequent customers see the different levels of service offered to different tiers of 'loyal' customers, even though from their perspective they have made a notable number of purchases. Moving beyond this is the issue of newly recruited customers appearing to get a better financial deal than those who have been tied into the brand for some time. This is evident in the mortgage and mobile telephone markets. Recognition of this has led some corporate brands to run campaigns along the lines of rewards not just being offered to new but also to existing customers.

4. To what extent do customers feel they lose control when interacting with the organization? If nothing else, just keeping customers informed while their purchase/service is being delivered reduces this sensation of vulnerability.

5. How much trust do customers have in staff consistently delivering the brand promise and being able to resolve a problem?

When monitoring the strength of the relationship the brand has with its stakeholders, it is as well to reflect on the benefits a stakeholder group is seeking from the relationship. For example, the Co-operative Bank provides a good example of relationship building. It talks about 'partners' rather than stakeholders, and in its quest to deliver better value to its partners it gets them to define value, then devises performance standards to meet its partners' views. Ways of categorizing benefits from a relationship include:

- social – for example, friendship and personal recognition
- psychological – for example, reduced anxiety, trust or greater confidence
- economic – for example, time or cost savings
- personalization – for example, preferential treatment.

With increasing experience buyers' expectations rise, and that which may be regarded as added value today is taken for granted tomorrow. By monitoring the changes in benefits being sought from a relationship, the brand's team can reconsider brand augmentations in order to protect its relationships.

However, once a review has been completed about the strength of the customer–brand relationships, before embarking on an investment programme across all customers, consideration about costs versus benefits may prove insightful. As a result of different customers having different levels of brand usage, brand profitability varies across customer groups (Hallberg 1995).

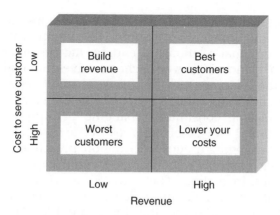

Figure 9.9   *Balancing the investment versus gains from different customers (Source: Piercy 2000)*

Furthermore, some customers need more servicing than others and therefore costs vary across customers. Piercy (2000) combined these dimensions, and from his matrix (see Figure 9.9) implications for investing amongst different groups can be better appreciated.

When there is a need to strengthen relationships, the group that should be given first priority is the high-revenue customers who have historically placed minimal demands on the organization. By contrast, the least attractive group consists of the low-spending customers who demand a lot of attention.

Managers and staff need to recognize that ending customer relationships needs to be managed. Michalski (2004) undertook research amongst customers in the banking sector and identified six types of relationship ending.

First, there are forced relationship endings where both situational triggers (e.g. change in personal situation) and influential triggers (e.g. competitor launches a better service) come about. The implication is that managers should continually understand how their brand tactics might be badly impacted by aggressive competitor activity. A second type, sudden relationship endings, occurs when one major unacceptable interaction between staff and customers occurs – for example, knowing that a customer's cheque has just cleared, but not having formal notice of this and refusing to allow them, for that day, to use their credit card to guarantee a room booking. Empowered staff, who understand a customer's background and purchasing history, should be able to minimize this form of termination. A third type, creeping relationship ending, results from a notable number of instances where unsatisfactory, small incidents have occurred, but even when customers take the effort to enter into dialogue, little change results.

At all times, staff need to be attentive to any comments made by customers, and improvements should be communicated.

In an optional relationship ending, the customer no longer cultivates a relationship, as he or she perceives minimal value – for example, the customer may hold several credit cards and rarely use one of these, and cancels the card when the renewal notice is sent. By tracking consumers' changing perceptions about the value of a brand (i.e. the benefits relative to sacrifices) and being attentive to changing usage levels, a more proactive stance can be taken to managing the relationship. The fifth type is an involuntary relationship ending. This may occur when customers are seeking unfairly to shift the balance of benefits more in their favour, and the brand owner then terminates the relationship. The sixth type, planned relationship ending, might occur when consumers have a time-limited project and only during this will they interact with an organization – for example, a couple who have bought a house in need of considerable renovation may use a loyalty card with a DIY store only during the time when they are improving their home. When issuing a loyalty card, it is helpful for managers to understand whether the relationship will be of a short duration so they do not mail out further money-off promotions.

Enabling staff to build stronger relationships supported by technology

Staff who passionately believe in their brand's values will be committed to building consistent, genuine relationships with their stakeholders. By then considering how to use technology to free them from repetitive standard tasks, where they add little value, not only can staff devote more attention to engendering trust through their stakeholder relationships, but this also enhances their workplace satisfaction. Satisfied staff lead to satisfied customers (Schneider 2000). The implications from this can be appreciated from Figure 9.10, building on an interview with a management journalist.

In the top right-hand box of Figure 9.10 is the 'haven' sought by many organizations – staff committed to genuine relationships and further opportunities to strengthen these, by freeing time by using technology for standardized tasks. The bottom right-hand box, 'frustration', characterizes brands in the physical fitness market where personal trainers develop relationships with their clients, employing selected pieces of equipment to facilitate their clients' exercises. The challenge in this box is keeping staff, since, as they gain experience, they may feel there is little scope for self-development and, through frustration, leave. The top left-hand

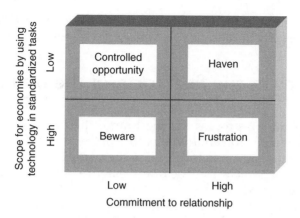

Figure 9.10 *Capitalizing on technology and relationships*

box, 'controlled opportunity', is likely to characterize superficial value brands which are not taking full advantage of greater use of technology. When incorporating more technology into the value delivery system, because these employees have little commitment to their brand's values there is little scope for them strengthening stakeholder relationships. The emphasis will continue to be controlling, scripting their roles and searching for further cost-reduction opportunities. The bottom left-hand box, 'beware', describes those organizations that are technology astute and have continually capitalized on new technologies with a production-line approach to staff involvement, primarily because their brands are standardized, low-cost offerings. Caution is needed in this box, since staff may feel subservient to technology, leading to high staff turnover.

Some organizations defend their views about not investing more in empowering staff to build stronger relationships, citing apparently satisfactory customer loyalty data. However, the assumptions about using these loyalty data may be questionable. Some brands represent serial, one-off, short-term customer–brand relationships – for example, a customer buying a new car is forced to consider their brand relationship. There is a notable association between their attitude and their resulting behaviour. However, for other brands, such as in financial services and telecommunications, customers are not forced to consider their brand relationship whenever they undertake a transaction. If anything, because of the high exit barriers when trying to leave the brand, they are less likely to review their relationship until such time as a renewal or a major problem occurs. In these situations, depending on the height of the exit barriers, the association between forming negative attitudes and changing behaviours (i.e. switching brands) is not notable. In this latter category of brands, loyalty should not be confused with inertia.

Arriving at the final form of the brand

In the planning process for the brand, the brand essence provides clear direction about the nature of the brand. The challenge for the brand's team is to translate the plans for the brand pyramid, which characterizes the brand essence, into a final form that is well resourced.

To enact the brand essence, a particular combination of resources is required. Just as a marketing strategy is characterized by a particular marketing mix, so the brand essence is characterized by the elements of the atomic model of the brand. This was originally devised by de Chernatony (1993), was validated in interviews with leading-edge brand consultants (de Chernatony and Dall'Olmo Riley 1997) and, as a consequence of its application in brand management workshops, has been further refined.

As will next be considered, to match the brand essence, the appropriate combination of components can be blended from the atomic model of the brand. When combining these components, an iterative process is followed, not only back to the brand essence stage in Figure 9.1, but also to the brand implementation stage to check the suitability of the internal delivery system.

The atomic model of the brand

Figure 9.11, using the analogy of an atom, illustrates a model that helps managers to develop a suitable resourcing package reflecting the desired brand essence. At the nucleus of any brand is its brand essence, portrayed by the five levels of the brand pyramid in Figure 8.2. Surrounding the brand essence are eight components (cf. electrons) whose trajectories are defined by the brand essence. For example, if the brand essence places considerable emphasis on the functional values of the brand, there is then a strong attractive force with the functional capabilities component in Figure 9.11. Working in a clockwise direction, each of the eight orbiting elements in the atomic brand model will be discussed.

Distinctive name and sign of ownership

For customers to recognize and be able to order a brand, it needs to have an easily pronounceable name, preferably evoking the

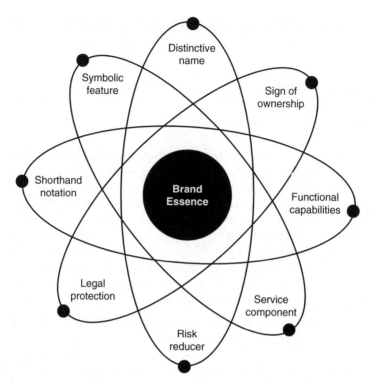

Figure 9.11   *The eight components of the atomic model of the brand characterizing the brand essence*

benefit of the brand – e.g. Timex, Lastminute.com. There are some instances where the values of the brand are distinctly different from the values of the corporation, thus we see a dominant distinctive name component and no immediately apparent presence of the corporation's name (i.e. sign of ownership). This is a strategy followed by organizations such as Unilever and Procter & Gamble with their fabric-care ranges. They have identified subtle differences in consumers' needs and, to meet these different segments, have developed brands such as Persil, Comfort and Surf (all from Unilever) and Ariel, Bold, Daz and Tide (all from Procter & Gamble). Each of these majors on its distinctive name with no sign of ownership.

By contrast, there are instances where there are significant commonalities between the values of the brand and those of the corporation. Here we see an equi-balanced combination of distinctive name and sign of ownership. Examples are Cadbury's Dairy Milk, Cadbury's Fruit & Nut, Cadbury's Flake and Cadbury's Milk Tray.

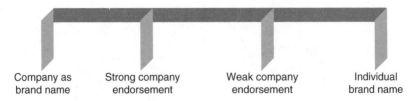

| Company as brand name | Strong company endorsement | Weak company endorsement | Individual brand name |

Figure 9.12   *Brand name spectrum*

There is a variety of combinations of the relative contributions from the distinctive name and sign of ownership components, and these can be appreciated from the brand name spectrum in Figure 9.12. Different writers have alternative reviews, and Kapferer (2004) has a much finer gradation of the brand name spectrum.

Some organizations' naming policies have historically majored on the sign of ownership component rather than the distinctive name – for example, financial services organizations. As firms develop new brands, they should not rely on historical precedents, but rather should consider:

- the extent to which there are similarities between the values of the corporation and the brand
- whether the new brand will create a new category that will expand with related offerings – e.g. Gillette Mach 3 Turbo, Gillette M3 Power, Gillette Mach 3 Turbo Gel, Gillette Complete Skincare.

This second criterion encourages the brand's team to take a longer-term perspective. By evaluating the overlap of values between

- corporation and newly developed brand
- newly developed brand and future new brands

a decision can be taken about the first two components of the atomic brand.

In addition to considering the overlap between the values of the new brand and the values of the corporation, managers also need to take into consideration the strengths and weaknesses of being reliant on the corporate name (sign of ownership) or unique brand names (distinctive name). Emphasizing sign of ownership may enable the new brand to capitalize on goodwill, consumer confidence and communication economies of scale. However, continually launching brands that draw on sign of ownership can dilute perceptions of the corporation's core benefits, and if there is a problem with the new brand this may damage the corporation. Minimizing the sign of ownership component and majoring on the distinctive name allows an organization to be more adventurous with its brands, enables several segments of the market to be covered and allows entry into numerous different markets.

There is, however, need for greater communication investment to overcome consumer reticence to try unknown brands. Readers interested in delving deeper into the principles of naming brands might like to consult de Chernatony and McDonald (2003).

Activity 9.6

Can you recall an example when an organization launched a brand that drew heavily on the sign of ownership component, and subsequently experienced a fall in its esteem due to problems with the new brand?

Discussion

Continental Airlines was inspired by the pioneer of budget air travel, Southwest Airlines, and decided to enter the low-budget, no-frills, cheap flight market using the brand Continental Lite. However, it continued to offer a full service under the Continental brand. They believed it was possible to serve both markets, and ignored the inevitable trade-offs on cost, service and efficiency. When Continental Lite was forced to withdraw from the market, consumers were aware of the failure of this venture, which reflected back on the parent corporation.

Functional capabilities

From the lower levels of the brand essence pyramid emerges a short, clear expression about the brand's functional advantages. The value delivery process, along with other factors such as packaging and communication, needs to be developed in such a way that everyone strives to ensure these functional capabilities are delivered and are instantly recognized by consumers. Having a clear positioning statement, through using the material in Chapters 7 and 8, facilitates not only consumers' recognition of the brand's functional advantage but also staff's appreciation of what is unique about the brand and thus how they should be contributing.

The brand pyramid may imply that the brand's competitive advantage is quality. Translating the concept of quality into a brand strategy can sometimes cause problems, as the term has a variety of interpretations. In the case of product-based brands, Garvin's (1987) work is helpful. He identified eight traits that characterize quality, thus enabling the brand's team to be more specific about their brand's quality. The traits include:

1. Performance, e.g. acceleration and top speed for a new brand of car
2. Features, e.g. the type of satellite navigation system in a car
3. Reliability, e.g. will the new brand start first time every time, regardless of the weather?

4. Conformance, e.g. if the new car brand is rated at 10 kilometres per litre of petrol, all drivers should have no problems achieving this
5. Durability, e.g. the economic lifetime of the brand
6. Serviceability, e.g. the intervals between servicing the car
7. Aesthetics, e.g. the design of the car
8. Perceived quality, e.g. as consumers find it difficult to understand the technicalities of a car, they form inferences about its quality from clues such as the brand name, advertising and price.

For services brands, the five SERVQUAL (services quality) dimensions from Parasuraman *et al.* (1988) provide a useful way of specifying and enacting quality. Issues to be considered here include:

1. Tangibles. As services are intangible promises, firms pay attention to the tangible components that are associated with the brand to enable consumers to recognize their quality. Thus the style of dress of staff, their logos and the design of their offices are the source of much management attention, as these give clues about the quality of the services brand.
2. Reliability. Since services are delivered by staff, one of the key concerns is to ensure that all staff have good technical knowledge about the brand. Thus, regardless of who is serving the consumer, they should all be competent to provide accurate information.
3. Responsiveness. For some services brands, firms pride themselves on the speed with which they can answer consumers' enquiries. A good example is FedEx, which uses bar coding on every package so that, through a sophisticated tracking system, its staff can rapidly interrogate the computer database to state where in the delivery system the package is.
4. Assurance. In services brands, a competitive advantage can result from staff being courteous and able to inspire trust and confidence.
5. Empathy. This relates to the care and individual attention provided by staff.

Activity 9.7

If a firm of architects wishes to develop its brand so that it is recognized for its quality, using the SERVQUAL dimensions, how might this be enacted?

Discussion

If this is to be regarded as a quality brand, it could be enacted through:

1. Tangibles – producing plans on high quality paper, having prestigious offices

2. Reliability – delivering drawings when promised with building solutions that continually stay within budget
3. Responsiveness – all the partners giving clients their mobile phone numbers and returning phone calls promptly
4. Assurance – having design awards hung in the reception area and the architects taking time to get to know their clients
5. Empathy – being able continually to revise designs without complaining, in response to changes in the client's evolving thinking.

Besides using the five dimensions as a basis for enacting the functional aspects of a service brand's essence, it can be used to evaluate consumers' perceptions of the brand's service quality and thus, where customer research shows this to be unsatisfactory, changes can be instigated. A generic twenty-two-item questionnaire covering the five dimensions can be administered, using a seven-point Likert scale from 1 (strongly agree) to 7 (strongly disagree). Consumers are first asked to give their expectations about the service brand, then the questionnaire asks them to provide their perceptions of the brand. Differences in scores between expectations and perceptions indicate gaps for improvement.

Criticisms have been levelled against SERVQUAL, even though it is widely accepted and popular. For example, there is a question about whether it is appropriate to ask consumers about their expectations immediately before consumption, and their perceptions of performance immediately after, and also whether gap scores should be used rather than perception scores alone (Palmer 2005). A more detailed critique is provided by Morrison Coulthard (2004).

Service component

To enable customers to gain the full benefit from the brand, it needs periodically to be serviced. Provision needs to be made for after-sales service when the brand unexpectedly fails and the organization needs to ensure rapid recovery of any problems. If the brand essence makes the claim of reliability, to some customers this is appreciated when servicing is carried out rapidly, courteously and competently. Serviceability is also assessed in terms of promptness of keeping appointments and the duration of the downtime of the brand.

When there is poor service backing the brand, a low proportion of customers complain. Unfortunately, it is not the majority who complain, as often customers do not think they will achieve anything and that it is easier to change brands. In effect, customers who complain when there is poor service recovery are not only giving the organization a second chance, they are also providing helpful brand information. As Piercy (2000) explained, when complaints about poor service recovery are satisfactorily resolved, customers tend to be more loyal than those who did not experience a problem. The brand's team needs to ensure that it is easy for customers to have contact with the organization to complain. Furthermore, complaints should be gratefully received, since they provide guidance about making improvements.

Risk reducer component

As discussed in Chapter 2, when people buy brands they are not necessarily concerned with maximizing their utility but rather with minimizing their perception of risk. Perceived risk is a multi-component concept that consists of:

- performance risk
- financial risk
- time risk
- social risk
- psychological risk.

The brand's team needs to consider the customer research completed when auditing the brandsphere (Chapter 7) to appreciate which of the five components of perceived risk evokes most anxiety amongst customers. Focusing on the risk component that causes customers most anxiety, the brand's team has an opportunity to consider how the benefits and the emotional rewards defined in the brand pyramid might be used to allay customers' concerns about the brand.

Activity 9.8

If one of the benefits of a small family car is a sensation that it responds like a high-performance car and the emotional reward is exciting, how could the brand be presented in an advertisement as a reducer of the prime risk component, financial risk?

Discussion

One way of minimizing financial risk would be to compare the brand with a high-performance car, contrasting the savings on car insurance from owning the small family car, yet reminding the audience of the fun of driving the cheaper-to-insure car.

Legal protection component

Taking action to register the brand provides legal protection against competitors developing counterfeit brands, who can then be prosecuted. However, while legal protection is a strong barrier, a more sustainable barrier is from the emotional values of the brand, driven by the culture of the organization.

To reduce the scope for counterfeiters, the brand's team needs to consider investing in registering their trademarks, employing firms to track down copiers, and devising more sophisticated packaging and batch-numbering processes. While these will deter counterfeiters, the more creative ones will continue to find ways of circumventing these barriers!

A balance needs to be struck between the distinctiveness of the brand name and the extent to which it describes the goods. The more descriptive the name, the more difficult it is to register. PaperMate launched an erasable ballpoint pen, branded Replay, which suggested the rational benefit from its brand essence yet was not so descriptive as to be unregistrable.

To ensure their brand name is not being infringed, some firms employ staff to monitor retail activities. For example, Coca-Cola staff visit outlets and order their brand without identifying themselves, then send samples for chemical analysis. If it transpires that the outlet was not in fact selling Coca-Cola, it is asked to refrain from such action or face legal action.

Shorthand notation component

As discussed in the 'End consumers' section of the brandsphere audit in Chapter 7, consumers rarely use all the available information to make a brand purchase decision. Jacoby *et al.* (1978) showed that consumers typically use less than 4 per cent of the information available to make a brand selection decision. The most sought on-pack information is the brand name, since for existing brands this enables consumers rapidly to interrogate memory and recall associations. Consumers prefer less *quantity* of information, and the few pieces of information presented should be of high *quality*. For example, someone who is on a diet and scanning competing cans of soup may feel in awe of the significant nutritional information on the packs, seeking to know primarily the calorific content.

The implications are that the brand name should be prominently displayed and the brand's team should resist the temptation to surround the brand name with numerous claims. Rather, using the earlier work by the brand's team on brand positioning, incorporated within the brand pyramid (see Chapter 8), the brand name needs to be associated with no more than three rational benefits that make the brand superior to competitors.

Activity 9.9

Take a brand that is familiar to you and examine its packaging and any promotional material. Write down the possible positioning claims being made. How many pieces of information are supporting the brand?

Discussion

Hopefully you only identified one or two positioning claims, and no more than around seven pieces of information were prominently portrayed. If you had more than three functional benefits competing for the positioning statement, and more than about seven pieces of information, this suggests a need for crisper communication.

To enable the brand to be an effective shorthand device, the brand's team members need to work with their designers and communications agencies to cut back the peripheral 'noise' they are introducing. There is a benefit in taking the positioning statement and checking each piece of information against this to arrive at a view about what is essential and what it is nice to have. The latter category of information should then be further assessed in terms of information that is legally necessary, and the remainder be a serious contender for being cut.

Symbolic feature component

From the upper part of the brand pyramid the brand's team can decide upon the personality to represent the brand, recalling the discussion about this in Chapter 8. The symbolic feature component is about bringing the brand's values to life through association with a personality or a lifestyle situation. If this is successfully enacted it can help consumers to select the firm's brand, particularly if it represents values important to them.

The response of the consumer's peer group when the consumer buys or uses the brand gives more meaning to the brand, as Solomon (1983) argued when describing symbolic interactionism. A classic example of this is the way that a consultant, when alone, might pay for lunch using a Tesco Personal Finance Mastercard because of the discount this credit card offers on a future Tesco shopping trip. Yet when the same consultant is paying for lunch with a client he or she wishes to impress, a Jaguar Visa credit card may be used instead because of the associated prestige.

Even though clear ideas emerge about a suitable personality from the upper levels of the brand pyramid, once a communications programme has been devised to associate the brand with that personality, research can show how consumers have negotiated and constructed a meaning for the brand. Changes may be needed to the communications programme so the desired brand personality is recognized, and hopefully consumer interactions further endorse this.

The integrated brand

As a consequence of the logical progression in the process of building and sustaining brands in Figure 9.1, the brand's team may have completed some of the analysis for the eight components in the atomic model of the brand. This is deliberate, since the intention is to develop an integrated brand. There may be some tension between the ideas suggested at the brand essence stage and the components at the brand resourcing stage, which can be resolved by iterating between these parts of Figure 9.1 until resolved.

Having 'put together the pieces of the jigsaw' using the atomic model, the brand's team needs to ensure that each of the eight resourcing components reinforces the others and logically links into the brand essence. As a consequence of the brand's team having such detailed insight to the brand, at this stage it becomes appropriate to use market research and assess different stakeholders' views.

Conclusions

This chapter has focused on considering the internal implementation issues involved in designing the brand delivery system and then specifying the eight resourcing components needed to provide the detail about the final form of the brand. It took as its starting point the direction for the brand, as summarized in the brand essence based on the brand pyramid. As the detailed form of the brand emerges, so its appropriateness can be checked against the brand essence with a view to fine-tuning and iterating between the brand essence, internal implementation and brand resourcing stages in Figure 9.1 until an integrated brand results.

When designing a values delivery system, it is difficult to focus solely on the way the system must satisfy the functional values and then solely on the way it must satisfy the emotional values, since any system has an impact on both types of values. By considering the mechanistic inputs of a values delivery system this helps to focus primarily on achieving the functional values, while the staff inputs primarily aid thinking about achieving the emotional values. However, the term 'primarily' should be noted, since neither the mechanistic nor the staff-based inputs solely drive functional or emotional values.

Porter's value chain can help to structure the brand delivery system and, through checking linkages, encourages a more integrated functional approach. The functional benefits of the brand are reinforced when, over time, the organization takes advantage of learning to strengthen its core competencies and adopts a strategic approach to outsourcing other activities. Services organizations may prefer to use the service blueprint to map the values delivery process. Through using the critical incident technique to identify contact points causing customer dissatisfaction, revisions can be made using the service blueprint, to deliver better the brand's functional values.

When thinking about staff-based inputs, aspects such as values, empowerment and relationships help to grow the brand's emotional values. Recruiting staff whose values concur with those of their brand is likely to encourage the growth of genuine value brands that take a stance on issues and gain customer respect. Encouraging staff to discuss how they interpret the brand's values provides a clearer sense of direction about their individual roles, as do values-related rewards.

The extent to which staff can effectively be empowered will vary between organizations, and even then there are varying levels of staff involvement in decision-making. Empowerment can engender greater customer respect for a brand, particularly when staff are seen to respond to customers' needs and help deliver the brand promise.

Brands represent an opportunity as relationship builders. The values of a brand are reflected in the way the organization interacts with its stakeholders. Committed staff, recruited on the basis of their alignment with the brand's values, are more likely to form genuine relationships with stakeholders. There is a danger of organizations becoming complacent in their stakeholder interactions, necessitating regular auditing of the affinity between stakeholders and the brand. Technology can help staff to build more respected relationships with customers, and a strategic perspective is needed when considering which tasks should be completed by technology rather than staff.

The eight components of the atomic model of the brand enable the brand's team members to decide upon the detailed form of their brand, and to consider the appropriateness of the brand delivery system. This model offers the brand's team the opportunity to evaluate the extent to which the different components reinforce each other, in addition to following the direction provided by the brand essence.

Brand marketing action checklist

This chapter contains ideas and frameworks that can help organizations to strengthen and build brands. To capitalize upon these ideas, undertaking some of the following exercises may prove beneficial.

1. Walk your way through all those activities that take place from the moment a customer places an order through to delivery of the brand. Whenever a value-adding activity occurs, consider whether this activity reinforces the values in your brand pyramid or, because of the context within which the activity takes place, whether the situation makes it difficult to deliver the value. If there are situations where problems are occurring, it would be helpful to consider how the process could be amended to deliver the particular value better.

2. Using the concept of the generic value chain discussed earlier in this chapter, plot each of the activities supporting your brand into the appropriate boxes in either the primary or support activities. For each activity, trace the boxes where it has an impact. Is there any change that could be made to the activity at the start of this linkage exercise that would notably ease, improve or reduce the cost of activities in later parts of the value chain?

3. From the value chain identified in exercise (2), work with your suppliers and customers to define their value chains and then together consider where changes could be made to the activity, so later in the value chain linking supplier to producer to customer there is a notable impact on either enhancing the benefits or reducing the cost of the brand.

4. Again taking the value chain from exercise (2), against each of the activities consider where your organization's core competencies are being employed. For those activities that do not draw on your core competencies, identify whether there are organizations that could undertake this activity better or more cheaply than you can. Use the matrix in Figure 9.4 (potential for gaining a competitive edge versus vulnerability outsourcing an activity) to plot those activities that could be outsourced. From this matrix, you are in a stronger position to manage the outsourcing.

5.   If you have a services brand, the previous value chain exercises should help. However, scope for improvements may follow as a result of understanding interactions. Using the service blueprint material covered earlier in this chapter, devise the blueprint for your brand. Consider:
     - the extent to which the sequence of processes and interactions support the values of your brand
     - whether there is a need to re-order the sequence of processes to deliver the brand's values better.

6.   If you work for a services brand organization, you might like to consider assessing the brand delivery process currently being used against the critical incident technique. Recruit approximately 50 customers who have used your services brand within the past 14 days, and ask them (individually) to think of a time when, as a customer, they had a particularly satisfying or dissatisfying interaction with .... (brand). Then ask them:
     - When did the incident happen?
     - What specific circumstances led up to this situation?
     - Exactly what did the employee involved say or do?
     - What resulted that made you feel the interaction was satisfying or dissatisfying?
     - What should or could have been done differently?

     These interviews are able to highlight parts of your brand delivery process that are either well or badly received. By investigating themes, and plotting where comments about these themes are being made on the service blueprint, you are better equipped to consider making changes. By repeating this exercise with a sample of your customer-facing staff, you can help your employees:
     - to recognize that there are conflicting views about a particular interaction, where the customers' views count most
     - to improve the interactions by encouraging staff, with their detailed knowledge, to make suggestions about improvements.

7.   Liaising with your human resources director, check the procedures being followed during recruitment campaigns. If not already in place, engender support for including an assessment of the concurrence between applicants' values and the values of the brand they will be working on. Consider what is being done to make your organization an attractive employer brand. Is anything being done to facilitate staff co-operation through understanding each other's identities better?

8.   Liaising with your human resources director and departmental managers, devise a workshop that clarifies, in easy-to-understand terms, the values of your brand and that gets

new employees who have been with the organization for approximately four weeks to discuss and debate what the values mean in their specific jobs. This should help to induct new colleagues in the values you cherish and enable them to enact these better.

9. By drawing on the five contingencies of Bowen and Lawler (1992) described in Table 9.2, assess whether your strategy of following an empowerment or a production-line approach is appropriate. By then using knowledge about the different levels of empowerment from Figure 9.7 (Bowen and Lawler 1992), consider whether the type of empowerment is appropriate.

10. Working with departmental managers, encourage their staff to attend a personality-relationship workshop. At this workshop, explain how a brand's personality leads to particular relationships. Clarify the desired personality of your brand, then encourage the staff to consider what types of relationships would be expected with different stakeholders. Make explicit the relationship that should support your brand, and encourage these employees to recognize how their behaviour may need to change to enact this relationship.

11. To assess the strength of the relationship customers have with your brand, interview a sample of your customers, either personally or using a postal questionnaire. In particular, ask them how far they agree or disagree with the following statements.

	Strongly disagree	Disagree	Neither agree nor disagree	Agree	Strongly agree
I have a strong affection for this brand	1	2	3	4	5
This brand connects well with my personality	1	2	3	4	5
I would be lost without this brand	1	2	3	4	5
If another well-known firm introduced a similar brand, albeit 10 per cent cheaper, I would still stay loyal to this brand.	1	2	3	4	5
I feel I really know this brand	1	2	3	4	5
I almost feel this brand has become a good friend	1	2	3	4	5

By calculating the average overall score, a guide is provided about the strength of the relationship between the customer and your brand. Scores greater than four indicate relationships to be protected. By contrast, scores lower than three indicate the need for rapid action. For brands with weak relationships, an examination of the six facets should indicate the issues most in need of attention.

12. Using the matrix in Figure 9.10 (scope for economies by using technology in standardized tasks versus employees' commitment to relationships), work with your colleagues to identify the quadrant characterizing your brand. Consider the changes that could bring about cost savings through greater use of technology, freeing staff to develop more committed relationships.

13. Evaluate how appropriately your brand pyramid has been enacted, by using the atomic model of the brand. Place at the centre of this model the detailed five-level brand pyramid, then, working in a clockwise manner and starting at the distinctive name component, assess how each of the eight components is either helping or hindering delivery of the brand pyramid.

References and further reading

Ambler, T. and Barrow, S. (1996). The employer brand. *Journal of Brand Management*, **4** (3), 185–206.

Bateson, J. (1995). *Managing Services Marketing*. Fort Worth TX: The Dryden Press.

Berthon, P., Ewing, M. and Hah, L. L. (2005). Captivating company: dimensions of attractiveness in employer branding. *International Journal of Advertising*, **24** (2), 151–72.

Bitner, M. J. (1993). Managing the evidence of service. In *The Service Quality Handbook* (Scheuing, E. and Christopher, W., eds). New York: The American Management Association.

Bitner, M. J., Booms, B. and Tetreault, M. S. (1990). The service encounter: diagnosing favourable and unfavourable incidents. *Journal of Marketing*, **54**, 71–84.

Bowen, D. and Lawler, E. (1992). The empowerment of service workers: what, why, how and when. *Sloan Management Review*, **33** (3), 31–9.

Buchanan, D. and Huczynski, A. (2004). *Organizational Behaviour*. Harlow: FT Prentice Hall.

Buchanan, D. and Preston, D. (1992). Life in the cell: supervision and teamwork in a 'manufacturing systems engineering' environment. *Human Resource Management Journal*, **2** (4), 55–80.

Ciulla, J. (1999). The importance of leadership in shaping business values. *Long Range Planning*, **32** (2), 166–72.

Davidson, H. (1997). *Even More Offensive Marketing*. London: Penguin.

de Chernatony, L. (1993). Categorising brands: evolutionary processes underpinned by two key dimensions. *Journal of Marketing Management*, **9** (2), 173–88.

de Chernatony, L. and Dall' Olmo Riley, F. (1997). Modelling the components of the brand. *European Journal of Marketing*, **32** (11/12), 1074–90.

de Chernatony, L. and McDonald, M. (2003). *Creating Powerful Brands in Consumer, Service and Industrial Markets*, 3rd edn. Oxford: Elsevier.

Ewing, M., Pitt, L., de Bussy, N. and Berthon, P. (2002). Employment branding in the knowledge economy. *International Journal of Advertising*, **21** (1), 3–22.

Fournier, S. (1998). Consumers and their brands: developing relationship theory in consumer research. *Journal of Consumer Research*, **24** (4), 343–73.

Fournier, S., Dobscha, S. and Mick, D. G. (1998). Preventing the premature death of relationship marketing. *Harvard Business Review*, **January/February**, 42–51.

Free, C. (1999). The internal brand. *Journal of Brand Management*, **6** (4), 231–6.

Garvin, D. (1987). Competing on the eight dimensions of quality. *Harvard Business Review*, **November/December**, 101–9.

Gifford, D. (1997). Moving beyond loyalty. *Harvard Business Review*, **March/April**, 9–10.

Gordon, W. (1999). *Goodthinking*. Henley-on-Thames: Admap Publications.

Goyder, M. (1999). Value and values: lessons for tomorrow's company. *Long Range Planning*, **32** (2), 217–49.

Grönroos, C. (2000). *Service Management and Marketing*. Chichester: John Wiley & Sons.

Gummesson, E. (1999). *Total Relationship Marketing*. Oxford: Butterworth-Heinemann.

Hallberg, G. (1995). *All Consumers are Not Created Equal*. New York: John Wiley.

Hinde, R. (1995). A suggested structure for a science of relationships. *Personal Relationships*, **2**, 1–15.

Hooley, G., Saunders, J. and Piercy, N. (2004). *Marketing Strategy and Competitive Positioning*. Harlow: FT Prentice Hall.

Iacobucci, D. and Ostromn, A. (1996). Commercial and interpersonal relationships; using the structure of interpersonal relationships to understand individual-to-individual, individual-to-firm, and firm-to-firm relationships in commerce. *International Journal of Research in Marketing*, **13**, 53–72.

Jacoby, J., Chestnut, R. and Fisher, W. (1978). A behavioural process approach to information acquisition in nondurable purchasing. *Journal of Marketing Research*, **15** (3), 532–44.

Kapferer, J.-N. (2004). *The New Strategic Brand Management*. London: Kogan Page.

Kunde, J. (2000). *Corporate Religion*. Harlow: Pearson Education.

Levitt, T. (1972). Production-line approach to service. *Harvard Business Review*, **September/October**, 41–52.

Lovelock, C., Vandermerwe, S. and Lewis, B. (1999). *Services Marketing*. Upper Saddle River NJ: Prentice Hall.

Maccoby, M. (1988). *Why Work: Motivating and Leading the New Generation*. New York: Simon & Schuster.

Michalski, S. (2004). Types of customer relationship ending processes. *Journal of Marketing Management*, **20** (9/10), 977–99.

Milton, L. and Westphal, J. (2005). Identity confirmation networks and cooperation in work groups. *Academy of Management Journal*, **48** (2), 191–212.

Morrison Coulthard, L. (2004). Measuring service quality. *International Journal of Market Research*, **46** (4), 479–97.

Packard, J. (1993). The real meaning of empowerment. *Personnel Management*, **November**, 28–32.

Palmer, A. (2005). *Principles of Services Marketing.* London: McGraw Hill.

Parasuraman, A, Zeithaml, V. and Berry, L. (1988). SERVQUAL: a multiple-item scale for measuring consumer perceptions of service quality. *Journal of Retailing,* **64** (1), 12–40.

Piercy, N. (1999). *Tales From the Marketplace.* Oxford: Butterworth-Heinemann.

Piercy, N. (2000). *Market-Led Strategic Change.* Oxford: Butterworth-Heinemann.

Pine, J. and Gilmore, J. (1998). Welcome to the experience economy. *Harvard Business Review,* **July/August**, 97–105.

Porter, M. (1985). *Competitive Advantage.* New York NY: The Free Press.

Quinn, J. (1999). Strategic outsourcing: leveraging knowledge capabilities. *Sloan Management Review,* **40** (4), 9–21.

Quinn, J. and Hilmer, F. (1994). Strategic outsourcing, *Sloan Management Review,* **35** (4), 43–55.

Reichheld, F. (1996). *The Loyalty Effect.* Boston MA: Harvard Business School Press.

Royal Society for the Encouragement of Arts, Manufactures and Commerce (1995). *Tomorrow's Company Inquiry.* London: Gower.

Schlesinger, L. and Heskett, J. (1991). Enfranchisement of service workers. *California Management Review,* **Summer**, 83–100.

Schneider, B. (2000). Brand image from the inside out: linking internal organization design to customer satisfaction. *Journal of Brand Management,* **7** (4), 233–40.

Solomon, M. (1983). The role of products as social stimuli: a symbolic interaction perspective. *Journal of Consumer Research,* **10**, 391–29.

Williamson, D. (2000). War of the words. *Revolution,* **7 June**, 4–41.

Wish, M., Deutsch, M. and Kaplan, S. (1976). Perceived dimensions of interpersonal relationships. *Journal of Personality and Social Psychology,* **33**, 409–20.

Zeithaml, V. and Bitner, M. J. (1996). *Services Marketing.* New York: McGraw Hill.

Chapter 10

Brand evaluation

Summary

This chapter focuses on the brand evaluation block of the process for building and sustaining brands (see Figure 10.1). Brands are multidimensional entities, and thus any brand evaluation needs to assess a variety of parameters. Using the relevant building blocks from the brand-planning process, criteria internal and external to an organization are identified which provide insight about the brand's health.

Multidimensional evaluation

If the brand's team has followed the sequential stages of the brand-building process illustrated in Figure 10.1, there is a high likelihood of there being an integrated brand that is respected by all stakeholder groups. At each stage in this brand-building/strengthening process, decisions have been taken about how the brand should be moulded to achieve specified objectives.

After launching the new brand, or enacting changes to an existing brand, its acceptability will become apparent over time as customers and other stakeholders respond to it. At the most fundamental level, tracking the brand's sales and profitability will provide some insight regarding the suitability of the brand. By tracking the brand against a broader set of measures, the brand's team is in a stronger position to fine-tune the brand.

Different writers have proposed alternative criteria for assessing brands. For example, the brand could be assessed by considering its financial value (Perrier 1997; Haigh and Knowles 2004; Kapferer 2004), or by considering the brand's equity (Aaker 1996;

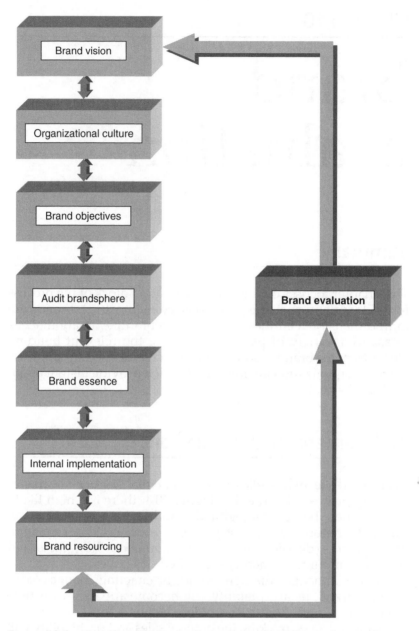

Figure 10.1 *Brand evaluation in the process of building and sustaining brands*

Ambler 2003) or through the brand report card (Keller 2000), amongst other methods. While these measures provide useful data about aspects of a brand's performance, and tap some of the building blocks in the flow process of Figure 10.1, they do not address all the relevant blocks. Therefore, the purpose of this chapter is to clarify a set of measures to evaluate all facets of the brand, as conceived through the brand-building process.

Brands are complex entities, and cannot be measured by just one parameter. An analogy may help. A man believed that jogging was the best way to keep fit and jogged every day. In his mid-30s he had a medical to evaluate his state of health. The doctor didn't just assess his heart and muscles, but did numerous tests. At the end he concluded, 'You have a very good cardiovascular system, but will shortly need a hip replacement operation as your jogging on the road has impacted on your bones.' Alas, by thinking of good health in terms of just one part of his body, he had overlooked the fact that it is based on many other parameters.

Research undertaken by de Chernatony *et al.* (1998), based on both a literature review and interviews with leading-edge brand consultants, showed that the success of a brand needs measuring using a combination of dimensions. In essence this research found that both business-based criteria and customer-based criteria are needed. One of the arguments developed in this book is that a more balanced perspective is needed in brand management, ensuring that both internal and external issues are addressed. As such any assessment of a brand's performance over time needs to be based on measuring changes amongst factors internal to an organization as well as those external to an organization.

Further justification for evaluating a brand over time by looking inside and outside an organization comes from considering one of the desired outcomes from a brand. If a brand is successful, it generates a favourable reputation (Fombrun 1996; Davies *et al.* 2003; Larkin 2003). Drawing on Fombrun *et al.* (2000: 243), a brand's reputation calibrates its relative standing internally with employees and externally with other stakeholders, and is a collective assessment of a brand's 'ability to provide valued outcomes to a representative group of stakeholders'.

In view of the argument that brands must meet the needs of stakeholders inside and outside the organization, and because of the rationale underpinning the way a brand is built by following the flow process of Figure 10.1, each of the stages contributes to strengthening a brand. Thus the impact of each of the blocks in the flow process needs assessing to identify the effect it has had on the brand. The intent is that if the strategy behind the brand is successful, there should be a positive impact from each block. The brand-planning process is concerned with defining the shape of the brand, and thus by returning to the process in Figure 10.1 a basis is provided for evaluating a brand's performance.

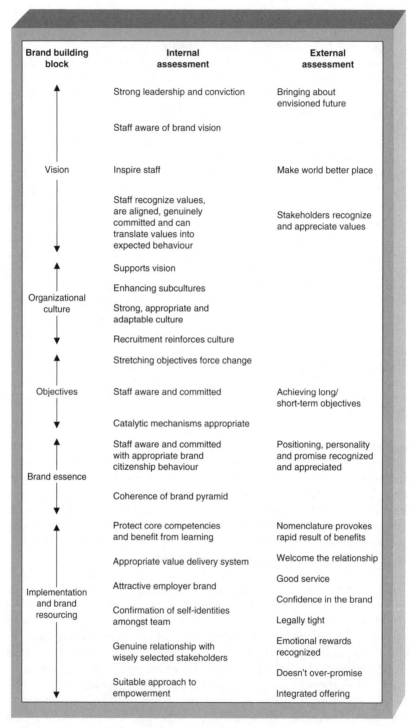

Figure 10.2 *A holistic approach to brand evaluation*

In Figure 10.2, a summary is provided of the criteria to evaluate a brand's performance. By monitoring a brand against these criteria, the brand's team is better able to identify areas where the brand is underperforming and changes can be made to strengthen the brand's performance.

This chapter will consider the diagnostics to evaluate the brand's performance. The breadth of issues addressed has the advantage of gauging the brand's health amongst staff, customers and other stakeholders. Furthermore, the evaluation is a thorough assessment, going beyond the minimum requirements of achieving sales targets and providing impressive levels of profitability. The disadvantage is that it takes time to complete this assessment, and may well necessitate extra financial and manpower resources to complete it.

Each of the relevant blocks of the brand-building process will be addressed to identify the questions that need asking in order to evaluate the brand's performance.

Brand vision

Issues to be assessed internally are:

1. How strong is the leadership provided either by the most senior influential person (typically the chair, or managing director) or the brand's team?
2. How involved are staff in brand visioning?
3. What level of awareness is there amongst staff about the brand's vision?
4. How committed is the senior team to the brand vision?
5. To what extent does the most senior influential person, or the brand's team, inspire staff about their roles as brand-builders?
6. To what extent do staff know the values of the brand they support?
7. How committed are staff to their brand's values?
8. To what extent do the values of the brand concur with the values of staff working on that brand?
9. How closely do the actions of the senior managers and other employees reflect the values being espoused?
10. How confident are staff in translating the values of their brand into actions they should undertake in their daily roles?

Issues to be evaluated amongst external stakeholders are:

11. What progress is being made in bringing about a welcomed envisioned future?

12. Thinking of the domain where the brand seeks to add value to people's lives, to what extent is the brand making their world a better place?
13. How accurate are the assessments of stakeholders about the brand's values?
14. When told the brand's values, how much do stakeholders appreciate these values?

Organizational culture

The internal issues to be evaluated are:

15. How well do the artefacts of the organizational culture support the brand vision?
16. How well do the values of the organizational culture support the brand vision?
17. How well do the assumptions of the organizational culture support the brand vision?
18. When considering the subcultures that exist in different parts of the organization, what proportions are
    - enhancing subcultures?
    - orthogonal subcultures?
    - counter-subcultures?
19. To what extent is the organizational culture
    - appropriate for the current environment?
    - adaptable to environmental change?
    - respectful of leadership at all levels?
    - attentive to satisfying the needs of staff, customers and shareholders?
20. How do recruitment programmes reinforce the desired culture?

Brand objectives

The internal issues to be evaluated are:

21. How stretching are the brand objectives?
22. What must be done differently to achieve the brand objectives?
23. How aware are staff of the brand's
    - long-term objectives?
    - short-term objectives?
24. How committed are staff to helping achieve the brand's
    - long-term objectives?
    - short-term objectives?

25. How appropriate are the catalytic mechanisms in guiding management and employees to achieve the brand objectives?

The external issues to be evaluated are:

26. To what extent is the brand under- or over-achieving on its
    • short-term objectives?
    • long-term objectives?

Brand essence

The internal issues to be addressed are:

27. How aware are staff of the elements of the brand pyramid and the resulting brand promise?
28. How committed are staff to delivering the promise inherent in the brand pyramid?
29. How coherent are the elements of the brand pyramid?
30. How supportive is the brand citizenship behaviour of employees?

The external issues to be assessed are:

31. How well do customers' perceptions of the brand's positioning match the benefits in the bottom part of the brand pyramid?
32. How much does the brand's target market welcome the brand's functional benefits?
33. How well do customers' perceptions of the brand's personality match the personality traits or personality at the top of the brand pyramid?
34. How much does the brand's target market welcome the brand's personality traits?
35. How well do customers associate the brand with its promise?
36. How much do customers welcome the brand's promise?

Implementation and brand resourcing

The internal issues to be evaluated are:

37. To what extent are the core competencies underpinning the brand benefiting from organizational learning and being protected against outsourcing?
38. How appropriate is the value delivery system (i.e. either the value chain or the service blueprint) for the brand?
39. How attractive is the employer brand?

40. How much do team members confirm each other's self-identities?
41. How appropriate is the policy on empowerment for the brand?
42. How genuine are staff when building relationships with their stakeholders?
43. How well managed are the terminations of relationships?

The external issues to be evaluated are:

44. How well does the brand nomenclature provide rapid recall of the brand's benefits?
45. How strong is the brand's relationship with its external stakeholders?
46. How well rated is the service supporting the brand?
47. How confident are stakeholders with the brand?
48. To what extent is the brand able to take legal action against infringes?
49. How well are the emotional rewards correctly recognized?
50. To what degree do stakeholders perceive any conflicts between the brand's promise and their experiences with the brand?
51. To what extent do elements of the brand reinforces the brand promise?

Summarizing the brand's health

The brand evaluation process just described will unearth many data, which can be synthesized by scoring each of the questions on five-point scales. This has the advantage of making members of the brand's team aware of areas where the brand is particularly strong or weak. However, some people may feel overwhelmed by the quantity of data. The evaluation data can be further summarized, as will now be described.

Five categories were specified in Figure 10.1 (i.e. brand vision, organizational culture, objectives, brand essence, and implementation and brand resourcing) within which detailed questions will have been answered. For each of these categories separately, the average score for that category can be calculated. This is done by adding the scores for the questions about internal issues to the scores for the external issues and dividing by the total number of questions about that category (for example, dividing by fourteen for the brand vision category). Having done this, the overall evaluation can be presented in the template shown in Figure 10.3.

The bar chart enables people to rapidly appreciate the brand's health. In the hypothetical example displayed in Figure 10.3, this

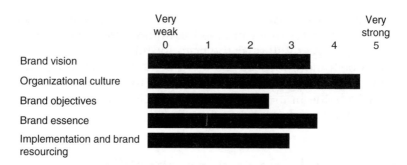

Figure 10.3 *A template for the brand health bar chart, with a hypothetical example*

brand has a very supportive organizational culture but has problems in terms of its brand objectives (or, more to the point, in not achieving these!). By then looking into the detail of the profiles that constitute each of the five summary assessments, the brand's team can identify where action needs taking.

The brand health bar chart provides a top-line picture at a point in time. By undertaking this evaluation on an annual basis and then displaying year-on-year changes, trends can be noted and further supportive activities implemented.

Conclusions

By considering the measures identified in each of the blocks just reviewed, the brand's team members should be in a better position to evaluate and monitor their brand. Checking the results against the aims originally specified for the brand should provide inspiration about changes to help the brand achieve its goals. Displaying the findings using the brand health bar chart enables people to understand the strengths and weaknesses of the brand.

The journey in this book has reached its conclusion. The reader should now have a better appreciation of the issues involved in building and strengthening brands. This journey has exposed the reader to a more balanced perspective on brand-building by looking inside and outside organizations. It has drawn attention to the diversity of interpretations about the brand, and has sought to help encourage the evolution of more integrated brands. Through the use of the sequential stages of the brand-building process, this book has attempted to help managers and students to devise more coherent brands that gain the respect of all stakeholder groups. A systematic approach has been advocated to help readers become more efficient in their use of brand-building resources and to minimize the out-of-context tangential debates that can take the brand's team off track. The planning process will raise the need for internal debate, but this should be a more focused debate. The hope is that the creative members of the brand's team will be able to devise the necessary 'magic' for the brand, which the strategists can then integrate within their brand plans.

Brand marketing action checklist

The thrust of this chapter has been to cover the issues that need assessing in order to evaluate the brand's health. By working through the questions in this chapter, the brand's team members can better evaluate their brand. This can be done by using the five-point scoring approach to each of the questions, then the detailed data can be presented on the brand health bar chart. Those topics scoring two or less indicate weaknesses that should be addressed. By contrast, those topics scoring four or more indicate brand strengths that should be protected.

References and further reading

Aaker, D. (1996). *Building Strong Brands*. New York: The Free Press.

Ambler, T. (2003). *Marketing and The Bottom Line*. London: FT Prentice Hall.

Davies, G., Chun, R., Vinhas da Silva, R. and Roper, S. (2003). *Corporate Reputation and Competitiveness*. London: Routledge.

de Chernatony, L., Dall'Olmo Riley, R. and Harris, F. (1998). Criteria to assess brand success. *Journal of Marketing Management*, **14** (7), 765–81.

Feldwick, P. (2002). *What is brand equity anyway, and how do you measure it?* Henley on Thames: World Advertising Research Centre.

Fombrun, C. (1996). *Reputation: Realizing Value from the Corporate Image*. Boston MA: Harvard Business School Press.

Fombrun, C., Gardberg, N. and Sever, J. (2000). The Reputation Quotient™: a multi-stakeholder measure of corporate reputation. *Journal of Brand Management*, **7** (4), 241–56.

Haigh, D. and Knowles, J. (2004). How to define your brand and determine its value. *Marketing Management*, **May/June**, 22–8.

Kapferer, J.-N. (2004). *The New Strategic Brand Management*. London: Kogan Page.

Keller, K. L. (2000). The brand report card. *Harvard Business Review*, **January/ February**, 147–57.

Larkin, J. (2003). *Strategic Reputation Risk Management*. Basingstoke: Palgrave Macmillan.

Perrier, R. (1997). *Brand Valuation*. London: Premier Books.

Index